Tanglewood

Tanglewood

A Group Memoir

by Peggy Daniel

AMADEUS
PRESS

An Imprint of Hal Leonard Corporation
New York

Published in 2008 by Amadeus Press
An Imprint of Hal Leonard Corporation
7777 West Bluemound Road
Milwaukee, WI 53213

Trade Book Division Editorial Offices
19 West 21st Street, New York, NY 10010

Printed in the United States of America

Book design by Snow Creative Services

Credits can be found on pages 243 to 244, which constitute an extension of this copyright page.

Library of Congress Cataloging-in-Publication Data is available upon request.

ISBN 978-1-57467-167-4

www.amadeuspress.com

For Dan Gustin and Richard Ortner,

the real Tanglewood historians

Contents

Foreword

I fell in love with Tanglewood the first time I saw it. I was thirteen years old, spending the summer at the Marlboro Music Festival, and went to hear Rudolf Serkin (with whom I was studying piano) play the Schumann concerto with Charles Munch and the Boston Symphony Orchestra. That was in 1956. As things turned out, my next visit to Tanglewood—as a guest conductor of the BSO!—was not until 1972, but the spell of the place stayed with me all those years. Whatever one's reason for being there—whether on stage or in the audience, whether working or relaxing—there's no escaping that special atmosphere. It's such an extraordinarily beautiful and inspiring setting; it's no wonder that what happens there is equally inspired.

The "work" at Tanglewood is of many kinds. Most immediately visible to audiences, of course, is the work of the Boston Symphony Orchestra. But equally important is the work of the 200 or so young musicians on the verge of professional careers who spend eight or nine weeks each summer at Tanglewood honing their skills by studying with members of the orchestra, its conductors, and many of the guest artists who come to work with the BSO. These young musicians are the "fellows" of the Tanglewood Music Center, founded in 1940 (as the Berkshire Music Center) by Serge Koussevitzky, just a few years after the BSO's first Tanglewood Festival in 1937.

From the start, it was Koussevitzky's intention that Tanglewood be a place of learning as well as a place of performance, an ideal that not only continues to this day but has set an example for many other summer festivals throughout the United States. For me, the opportunity to work with both the Boston Symphony itself and the musicians of the Tanglewood Music Center—not only participating in but also helping to perpetuate Koussevitzky's dream—has provided a personal pleasure and excitement that can hardly be described in words. But Peggy Daniel has done it. Thanks to her, we get a marvelous sense here, through the words of participants and observers over the years, of what Tanglewood has meant from the very beginning, and what it will surely mean for years to come. This is *the* book on the subject for everyone—those who know Tanglewood intimately, and those who have yet to discover its unique magic.

—James Levine
Music Director, Boston Symphony Orchestra

Preface

I was eighteen. I had just graduated from high school. I was more than ready to begin my life as a mature adult.

The precipitating event: Lucie Hill, a boarding school classmate, had invited three girls from school to visit her for a week in Connecticut that summer. The idea was that we would borrow her family's car and, if at all possible, her father's gasoline credit card, and head off to Tanglewood for a weekend of music and adventure. None of us had ever been *anywhere* without our parents, so this promised to be a major benchmark in the growing-up department.

I was particularly excited, since I had been devouring music—especially classical music—for a long time. Before my tenth birthday, I smugly informed my mother that the only present I wanted was a recording of the *Moonlight* Sonata, and it *had* to be played by Rudolf Serkin. You get the idea.

To ratchet up the excitement level, Lucie had recently vacationed in Bermuda with her family, where she met an "older man"—a marine in his early twenties just back from a tour of duty in Korea. I guess her parents approved of him, because he joined us on the trip.

Saturday night, we three girls and the marine arrived at the Tanglewood Main Gate, picnic baskets in hand. While we were stretched out on the lawn before the concert started, the marine—unfortunately, I have forgotten his name after all these years—proudly informed us that in Korea a woman had walked barefoot on his back, a traditional form of massage in that country. What an intriguing idea! Nothing would do but that we should try this out on him right then and there on the Tanglewood lawn. Does it get any better than this?

Well, yes, it did! It soon became dark. An amazing number of stars appeared in the sky, but to me, the brightest star of all was Leonard Bernstein. He conducted Beethoven's *Missa Solemnis*, a piece I had never even heard of, much less heard. When the violin solo in the second movement began, *ecstasy* is the only word in the dictionary that comes to mind to describe how I felt.

Some decades later, I had become a veteran public television producer with dozens of classical music specials to my credit. My feelings about music hadn't changed much. Neither had my attachment to Tanglewood, which I had been visiting a lot over the years. All that time I had been harboring a secret ambition to spend an entire summer living and breathing music at Tanglewood.

Nineteen ninety-six marked the fiftieth anniversary of the original Tanglewood production of *Peter Grimes*, the landmark opera Serge Koussevitzky had commissioned Benjamin Britten to write for his Music Center students. What a golden opportunity, I thought, for me to worm my way into the inner sanctum.

Two years before, while working on a documentary for Sony Classical on the opening of Seiji Ozawa Hall, I had met Richard Ortner, then the administrator of the Tanglewood Music Center. Who better to go to for a job there? It took me several months of serious arm-twisting, but eventually he saw it my way and hired me to work in the vocal department.

During production, television producers work long, grueling hours. But nothing could compare to the amount of work I put in that summer. No days off, with well over a hundred concerts presented in a scant two months, plus the Festival of Contemporary Music, which consumed every waking hour of both staff and student body. Believe me, there was plenty of stress to go around.

My way of taking a little break from all this turmoil was to go over to the Aaron Copland Library and root around in the music books for a few minutes. One day I came across a charming memoir written by composer Nicolas Nabokov, *Old Friends and New Music*, describing a moving encounter he had had with Koussevitzky—an old family friend from Russia—immediately after the end of World War II. Early in the morning on Nabokov's first day back from bombed-out Berlin, Western Union woke him up in his New York hotel with a telegraph message from the maestro, inviting him to spend the weekend at Seranak, Koussevitzky's house in Tanglewood, to discuss a symphonic commission. This was good news to Nabokov, who had not had a commission for quite a while.

When two deeply emotional Russian musicians get together, matters of the soul are bound to be discussed. Indeed they were, and I was charmed by Nabokov's account. He had a way of describing Tanglewood that pungently evoked its 1940s ambience. So I began to wonder whether other musicians—many of whom regard Tanglewood as a second home, even a shrine—had put their feelings for Tanglewood down on paper.

Yes they had, and the idea for this book was born.

—Peggy Daniel
The New York Society Library

Tanglewood

One day he [George Edman, county editor of the *Berkshire Evening Eagle*] came home and said, "I had an interesting thing happen today. A man came in who wants to start concerts in Berkshire County and call it Music Under the Moon. It was either Howard or Harold Chandler. He was a salesman out of a job. . . . He had a wife who was a singer, and she was a friend of Henry Hadley, who also was out of a job. He was a well-known conductor in New York. They both wanted a job for the summer.

—Alice Edman (Mrs. George W.)

CHAPTER 1

Music
Under the
Moon

The Early Days of the Berkshire Music Festival

Odd, isn't it, that Tanglewood—America's foremost music festival, a bastion of Boston Brahmins and Mrs. Astor's 400 set, the elegant summer home of the world-renowned Boston Symphony Orchestra—began life as a means of providing employment for a sales-man and an entrepreneurial musician from New York.

Well, that depends! In some part of its being, Tanglewood—like New England—has always been a touch unconventional.

After all, Gertrude Robinson Smith—its founder—was a frumpy, unmarried, middle-aged, socially prominent woman from New York, well known in her circle as a crusader for social causes. Had she lived fifty years later, she might well have been the high-powered CEO of an international conglomerate. Some of the earliest musicians who came to world prominence at Tanglewood were either black, women, or—most shocking of all—American-born soloists. Serge Koussevitzky, the conductor who brought Tanglewood to musical preeminence, was in his day the world's foremost champion of contemporary American and European composers—not necessarily the music symphonic audiences are most eager to hear.

Since its earliest days, even while being supported by the East Coast social, financial, and intellectual elite, Tanglewood has always maintained a streak of adventurousness, com-mingled with a sincere dedication to "the middle of the road."

Its beginnings were very much a homegrown affair, the joint effort of well-off summer residents in the Berkshires and the local movers and shakers.

The local paper, the Berkshire Eagle *and its offshoot editions, has to this day been one of the Festival's most enthusiastic supporters. In 1955 it published* Music Under the Moon: A History of the Berkshire Symphonic Festival, Inc *by John G. W. Mahanna, who, like George Edman before him, was county editor of the* Berkshire Evening Eagle.

The Berkshire Symphonic Festival Incorporated, a pioneer organization in the field of music, got its start in 1934—a time when the future was heavily clouded.

Here in the United States, the unemployment problem was becoming more desperate every day.

President Franklin D. Roosevelt had established the Civil Works Emergency Relief Administration. Adolf Hitler had been chancellor of Germany only a short time. In Canada the Dionne quintuplets had been born. The United States had recognized the Soviet government, bringing to an end a long period of estrangement. After sixteen years of political power in New York, Tammany Hall had lost control. Prohibition had been repealed. Uncle Sam was walking a tightwire.

At this time, Dr. Henry Hadley, noted conductor-composer of the period, made known to Miss Gertrude Robinson Smith of Stockbridge, Massachusetts, a widely known summer resident of the Berkshires, his dream to give symphony concerts in the Berkshires "under the stars." Dr. Hadley revealed his wish to her one afternoon in May 1934.

Thrilled with the idea, Miss Robinson Smith reserved her decision until she had time to confer with two close friends, Mrs. Owen Johnson, wife of the late novelist [*Stover at Yale*], who lived nearby, and Mrs. William Felton Barrett of South Egremont, a summer resident of the Berkshires. They took a compass, set it on a New England highway map, drew a circle covering a forty-mile radius of Stockbridge, and decided to draw on that section for support.

On her personal stationery, Miss Robinson Smith drew up a letter dated June 18, 1934, which was sent to 150 representative people within this radius, inviting them to a meeting at her Stockbridge residence to hear Dr. Hadley outline his proposal.

> Dear Mrs. Taylor:
>
> I am sure you will agree with me that there are few things artistically more enchanting than listening to a beautiful symphony orchestra on a summer evening outdoors under the stars.
>
> Such an opportunity is being offered the Berkshires by Mr. Henry Hadley, our own American composer and conductor, provided we can interest the necessary audience. The plan is to have the concerts at the Hanna Farm on Route 41 between Stockbridge and Lenox on August 23, 25, and 26. The subscription prices covering the entire Festival of three concerts would be $5 and $3 depending on location. Mr. Hadley will bring an orchestra of sixty-four men from the New York Philharmonic Symphony Orchestra and hopes at two of the concerts to be able to have well-known soloists.
>
> As the concerts seem to be of great interest to our community, I am asking a representative woman from each locality to come to my house on Tuesday, June 26, at four o'clock to hear Mr. Hadley outline the plan. There will be no guarantee funds asked from anyone. If, after careful discussion, we all agree that we want the concerts, then we will organize to dispose of the moderately priced subscriptions to insure success.
>
> It is my privilege to have been asked by Mr. Hadley to present this idea to our community. I am more than happy to do so and I hope that you will be interested and able to come to the meeting on the 26th.

The response was most gratifying. Sixty-four men and women gathered at the first meeting, many quickly setting to work as chairmen in their own localities. An executive committee was elected to spearhead a drive for additional Festival support.

Mr. Mahanna continues his account.

Weekly report meetings were held. Men and women from all area towns traveled up and down the country, meeting the challenge to interest enough people to assure in advance the success of the concert series, tentatively planned for August 23, 25, and 26 at the Hanna Farm in Interlaken, between Stockbridge and Lenox.

The *Berkshire Evening Eagle*, published in Pittsfield, Massachusetts, the county seat, opened its columns from the start to the concert idea. Through some well-planned publicity, engineered by the newspaper's county editor, George W. Edman, now serving with the information service of the State Department, the Festival story began to reach home. His newspaper articles and press releases found their way into the pages of the metropolitan press and a few trickled into some magazines.

On the home front, the *Eagle* directed its editorials to the resort towns of Lenox and Stockbridge, the two communities that needed a new industry after the great depression in 1929 had left its mark on the area.

Encouraging letters began arriving and other cultural enterprises in the Berkshires began to lend their support. F. Cowles Strickland, then director of the Berkshire Playhouse at Stockbridge, and Ted Shawn, director of the Jacob's Pillow Dance Festival in Becket, offered their services.

Subscription teams were given until July 30, 1934, to show whether the Berkshire people would accept this project—symphony concerts out of doors.

"Every effort is being made to keep the concerts within the reach of everyone," echoed the workers in their jaunts through the village, towns, and cities of the Berkshire area. They addressed civic organizations, garden clubs, Granges, service groups like Rotary, Kiwanis, and the Lions, chambers of commerce, fraternal groups, and anyone who would listen to them. As an added inducement, they assured everyone that if the drive failed, the subscribers would be refunded their money.

An account was opened in the Housatonic National Bank at Stockbridge. Funds were received from neighboring communities, but the goal was a long way off. Estimated expenses for the first Festival concerts amounted to $11,420. Subscription prices, covering the series of three concerts, ran from $2.75 to $5.50; a limited number of tickets were offered for reserved seats at $7.50 for the three performances.

The million-dollar Hotel Aspinwall fire in Lenox in April 1931 had resulted in a heavy financial loss to the town and county. The owners of palatial estates in Stockbridge and Lenox had been economizing since the 1929 crash.

Some put their Rolls-Royce, Pierce-Arrow, and other luxurious limousines in dry storage. A few discharged their faithful and longtime chauffeurs and footmen, some of whom had been with them since the days before the horseless carriage. These were not the only employees on the great estates who began to feel the pinch. Skilled workmen, gardeners, laborers, and other employees in the area soon joined the army of the unemployed.

The biggest industries in Berkshire County like the General Electric Company in Pittsfield, the paper mills in Lee, the textile plants in Housatonic, Adams, North Adams, and Pittsfield, and a number of smaller manufacturers felt the pressure of the times. Relief rolls continued to mount in every section. There were no bread lines, but it was a gloomy picture.

The Berkshire Symphonic Festival idea was accepted in some sectors as a miracle. It gave new hope, new faith for the small businessmen and homeowners who were facing disaster.

Outdoor concerts by a huge symphony orchestra? That was something new for the Berkshires. Mrs. Elizabeth Sprague Coolidge, the fairy godmother of chamber music, had put Pittsfield on the musical map of the country with her chamber concerts at the South Mountain Music Temple, but an outdoor concert by a great symphony orchestra seemed to offer so much more to the cultural life of the Berkshires.

Knowing the Berkshire residents had to be sold to [*sic*] the Festival idea by giving them the opportunity to enjoy fine music out of doors, the *Berkshire Evening Eagle* on June 28, 1934, commented editorially on the plan.

Under the heading "Music Under the Moon," the *Eagle* editorial said:

> Anyone who was fortunate enough this spring to hear, either at Carnegie Hall or over the radio, the music of Richard Wagner—the love music from *Tristan* or the breathtaking conclusion of *Gotterdammerung*—as interpreted by the New York Philharmonic, under Maestro Arturo Toscanini, knows to what incomparable heights that great orchestra is capable of rising. And it seems almost too good to be true that members of the Philharmonic, conducted by Henry Hadley, frequent guest conductor of the Philharmonic Society in New York, will give concerts for three days beginning August 23 in Stockbridge.
>
> Wagner, Beethoven, Liszt, and the more modern European and American composers will be offered, so the taste of the oldsters, who are convinced that no music worth listening to has been written since Wagner laid down his pen in 1883, and the taste of the youngsters, who look with easy tolerance on the nineteenth century, but who, of course, cannot enthuse over anyone more antiquated than Richard Strauss, will both be satisfied.
>
> In recommending the summer concert season at the Lewisohn Stadium in New York, Lawrence Gilman, erudite critic of the *Herald Tribune*, says it should be relished especially by "those who enjoy listening to music in what Beethoven so delectably called an 'unbuttoned humor.'" What marvelous advantages will be given this 'unbuttoned humor' at Stockbridge! Not only will the concerts take place in an open-air amphitheatre

on the Dan R. Hanna estate, but all the lights will be turned off, allowing the listener unlimited opportunities for the flight of his imagination and the comfort of his body. The moon, by way of reassurance, will be full during the concerts.

Owen Johnson, who was close to the Roosevelt Administration, had succeeded in getting federal aid. The Civil Works Emergency Relief Administration agreed to provide labor to build the stage and shell for the orchestra and benches for the audience in a horse show ring on the Hanna Farm in Interlaken. (Once the home of Dan R. Hanna, son of U.S. Senator Mark Hanna, the property is now the Stockbridge School, a private institution.) [Later, it became the DeSisto School, which closed in 2004.]

Unemployed electricians, carpenters, plumbers, and laborers from Stockbridge, Lee, and Lenox were ready for the symphony concerts. Assisting Mr. Johnson with the work were two Stockbridge residents, Frank Reusch, who was named foreman, and Richard K. Thorsell, the ERA representative. . . .

Police, headed by Chief Walter Stannard, and firemen, under the direction of Chief Edward Pilling from Stockbridge, arrived early to assist state police in handling the traffic and parking. Program girls, dressed attractively in evening dresses, took their places at strategic spots in the horse show ring, eager to exhaust their supplies of concert material. Young men, wearing dark jackets and white trousers, manned their stations to usher ticket holders to their seats.

One by one the cars started to enter the makeshift parking lot, which only a few days before had been a favorite grazing ground for cows from nearby farms.

In the distance, early arrivals could hear the screeching of sirens. State police were opening the way to the Festival grounds for the chief executive of the Commonwealth, Governor Joseph B. Ely, and Mrs. Ely. From another direction, police furnished an escort for United States Ambassador-at-Large Norman Davis and Mrs. Davis from their estate on Prospect Hill in Stockbridge (now the Indian Hill Music Workshop).

Soon the pattern began to take shape. The serious-minded music lovers selected choice seats toward the middle of the outdoor concert hall; the more curious either sat in the front section, where they could watch every movement of the conductor, or walked aimlessly about to get a glimpse of the notables. A few were intrigued with the glistening jewels and gowns of many of the wealthy with whom they were rubbing elbows.

The weatherman had been kind. Shining brightly above the amphitheater was the moon, full in all its splendor. The sponsors had made good their promise of "Music Under the Moon."

When Dr. Hadley lifted his baton to open the first performance with Berlioz's "Overture," *Carnaval Romain*, there were close to 3,000 persons in the audience. Many had never listened to a symphony concert, except over the radio or on recordings, but they were a serious, intent crowd. Some applauded between movements, but the more experienced concertgoers tried to ignore the outbursts of well-meaning enthusiasm. It was a new experience for the Berkshire folk, but they seemed to like it. . . .

The fairy godmother of the South Mountain concerts may have been Elizabeth Sprague Coolidge, but the principle motivating force behind the Berkshire Symphonic Festival was Gertrude Robinson Smith.

A Berkshire Magazine [now defunct] profile of her by Alessandra Bianchi gave an interesting appraisal of Miss Robinson Smith from the feminist vantage point of the late twentieth century.

Robinson Smith—she always used both names, to avoid confusion with the mere "Smiths"—had by this time devoted a good deal of her life to realizing dreams and, at fifty-three, she needed a new project. . . .

The oldest child in a privileged household, Gertrude was exposed early to classical music and its makers. Frequent dinner guests at her mother's homes in New York and Paris included Gustav Mahler, soprano Emma Calvé, and pianist Nadia Boulanger (with whom Robinson Smith maintained a lifelong correspondence). But those factors alone did not create Tanglewood: that task required toughness, tenacity, and business acumen, qualities women were not supposed to have during her day but which Gertrude possessed in more than full measure.

Her nephew David Stowe, now seventy-three, remembers Robinson Smith as a woman who prided herself on what he calls her "mannish skills" and welcomed every opportunity to demonstrate them. Stowe recalls his aunt livening up a particularly "dull Sunday luncheon" by inviting all the young boys in attendance onto the lawn, where she demonstrated her curveball, which she said she picked up "playing ball on the sandlots" in Brooklyn as a young girl. His aunt was also a good auto mechanic, Stowe says, who once took apart her 1913 Buick roadster on the residence lawn and put it back together on a dare from her New York City pals. . . .

David Stowe's younger brother, Robinson Beecher Stowe, speculates that if his aunt were alive today "she'd be president of General Motors." [Thomas D.] Perry, formerly of the BSO and now retired in West Stockbridge, worked with Robinson Smith for years and likens her to "a cannonball in both appearance and personality."

Amy Bess Miller, who met Robinson Smith in the early 1930s, agrees with the cannonball moniker, but said her friend also "had a very sweet side when you broke into it." She recalls the time Robinson Smith arrived early at a coming-out party for Miller's daughter, an outdoor tea, and sat politely in her car because she had arrived too early.

Miller, whose husband Lawrence "Pete" Miller worked closely with Robinson Smith by providing the support of his newspaper, the *Eagle*, sums up her managerial style: "If you were working with her, as my husband was, she kept you up to date on all the ins and outs. I mean she really was a great leader and chairmadame, a near genius in the way she manipulated things. She had a real instinct for people who could help her. . . .

Robinson Smith wrote a letter to George Edman, a leading trustee and clerk of the Berkshire Music Festival, that leaves little doubt as to her organizational abilities, not to mention her tenacity.

This is just a hurried note to tell you of my immediate plans.

First of all, I am going to Boston on Tuesday and will be spending the night with Mrs. Harold Russell, 685 Chestnut Hill, Brookline, telephone: Longwood 2654. On Wednesday, I will try to see the publicity man for the New England Council as I have been in touch here in New York with Mr. Underhill of Batten, Barton, Durstine & Osborne, and he thinks there is a very good chance and every reason why they should advertise the Festival in their newspaper advertising as well as in their broadcasts. I may also try to see some of the newspapermen again—particularly our friend Moses Smith [for many years music critic of the *Boston Evening Transcript* and later a biographer of Serge Koussevitzky].

In the afternoon I shall go to the reception being given for the friends of the Boston Symphony Orchestra. Olin Downes [chief music critic of the *New York Times*] is to be the guest of honor. On this occasion I shall have the opportunity of meeting some of the trustees. Mr. Judd is very anxious that I should be there and hopes that the personal contact will make things even more pleasant than they are at the present time.

The chances are that I will dine with Dr. and Mrs. Koussevitzky and I understand that Olin Downes will also be there. Mr. Judd is very anxious that we should put over a plan that Dr. Koussevitzky has in mind connected with Olin Downes. I shall, of course, know more of this after Wednesday evening and it is, naturally, one of the things I want to discuss with you in detail.

On Thursday morning, I shall go to the rehearsal of the orchestra and then go to Stockbridge, where I plan being for several days. I am sorry Mr. Lynch will not be there, but I think it is of vital importance that you and I should have a long conference. I will keep time in Stockbridge free until I hear when we can get together. If agreeable, I would suggest that you come over to my place on Friday afternoon and remain for dinner so we can have a long, quiet talk. If Mrs. Edman felt well enough to come, you know how glad I would be to have her also.

Will you try to line up information regarding all the various problems that we will have to discuss such as buses, hotels, etc., etc.? What hope is there of the Berkshire Hills conference doing anything for us? As I have not very much time just now, would you be good enough to telephone to Elizabeth and ask her to get up a complete detailed report of everything in the office for me? I shall probably try to see her Friday morning.

Dr. Koussevitzky played the second Sibelius symphony last night. It was magnificent and I am sure it will carry our public off its feet. Perhaps you will have time to write me a line here before I leave—otherwise, you can get me in care of Mrs. Russell.

With all good wishes to you both, believe me,
G. R. S.

As this letter makes apparent, after its second year Henry Hadley had given up conducting the Berkshire Symphonic Festival's orchestra due to failing health and a certain dissatisfaction amongst the more sophisticated Berkshire concertgoers with his rather ordinary conducting and music programming.

Before Koussevitzky was hired, however, another conductor was approached to take Hadley's place. Johanna Fiedler, author of Papa, the Pops and Me, *lets us in on a little secret.*

In 1936, a much more substantial and tantalizing project was proposed to Papa. A group of affluent music lovers from both Boston and New York approached him with the idea of starting a summer music festival in the Berkshires. There already existed a modest series of concerts in Stockbridge, Massachusetts, and the local summer residents had been impressed by the success of Papa's innovative Esplanade Concerts.

Nineteen thirty-six was the year that my father's own father and sisters left Berlin and moved to Boston. Papa, who had spent his summers in Europe up to this point, was delighted with the idea of a summer season in the Berkshires after the Esplanade Concerts ended. Since the orchestra in Stockbridge would be made up of Boston Symphony musicians, my father again went dutifully to the orchestra's management to clear the project in advance.

The management was quick to see the possibilities of this proposal, especially in extending the annual employment for the musicians. They told my father that their initial response was positive but asked that, as a matter of courtesy, the project first be presented to Koussevitzky. No one thought that the orchestra's music director would be the least bit interested in the Berkshire concerts. He always spent the summer in Europe and would seemingly have little interest in a rustic festival in western Massachusetts.

Koussevitzky was nothing if not unpredictable. Whether he knew that the proposal had first been made to my father and this fact influenced his decision is a matter of speculation, but he certainly saw signs that Europe was becoming unstable. Papa had already foreseen the Berkshire performances as much more traditionally classical concerts than the Pops or the Esplanade, but the Russian conductor considered this repertoire his bailiwick. Visions of an American Salzburg Festival seemed most appealing to Koussevitzky, and he decided to take over the Berkshire Festival himself, although even he could not have foretold the growth of what was to become Tanglewood. Of course Papa was disappointed at losing another opportunity to expand his repertoire, but he too didn't see the wider implications. He could not possibly have known that Tanglewood as it grew would not only be closed to him but would nearly destroy his beloved Esplanade Concerts.

When Serge Koussevitzky and the Boston Symphony were invited to replace the New York orchestra, a sea change was about to take place.

Olin Downes, the distinguished chief music critic of the New York Times *and, later on, a regular lecturer-in-residence at Tanglewood, reviewed the first Boston Symphony concert in the Berkshires on August 23, 1936, in a* New York Times *piece. Unlike Mr. Fiedler, Downes saw the future very clearly.*

The character of the performances given by Dr. Koussevitzky and his men were of a quality to set them wholly apart from any others the writer has heard at summer concerts in America. This was due to three things: to the presence of one of the two or three most distinguished conductors in the world, who gave of his very best; to the qualities of a celebrated symphony orchestra of the same rank, appearing as a unit for the first time outside its concert series of the winter series; and to the determination on the part of all concerned to spare no pains in preparing the kind of performances which usually are reserved for the climaxes of the winter season.

It should be added that the time is ripe in America for such a festival to be instituted. The public is ready for it. The resources are here, and returning prosperity will increase them. The nucleus of a very great artistic achievement is available in the form of the Boston Symphony Orchestra and its wholly exceptional leader. Furthermore, if this thing which can be done in the Berkshires is not done there, it soon will be undertaken somewhere else. There is very little doubt that in the next twenty-five years the significant advance in music will be in America. It only remains to be seen what particular places and what particular people will lead.

Years later, on August 18, 1974, in an article celebrating the one hundredth anniversary of Koussevitzky's birth, Harold C. Schonberg, another eminent music critic at the New York Times*, gave an astute analysis of why Koussevitzky was able to create such an outstanding institution as Tanglewood.*

The man was a force of nature. In the quarter century between 1925 and 1950, there were three superstar conductors active in America. Stokowski had the Philadelphia Orchestra and, during that period, other groups. Toscanini was active in New York, with the Philharmonic and then the NBC Symphony. Koussevitzky was in Boston; he had been named conductor in 1924.

Three more dissimilar conductors never existed. Toscanini was the literalist, the perfectionist, content to play a relatively limited repertory over and over again. Stokowski was the super-showman, always interested in effect, the virtuoso of virtuosos, the electrifying magician who also tried to pull his audiences into the twentieth century. But neither Toscanini nor Stokowski came anywhere near making Koussevitzky's impact on the development of music in the United States.

For it was Koussevitzky who nourished the emergent American school—the then new and, often, avant-garde American composer. Copland, [Roy] Harris, [Walter] Piston, [Samuel] Barber, [William] Schuman, [Howard] Hanson, and dozens of others were Koussevitzky's pets. And while Stokowski and Toscanini did not teach, Koussevitzky gathered unto himself a brilliant group of baton wielders, including Leonard Bernstein, Lukas Foss, and Walter Hendl, and did his best to help them along.

It is not as though Koussevitzky was only an organizer and a pedagogue. He was as brilliant and exciting a conductor in his way as Stokowski and Toscanini were in theirs. His specialty was Russian and French music, and there he was unique. Who can ever forget the sight of Koussevitzky on the podium? His beat was the most amazing thing since the great days of Furtwängler. One wondered how his players ever achieved such unanimity in attack and release. There stood Koussevitzky, making those nervous-looking, trembling gestures, the prominent vein in his forehead beating away, his great orchestra achieving a mixture of color, power, and nuance that was unique to its conductor.

He represented a fairly free school of interpretation. In that, he was midway between Toscanini's objectivity and Stokowski's egocentricity. He was an extraordinary colorist. His Ravel and Debussy positively shimmered. And the personality he brought to Russian music! Nobody has conducted the Tchaikovsky symphonies, or some of the other Russians of whom he was so fond (he did great things with Rimsky-Korsakov's "Antar" Symphony), with an equivalent mixture of flexibility and imagination.

Some considered him a dilettante. He had started out as a double bass player (RCA Victor once brought out a private recording of Koussevitzky as bass soloist), married money, and bought himself an orchestra. There were some gaps in his musicianship. Everybody knew he was a poor score reader; it was no particular secret that a new score had to be played to him by a pianist until he had the contours in his ears. Musicians, who are apt to be snobbish, would talk about this behind his back. As if it made any difference! Koussevitzky was blessed with an extraordinary memory and an infallible ear. Once he had a piece of music in his mind, he had it for life. . . .

Koussevitzky left records too, and many of them are glorious. But he also has left a permanent memorial in Tanglewood that continues to carry on, year after year, the work that he started so many decades ago.

But let's return to the chronology of our story. At this point, Koussevitzky and the Boston have given one very impressive summer season in the Berkshires. So impressive, in fact, that Mrs. Gorham Brooks has donated Tanglewood, her summer estate overlooking the Stockbridge Bowl, to the Boston Symphony. According to writer Edmund Wilson, a frequent visitor to the Festival, Koussevitzky "received it with gracious thanks, but did not have any notion as to what it was proposed to give him. He had to go to Mr. George E. Judd, the manager of the orchestra. 'Tanglewood?' cried Mr. Judd. 'Every child knows what Tanglewood is!' and the present was accepted with alacrity."

That Mrs. Brooks did not give the estate to the Berkshire Symphonic Festival was a decision that would have grave repercussions in only a few years.

The orchestra no longer played under the moon, but was now sheltered by a tent, much to Koussevitzky's disgust. He was adamant that a permanent structure be built to house the concerts, a proposition, in his opinion, that the Berkshire Symphonic Festival was slow to address. He had already suggested to Robinson Smith that they retain his friend, Eliel Saarinen, the renowned Finnish architect and a mutual friend of Koussevitzky and Sibelius, to design the pavilion.

Miss Robinson Smith recognized early on that the fundraising efforts to build the Shed were being hampered by the hesitancy of the local Berkshire committee members, an opinion she expressed in a personal letter to George Judd, manager of the Boston Symphony, on October 27, 1936.

I did not telephone you yesterday because the meeting was too discouraging. It was of course suggested that I ask Dr. Koussevitzky for an extension of time, but I feared that even with two weeks more the businessmen wouldn't get much further. It was more than obvious that everyone wanted to have the Festival, and that they deeply appreciated Dr. Koussevitzky's interest and wanted to cooperate toward the fulfillment of his own dream—but the expressions from each and every one showed they thought the development of a Shed costing $100,000 for this second year was too great a jump.

They asked me if I thought he would be willing to hold the concerts another year in a tent, provided a proper stage could be constructed. This they thought would give them time to raise the necessary money before the third year. My answer was "positively not," and then I explained why it was that Dr. Koussevitzky wanted the Shed.

As you must realize, these businessmen of the Berkshires do not see things in the big way that many of us do, nor have they the habit of thinking and acting along imaginative lines.

All this is just to prepare you for what I think will be the inevitable answer of our executive committee on Saturday after we have received the report from the business men.

That I am heartbroken is putting it mildly, but this last statement is for you alone, and I'm sure you realize the cruel hurt it is to me to see a great institution headed by the greatest conductor and the most intelligent and clear-visioned of men go by the board.

Thank you for all you have done, and I will write you officially after the meeting on Saturday.

In fact, Koussevitzky had threatened to quit the Berkshire Symphonic Festival if he had to conduct another season under such primitive and acoustically imperfect conditions.

However, one evening during a concert, a fateful event occurred. Fortunately for us, Sylvia G. Dreyfus, a fledgling author and the wife of Boston publisher Carl Dreyfus—both old friends of the Koussevitzkys—wrote a contemporary account. Her explicit purpose was to create a permanent record to be placed in the archives of the Boston Symphony, where I found it. In the ensuing years, she published several magazine articles about the Festival.

I hope the Festival committee and, above all, Mr. Koussevitzky will forgive me when I say that the dominant memory of the 1937 season was the weather. And as the weather played such a decisive part in the development of the Festival, I dare say I shall be forgiven. You have all heard the story of the all-Wagner program and the storm. You know how the rain held off until the audience was assembled in the tent and, perhaps five minutes before eight-thirty, began to pour. There was thunder and lightning. Shortly after the scheduled starting time, K. took his place on the podium. The rain stopped. He raised his baton for the beginning of the *Rienzi* Overture and played a few bars. The downpour started again, steady, loud, resounding on the wet canvas top like drumbeats or machine-gun fire. K. stopped. A lull. He started again and managed to get through the overture; but with the opening measures of the *Siegfried Idyll* the rain began once more, a deluge.

With a gesture of despair, K. left the platform. For half an hour we awaited the pleasure of the storm. The audience began to get wet, and people kept shifting to different seats to escape the water, which dripped through the joints in the tent and through the holes around the great upright poles. Nobody could leave—the downpour was too heavy. Everyone was good-natured, including the conductor, who proved not only that he had an indomitable will but that he was really a good sport. Eventually he played all the noisier numbers (Wagner lovers, forgive me for the word *noisy*) regardless of the order of the program. You would be surprised to know how exciting the "Ride of the Valkyries" sounded against the elements that were really the appropriate setting for those dauntless ladies. The program ended with "Tristan und Isolde," instead of Tannhauser, but by that time the rain had stopped. The conductor was cheered to the skies that wept no longer.

Later that night, four or five of us were sitting in the deserted so-called bar of the Berkshire Hunt Club when K. stopped in to say good night to us. He was bedraggled and weary, but triumphant. "So," he said gaily, "here I am. You see, not fire nor water shall drive me out. *But* not again will I do this. I will not conduct here next year if there is no protection against storms. It is not fair to my orchestra. It is not fair to my audience. It is not fair to music."

During one of the many forced intermissions caused by the storm, Gertrude Robinson Smith took the stage and announced to the audience that "this storm has proved conclusively the need for a Shed. We must raise the $100,000 to build it!" Thirty thousand dollars were donated on the spot by the shivering, wet members of the audience.

The die was now cast and the Festival board forced into action. From the minutes of the BSF board meeting on February 24, 1937:

Mr. Edman: We have an invitation to send letters to every member of the Boston Symphony Orchestra board of trustees, asking them if they would not like to contribute to the building fund. There are several members of the board of trustees of the Boston Symphony Orchestra who might want to help.

Mr. [Philip Marshall] Brown: I suspect these people in Boston are waiting. They are a pretty canny lot.

Mr. Edman: I think they are waiting for us in the Berkshires to show a little initiative. As with a boy; if he shows initiative, you are willing to help him, but if he doesn't show initiative, you do not want to help him.

Miss Robinson Smith: I really think Mr. Dane [president of the BSO board of trustees] is awfully interested. If we show any initiative at all, I shouldn't be a bit surprised if Mr. Dane did something. I think he is very vitally interested in it. . . . I believe it is going to be a pretty fine building, isn't it?

Mr. Edman: Yes. Last December I went west with the Boston Symphony Orchestra, with Dr. Koussevitzky and Mr. Judd, to Bloomfield Hills, Michigan, to see Mr. Saarinen, who is head of the Cranbrook Academy of Art. He and Dr. Koussevitzky are friends and were mutual friends of Sibelius. His name is international. He was the architect for that great development for which Mr. Booth gave $10 million. It is a beautiful layout—modern art, but beautiful. He came east and spent a day with Mr. Judd and Mr. Lynch and me and we went over Tanglewood. The minute he struck that section of Berkshire County he said, "What we must do here is something entirely in keeping with the New England atmosphere, something that will be beautiful, something that seems to belong here." Of course he is working on something of a permanent nature. However, just because he submits a drawing is no reason why we should accept it. We are not bound to him.

Mrs. [John Bross] Lloyd: Don't you think a man of his reputation would give us something very nice?

Mr. Edman: Yes. However, we should not be so gullible as to say, just because he is a famous man, that we should take anything he proposes.

Eliel Saarinen did give them something nice. In fact, it was so nice that it exceeded the expected costs and had to be modified by an addition of three interior columns to hold up the structure, which was designed by Joseph Franz, a local engineer and a member of the Festival board. The architect was understandably upset by the changes to his plan and told Robinson Smith so in this letter of March 21, 1938.

After all the controversies that have happened since then [over the placement of the Shed, the architect's fees, and—most importantly—the anticipated budget of $300,000], I am more than glad to have been forced out of a picture which, contrary to my advice, has developed to all but me architecturally satisfactory. My sincere wish, therefore, is to be in any way free from the whole affair, even as concerns money due to me. Accordingly, I have not included in my bill any compensation for the latter part of the work. . . .

I am sorry to have to write this letter. I hoped that the finale had been as harmonious as was the prelude, in spite of the many discords in the central movement.

At this point, I would like to dispute a popular anecdote often told at Tanglewood. When Koussevitzky heard about the changes to be made in the Saarinen design, he derisively hypothesized that the structure would only be "a Shed!" (Sometimes Saarinen gets the credit for this remark.)

However, charming though this story might be, the building seems always to be referred to as the Shed from the very start. Think back to Miss Robinson Smith's little speech during the storm.

According to Moses Smith in his biography Koussevitzky, *the maestro was pleased with the acoustical results.*

I remember Koussevitzky's first inspection of the Shed. On a day in June a party of us drove to Tanglewood from Boston—Koussevitzky; George E. Judd, manager of the orchestra; John Burk, the orchestra's program annotator; and myself. The first sight of the Shed was breathtaking: the structure was boldly conceived and boldly executed. Koussevitzky made rudimentary tests of the acoustics, clapping his hands at different locations, shouting and singing from the stage, as the rest of us listened at different points and then compared notes with him. When his turn to listen came I went onstage and began to whistle the opening theme of the Fourth Symphony of Brahms. "Out of tune!" yelled Koussevitzky promptly in the role not of conductor but of critic.

On the whole he seemed satisfied. He grumbled a little, though, at the hardheaded economy of the Berkshire-ites. Saarinen's original plan had been that the huge roof of the Shed be supported entirely from the sides, so that no posts would interfere with the view of the stage. The plan had been changed so that a row of steel pillars ran across the middle of the "auditorium." In an aside Koussevitzky snorted, "Money! They save $25,000 and spoil the Shed."

It was clear that the Shed had admirable, almost miraculous, acoustical properties. The lack of reflecting walls at the side and in back did not seem to affect the orchestra's characteristic resonance. Sometimes the sound seemed even better than at Symphony Hall. It carried well, also, to the clusters of people on the grass beyond the Shed. The crowds were so well behaved that even in later years, when the lawns were covered thick with people, a listener, sitting on the porch of the main Tanglewood house a couple of hundred yards away, could usually hear the faintest orchestral passages.

At the inaugural concert Koussevitzky made one of his characteristic little speeches. "I have selected Beethoven's Ninth Symphony," he said, "not only because it is the greatest masterpiece in musical literature, but because I wanted to hear the voice of Tanglewood singing Schiller's words calling all nations to the brotherhood of man."

With the Munich conference only two months away, he could hardly have chosen his words better.

Mrs. Dreyfus also reported on the Shed.

It is quite an achievement to seat 5,700 people safely under cover but out of doors. And you never for a moment lose that out-of-doors feeling, because the colonnade is so high and the openings so unobstructed and simply framed that they form a series of pictures wherever you look. The great trees, none of them, fortunately, damaged by the hurricane, surround the Shed with beauty. The grounds, with their lovely, ordered informality and broad vistas, are an integral part of the whole effect. . . .

K. likes the sonority of music played out of doors. The sound flows out into the open and doesn't come back, he says, and he feels this strongly when conducting. He told me once that he had come to the conclusion that it is the classical music which sounds best in the open—Mozart and the Beethoven "Apollonic" [music], for example, sound better than the romantics. . . .

When we arrived in Lenox for the 1938 Festival, the new building was ready. A visitor from the west remarked that he could not understand the temperament of the New Englander: sometimes he goes in for exaggeration, sometimes for understatement. How reconcile the facts that at South Mountain they call a barn a "temple of music" and at Tanglewood they call a temple a "shed."

Tanglewood itself was nothing if not socially forward-thinking. Under Koussevitzky and at a time when it was far from fashionable to do so—political correctness being far off in the future—women and minorities were always part of the performing, composing, and conducting scene at Tanglewood.

Nineteen thirty-eight brought with it the dramatic discovery of soprano Dorothy Maynor. At the peak of her career, she was one of the most sought-after and well-paid singers in symphonic and recital concerts. She appeared frequently on radio, and her recordings were best-sellers. Unfortunately, on account of her skin color, she never had the opportunity of performing on the opera stage, something she very much regretted. Mrs. Dreyfus, our faithful recorder, published an article about her in Liberty Magazine. I first saw her name in the lower left-hand corner of an invitation card in the spring of 1938 when Mrs. Gorham Brooks of Boston gave a small Sunday evening party "to hear Dorothy Maynor." Somebody had told me she was a Negro singer.

Her appearance that night was unprepossessing. She was short, dark, heavy, and badly dressed. But as soon as she began to sing we were attracted by her expressive eyes and beautiful mouth, a small, well-shaped mouth with a winning smile. The voice that poured forth from those lips swept me off my feet. Though her singing had not then reached its present beauty, I could not fail to recognize its potential greatness. But I did not believe that she could overcome the disadvantage of color and appearance and achieve an important place on the concert stage. Was there room for two Negro women singers? Could even this wonderful voice compete with Marian Anderson's talent, beauty, and popularity? . . .

Then she struck a gold mine of free publicity that could never have been planned or bought and which blazed her name across the continent. For a year her friends had tried to arrange an audition with Serge Koussevitzky, conductor of the Boston Symphony Orchestra. Last summer, while Koussevitzky was at Lenox for the Berkshire Festival, Mrs. Gorham Brooks wrote to ask if he could possibly find time to hear Dorothy. Mrs. Brooks is a personal friend of the Koussevitzkys; she is, moreover, the woman who presented her beautiful Lenox estate to the Boston Symphony as a permanent home for the Berkshire Festival. And she was tremendously enthusiastic about Dorothy's voice.

The audition took place on a hot Tuesday morning. Koussevitzky was tired. After a two-hour rehearsal he had had to listen to double-bass tryouts. The musicians had wandered off to rest and smoke. The huge Shed was empty. Dorothy stepped to the front of the stage and began, "O Sleep, why dost thou leave me?" from Handel's *Semele.* Mrs. Brooks, who was sitting directly behind Koussevitzky, saw him stiffen to attention. Then, as the song went on, she could see the back of his neck growing redder and redder with excitement. "Marvelous! Marvelous!" he exclaimed, and asked for more.

Then he declared, "The whole world must hear her!"—and made a start by asking her to sing at the picnic he was giving next day for the men of the orchestra.

The picnic was the second stroke of luck. The only professional critic present that afternoon was Noel Strauss of the *New York Times*, who on Thursday morning startled the music world out of its summer somnolence with a full column on Koussevitzky's "discovery," the sensational Negro soprano Dorothy Maynor. The Associated Press seized the story and spread it across the country. Before noon that day the big New York managers were telephoning frantic messages to Lenox offering contracts to Dorothy.

Three months later Dorothy Maynor made her debut at Town Hall before a house that had been sold out for weeks. "Everybody" was there. Never, since the debuts of Galli-Curci and of Heifetz had there been such excitement. At the end of the recital, crowds of people, white and black alike, rushed to the stage to kiss her. Since then she has sung with four major symphony orchestras, the Philharmonic, the Philadelphia, the Chicago, and the Boston. The whole of next season is heavily booked. And in August of this year, just a year after her audition in the empty Shed at Tanglewood, Dorothy Maynor appeared before an audience of 9,500 as one of the most brilliant features of the Berkshire Festival.

In its own inimitable way, the New Yorker *magazine also gave Tanglewood its seal of approval. The Talk of the Town paid a visit in August 1938.*

I was a shade suspicious of the Festival beforehand, for visitors had been talking about the event as some itinerants used to carry on about Salzburg. Everything proved to be okay, however, the only demurrer being that apparently somebody threw several bags of mosquitoes into the general vicinity of the audience. The Boston Symphony, led by Dr. Serge Koussevitzky, played with all of the accurate sonority that it reveals in Carnegie Hall, and the music Shed is one of the best concert places in the country. . . .

You can buy refreshments, printed music, and phonograph records on the lot, and cigarettes from pretty cigarette girls who don't expect tips. Almost everybody associated with the operation of the concerts is a volunteer, and volunteering is so popular in the Berkshires that there's always an amiable usher ready to escort you to the right seat, while your car will be parked with éclat by a member of the American Legion. . . .

If you're tempted to see and hear for yourself what happens in Tanglewood, two concerts are scheduled for this weekend. (Saturday evening, August 13, and the next afternoon). Rain won't make any difference. They have arranged the Shed so that the music comes out and the rain doesn't get in.

The Festival was indeed launched. Now what did Koussevitzky have up his sleeve?

And the great Koussevitzky was standing here talking to us. He was talking about commitment—commitment to art, devotion to music, dedication to one's work.

It was an "inspirational" kind of speech, full of phrases that I suppose today would be smiled at as old-fashioned clichés. Does anyone speak of "dedication" anymore, or "commitment?" Does one dare, in 1970, to speak of "values" or of "virtues" such as hard work, faith, mutual understanding, *patience*?

Well, the answer is yes; one does dare.

—Leonard Bernstein

CHAPTER 2

Koussevitzky's Dream

Early Days at the Berkshire Music Center

Koussevitzky was one of the most esteemed conductors of his time. Known for his impassioned symphonic interpretations, his charismatic posture on and off the podium, and his taste for the newest in music, who would have thought that one of his most cherished ambitions would be to start a school?

Not just a conservatory, but, as Aaron Copland would later describe it so perfectly . . .

. . . a summer school under the aegis of a symphony orchestra. No one had ever before heard of such a thing. But it was the dream of our former director to find some tangible way for the older and more experienced musicians to pass on a lifetime of experience to the young aspirant. Here talented young musicians might gather to engage in all kinds of ensemble playing and singing. Their very presence was to act as a stimulus among themselves and also to their teachers. Before long the plan was enlarged to include the departments of opera production, composition, and the study of the art of conducting. Beyond this—and here was a special love of Dr. Koussevitzky—a division of the school was to be set up for the musical enthusiast who wanted to spend a summer of "living and working in music."

But before he could realize his dream, Koussevitzky first had to convince the Boston Symphony trustees, not famous for undertaking risky and expensive educational ventures, that their orchestra had an obligation to the future of music in America. This 1939 speech, "Vision of a Music Center," was Koussevitzky's official communication to them of his plans.

Throughout my life I have envisioned the establishment of a great music and art center in the world. The United States of America can and are destined to have such a center. American freedom is the best soil for it. Rapid growth of American culture dictates its necessity, as a crowning peak of its unfolding, as a historical mission and perennial contribution of America to human art and culture.

We contemplate to establish an academy of music and art as a permanent institution. It has to be a creative musical center where the greatest living composers will teach the art of composition; the greatest virtuosi, the art of perfect performance and technique; the greatest conductors, the mystery of conducting orchestras and choruses. The most eminent thinkers and scholars will be teaching there, each in his field so far as it concerns art and music: musicologists; art psychologists and sociologists; art historians and philosophers. A free cooperation of such an elite shall certainly result in the creation of new and great values of art; in the radiation of the beams of high culture over a nation and the whole world; and finally in the education and training of a new generation of American artists. . . .

Such an institution will be, no doubt, unique and far greater than any similar institutions existing.

The central idea of our short summer work will be *interpretation*. You know that the art of interpretation is still very young. To attain perfection in interpretation will be our special aim. . . .

Our problem is to help artists with good training and knowledge to acquire a penetrating and vivid conception of the music they interpret; to stir their imagination to new heights and new depths, because imagination evokes in the interpreter the right intuition and emotions to conceive the inner meaning of the score and to reveal the emotion of the composer.

We want to be modest in our promises, but by no means do we want to be modest in our aspirations. We are confident that our students will receive the very best of our ability and practical experience, as well as our spiritual guidance.

The Boston Symphony trustees—albeit, somewhat reluctantly—went along with Koussevitzky's plan. However, one trustee, Jerome D. Greene, was a particular enthusiast. He went out of his way to secure a grant of $60,000 from the Rockefeller Foundation, where his friend, Raymond B. Fosdick, was president. A big infusion of money from the foundation would, Greene reasoned, go a long way to solidly establish the school in its initial two years.

Dr. David H. Stevens was the foundation's program officer, who shepherded the funding through the hierarchy. His November 15, 1939, report to Mr. Fosdick would prove prescient in its understanding of the coming importance of Koussevitzky's dream.

Re: Berkshire Music Festival and School

Mr. Judd, manager, and director Koussevitzky of the Boston Symphony Orchestra have gone far in establishing a plan for a six-week school in connection with the Berkshire Music Festival. They have been ably assisted by Mr. Jerome Greene, one of the trustees of the symphony. The symphony organization proposes to accept responsibility for the school and to recruit directors and lecturers from Harvard University and from New York City. . . .

Counted important that at least three schools (Juilliard, Curtis, and Eastman) endorse the plan heartily as outlet for their better students and graduates. The preliminary canvass produced 250 inquiries. It is sure that not less than that number will be available, and rigid selection probably would be needed in two or three years to keep the enrollment at 400. . . .

The director [Koussevitzky] has recognized American composers to a degree found nowhere else in the country. The last pages of the attached announcement for 1939–40 have a record of works by American composers given first productions by the symphony since October 1924. The concerts in New York this coming week are wholly American. The Negro singer Miss (Dorothy) Maynor, making her debut on November 19 at Town Hall, owes her advance into public notice entirely to the director. She was one of a large number given auditions during the Festival season of 1939, and this autumn sang in Boston under symphony sponsorship.

The director has unqualified enthusiasm over the present position of American music in its creative phases of growth. He says that this country not only is the only one with life but is at the peak of a growing power in creative writing and production. He of course would give prestige to the school and would devote all his energies to it. Undoubtedly as the time comes for division of his burden during the regular season, he will put more time on the summer plans and on constant advice to younger writers and directors. . . .

This is true also of the younger directors [i.e., student conductors], who will have personal instruction by Koussevitzky and a chance to direct under his observation.

The hope of the persons behind the plan is for at least two years of backing at the level of $25,000 a year. Then the plan would be scrutinized to see whether a tapering grant is essential.

Mr. Greene sent his own pitch letter to the foundation on November 17.

Mr. Judd has sent me a copy of his letter containing the formidable list of documents with which you have been supplied. I do hope that Raymond Fosdick, and the officers generally, will feel that our plans for the Berkshire Music Center present a really strategic opportunity for a splendid reinforcement not only of the growing interest in music, which is such a remarkable phenomenon, but also of our efforts to identify that movement with the highest standards of the art.

Excellency in any art must always be comparatively rare, but the existence of standards may mean all the difference between a popular and contented mediocrity and the constant struggle for excellence which art should inspire. The encouragement of young composers and the creation of a Koussevitzky school of picked conductors will also provide indispensable elements of musical progress.

Fortunately, Dr. Koussevitzky does not himself embody Lowell's "certain condescension in foreigners." Perhaps he is too sanguine, but how much greater his influence will be on young musicians if his work is inspired by optimism, rather than by conceiving his task as that of teaching the elements of civilization to American barbarians.

I am happy to report, and this is really the only excuse for my present effusion, which adds nothing to what you already know of our plans and hopes, that the trustees of the Berkshire Festival, at their meeting this week, voted to accept the three weeks' Festival with continued responsibility for financing that part of our program under the present contract. The resulting combination of Boston Symphony control of the entire program with civic interest and responsibility in promoting attendance seems to me to ensure the two complementary elements of cooperation that an enterprise of this kind ought to have.

July 8, 1940—the great day had arrived. The formal Opening Exercises of the Berkshire Music Center were held that afternoon in the Shed. Koussevitzky's moving speech to the assembled students and dignitaries reflected not only the idealistic spirit that was going to play such a crucial role at the Center, but underlining this spirit was the chilling fear of what Hitler's rampage across Europe would mean for Western culture.

The creation of a music center in America becomes more significant in these days than in any other time. For, indeed, so long as culture and art exist, there is hope for humanity; and all those who believe in the values and inheritance of culture and art should stand in the front rank. If there ever was a time to speak of music, it is now, in the New World.

Therefore, our feeling of appreciation and gratitude goes to the board of trustees of the Boston Symphony Orchestra, and especially to Mr. Dane, our president, for their deep understanding of the significance of a music center in America, and for helping to materialize the idea.

It is easier to conceive an idea than to bring it to existence. My vision of a music center is of long standing. In 1913 and '14, in a quiet, residential part of Moscow, I first contemplated a center of every branch of musical art. The assistance of great artists and brilliant minds of that epoch had been secured. Then came the world war and the Russian Revolution of 1917.

Only in America, many years later, when I became conductor of the Boston Symphony Orchestra, did I return to my lifelong dream. I felt that a music center in this country was not only possible, but definitely, absolutely necessary.

So the question was, how could it be materialized?

The first hope came in 1929, when I was asked by Mrs. Eugene Meyer to start a music and educational center in White Plains, New York, but the Depression set in, bringing a final stop to all further plans.

In 1936, Miss Robinson Smith, president of the Berkshire Music Festival, asked the Boston Symphony Orchestra and myself to participate in their summer Festival. I explained to Miss Robinson Smith that my idea was to create a great music festival of a national, and even international scope. Our first Festival was started; and a year later, Mrs. Gorham Brooks offered her beautiful family estate Tanglewood as a permanent home for the Festival.

It is then and there that my dream of a music center was revived.

At a meeting with the trustees of the Boston Symphony Orchestra, I spoke of my vision of a music center, its meaning in American life, and its influence on the arts and culture of this country. I shall never forget the words said by our president, Mr. Dane, when I unfolded my plan: "Go ahead—we cannot afford to lose it."

The support of the president and trustees of the Boston Symphony Orchestra; the support of the Rockefeller and Carnegie foundations, ASCAP, and other great American institutions proves the national significance of our undertaking.

Today, the ground is set and we lay the cornerstone of the Berkshire Music Center. I look into its future with faith and confidence.

My faith is justified because the leading forces of the musical world have joined our faculty. I am happy to present: Mr. [G. Wallace] Woodworth, Paul Hindemith, Olin Downes, Mr. [Aaron] Copland, Dr. [Herbert] Graf, Mr. [Richard] Burgin, Mr. Abram Chasins, Mr. [Stanley] Chapple; Mr. Holmes, Mr. [Georges] Laurent, Mr. [Fernand] Gillet, Mr. [Victor] Polatschek, Mr. [Georges] Mager, Mr. [Jean] Lefranc, Mr. [Jean] Bedetti, Mr. [Georges] Moleux, Mr. [Raymond] Allard, Mr. [Willem] Valkenier, Mr. [Jacob] Raichman, Mr. Bernard Zighera, Mr. [Jesús Maria] Sanromá, [all first-desk players of the orchestra] and Mr. E. Power Biggs [organist], and [Roman] Szulc.

My confidence is also justified by the splendid work on the part of our collaborators. I want to thank Mr. [George] Judd, our manager, for his invaluable assistance, and Dr. Margaret Grant, secretary of the Center, for her devotion to our common tasks and ideals.

As I have stated before, we want to be modest in our promises, but by no means do we want to be modest in our aspirations.

We feel it our duty to hand down the old treasures of Musical Culture to American Youth. Enriched by this culture, the young people of America will carry it further to new achievement.

After Dr. Koussevitzky's speech, the students and faculty made music together for the first time. Randall Thompson's Alleluia *had been especially composed for the occasion and to this day remains a revered Tanglewood tradition, sung at the end of every Berkshire Music Center Opening Exercises.*

G. Wallace Woodworth, conductor of choral music at Harvard and lecturer for many years at the Berkshire Music Center, described the proceedings in a 1948 Tanglewood program note.

When Dr. Koussevitzky was arranging for the Opening Exercises of the first summer of the Berkshire Music Center, he turned to Randall Thompson for a new choral work, written especially for the occasion.

In May or early June of 1940, Dr. Koussevitzky and I met to discuss the program for the formal Opening Exercises of the first session of the Berkshire Music Center. Clearly there would be speeches and an inaugural address by the director—but what about music? I suggested a classical overture or symphony by the twenty or thirty faculty members from the Boston Symphony Orchestra. "No," said Dr. Koussevitzky. "The whole school must participate, every member—it is their own opening session."

I suggested two or three of the noblest Bach chorales as fitting and, above all, practicable for the occasion. But I had not reckoned with Dr. Koussevitzky's imagination. "Bach would be fine, but we are an *American* music center, and a new one! We must have a new work, especially for the occasion. I will ask Randall Thompson." With only three weeks to write the music, Mr. Thompson accepted.

On Saturday, forty-eight hours before the formal opening, we had not heard from Thompson nor seen the music. Mr. Judd telephoned to Philadelphia; Thompson assured us that the score had just been printed and that three hundred copies would arrive in Lenox Monday morning.

At two o'clock on Monday afternoon the students assembled for the first time. In the corner of the barn I had secreted our collection of Bach chorales, for one mail after another had arrived at the Lenox post office during the morning without the package from Philadelphia. But at just five minutes before two, Mr. Judd came in with the music. I tried it over once on the piano, and the chorus of 250, assembled from all over our country for the first time, went to work. By two forty-five it was time to go to the Shed for the Exercises, and at three-thirty we had given the first performance of a work which has been heard hundreds of times in choral concerts from Boston to San Francisco. So sure was Thompson's technique, so expert his craftsmanship, and so masterly his grasp of the true genius of choral singing, that despite a blueprint of unique limitations, he had created one of the noblest pieces of choral music in the twentieth century.

Randall Thompson gave his own account of the Berkshire Music Center in this letter to his friends, the composer Douglas Moore and his wife, while on vacation in Encampment, Wyoming.

If I was one day late in visiting you, it was as nothing compared to the time I have taken to send you formal thanks for a lovely visit. Without that all-too-brief interlude I doubt whether I'd have pulled through the past month. I felt sorry for Douglas, with a movie score to write under such pressure, and no sooner did I get back to Phila. than a similar pressure descended on me. Thank heavens for the breather with you two.

First Wallenstein rang up and wanted an orchestral score for *Americana*. Then Koussevitzky sent word he'd like a choral piece for the Opening Exercises of the Berkshire Music Center. *Americana* ran to sixty-five pages of scoring. Than I saw Margaret and three of the children off for Wyoming, went home, and began the choral piece. It had to be of a kind that would fit a solemn occasion, and that could be performed after one rehearsal on the first day of the school. I enclose a copy of what I turned out.

On July 5, I turned the piece over to the lithographer and left for a long weekend at the Reiners' in Westport. I then returned to Bryn Mawr long enough to close the house and get Varney and head for the Berkshires. There I gave five lectures and fell swooning onto the train for the West!

The Music Center is truly marvelous—heavenly country and such a fine group of students and teachers. I was there the first week but already the place had such spirit and atmosphere. Most congenial, and stimulating to a degree. My *Alleluia* had been sung to perfection at the Opening Exercises, so my entrance into the place two days later was not so awkward as it might have been. I went to several of the institute ("professional" students) orchestra rehearsals, which gave its first concert on Friday night of the first week, opening (if you please) with a certain E minor Symph. led by Leonard Bernstein, a student from CIM [Curtis Institute of Music]. I confess I enjoyed this privilege because it was really a fine performance. Most of all I relished watching Koussevitzky sit directly behind the student conductors at all rehearsals, criticizing them at every turn. He has proved himself a fine teacher and—still more surprising—a most skillful administrator of the school. His outlook is very broad, and he seeks at every turn to do equal justice to the professional and nonprofessional students. There is no doubt in my mind that he has come out with a permanent institution of the greatest value and importance. It preserved the best in Mr. Surette's Summer School, with an added plus of a fine performing group, the presence of members of the BSO, and facilities of all kinds—little operas, masques, plays, large choral works, and a situation that is simply beautiful. You must go up, and so must the Giddings.

Enough. How did the movie music turn out? . . .

The school had begun. And Koussevitzky turned out to be a dedicated and inspiring teacher. His most famous pupil was Leonard Bernstein, who wrote this rave review in a letter to his family in Sharon, Massachusetts.

Dearest Folks,

I have never seen such a beautiful setup in my life. I've been conducting the orchestra every morning and I'm playing my first concert tomorrow night. Kouss gave me the hardest and longest number of all—the Second Symphony of Randall Thompson, thirty minutes long, a modern American work—as my first performance. And Kouss is so pleased with my work. He likes me and works very hard with me in our private sessions. He is the most marvelous man—a beautiful spirit that never lags or fails—that inspires me terrifically. And he told me he is convinced that I have a wonderful gift, and he is already making me a *great* conductor. (I actually rode in his car with him today!) He has wonderful teaching ability, which I never expected, and is very hard to please, so that when he says he is pleased, I know it means something. I am so thrilled—have never been more happy and satisfied. The orchestra likes me very much, best of all the conductors, and responds so beautifully in rehearsal. Of course, the concert tomorrow night (Shabbas, yet!) will tell whether I can keep my head in performance. We've been working very hard—you're always going like mad here, no time to think of how tired you are or how little you slept last night. The inspiration of this Center is terrific enough to keep you going with no sleep at all. I'm so excited about tomorrow night. I wish you could all be here—it's so important to me, and Kouss is banking on it to convince him that he's right. If it goes well, there's no telling what may happen. . . .

Please come up—I think I'll be conducting every Friday night and rehearsing every morning—please come up. . . .

All my love,
Lenny

Lenny remembered more about conducting the Thompson symphony in a remarkable verbatim interview with Herbert Kupferberg published in his book Tanglewood.

I remember that first week I was up here, very confused, not knowing what to do, never having conducted an orchestra at all, and there was this beautiful student-conductor orchestra ready to be conducted. I was very nervous, as I can tell you. I thought maybe I could get through *The Afternoon of a Faun* with some luck, or something like that. But he announced to me the first day that I would have to conduct Randall Thompson's Second Symphony, because Randall Thompson was up here then, having just written that famous *Alleluia* for the Opening Exercises, which has been sung every year since. And Randall was somebody I had been studying with at Curtis. And I'd studied orchestration with him at Curtis that same year I was with [Fritz] Reiner. Koussy said: "But how apropos! Of course you must conduct Randall's Second Symphony!" And I said, "All of it? All four movements?" And he said, "*All* of it." And I said, "When?" He said, "Well, Friday night. This is Monday—you have rehearsals Tuesday, Wednesday, Thursday." Just like that!

So I got hold of a score and went into the bushes somewhere and studied till I was blue in the face. The next day I had my first rehearsal with Koussy by my side. We had private sessions in between at which he gave me great long disquisitions on legato . . . and the sun coming out . . . "it must be *varm*, varm." He was so inspiring, so caring. And I must say I was in the sky somewhere. And I did that symphony on the Friday.

H. K.: How did it go?

L. B.: It was great. I couldn't believe it. It took a lot of doing. Koussevitzky was so thrilled.

At the end of the summer, in a letter to his first piano teacher and later longtime secretary, Miss Helen Coates, he waxes even more enthusiastic over Koussevitzky.

Dear Helen,

He seems to like me more all the time. He now wants me to study with him this winter in Boston. He said today that I will certainly be the *greatest!* conductor, if only I will work hard. Three years—that's all. He wants to mold me, etc. He says I have everything for it—of course, I have my usual reaction of self-abasement and get slightly depressed by that sort of confidence, but it's so wonderful here that I disregard it, and work, not even thinking of the horror of conscription that seems to be lurking in the fall. No matter—I must work while I can.

According to the Kupferberg interview, Bernstein had not as yet met Koussevitzky, but had seen an article in a newspaper saying . . .

. . . that Koussevitzky was opening a thing called the Berkshire Music Center, so I applied, like all the other kids. I mean, I had no particular in or anything. . . . And I came to Boston and met Koussevitzky for the first time in the green room at Symphony Hall after one of his concerts. We just sat there and talked, there was no audition or anything, and he suddenly said, "But of course, I vill accept you in my class," which was astonishing to me. I jumped for joy. . . .

I think that in those eleven years we had only one quarrel, or one time of tension. *Quarrel*'s not the right word. It was the first time I knew that I was really very important to him. He invited me to dinner at Seranak and began to make me a speech which obviously he had rehearsed in his mind. It had a certain formality about it. He was addressing me. And I remember the words very clearly. He said that he had been thinking a great deal about me and so on, and then he said: "It vill be open to you all the gates from the world." It was the first time I ever heard anybody speak in those terms—full of sentences about what I would be and become, and what I would signify for my country, and my people, and music. . . .

In the summer 1942, a young man by the name of Theodore Giddings, who lived at 55 Appleton Avenue in nearby Pittsfield, spent some time researching Koussevitzky as he conducted the student orchestra at Tanglewood. Mr. Giddings's notes somehow ended up in the archives of the Boston Symphony in Boston.

Koussevitzky, usually attired in sports shoes, slacks, and open-front shirt with sleeves rolled, sits on a high chair with cushioned back on the podium and conducts with a small baton. He sings or hums the music while conducting and gesticulates his commands mostly by expressions of the mouth. The players learn to read his lips, for he never shouts although giving the appearance of shouting.

The other day, in rehearsal, a violinist was late coming in several times. When Koussevitzky stopped the rehearsal, it was to show this player why he was late. The violinist was holding his bow improperly while in rest position. Illustrating by drawing his baton across his arm, Koussevitzky showed the dilatory player how to be in an alert position, thought resting, and thus come in on time.

Personal instruction is often given by Koussevitzky during rehearsal, but he never holds a student up to ridicule, and his criticism, though sharp, is constructive. . . .

When the students begin their orchestra training at Tanglewood, they are rehearsed one morning each week in sections by faculty leaders. This is a tremendous help to them in their orchestra work under Koussevitzky because they are "tipped off" and taught what to expect from him. The Boston Symphony faculty members, being Koussevitzky-trained themselves, are able to impart invaluable knowledge to the students.

There are no prima donnas in the student orchestra. The chairs are rotated between first-, second-, and third-chair players, so that the first-chair player today may find himself in the third spot tomorrow or vice versa.

"It doesn't sound, it doesn't sound," he will say frequently during rehearsals, "but we will arrive, we will arrive." (He uses *arrive* continually when he means *succeed*.)

It is this continual encouragement that makes the students work harder than ever to deliver the goods for Koussevitzky. . . .

"Dr. Koussevitzky insists on the greatest amount of sonority and tone, " said Miss Barbara La Couline, nineteen, of Springfield, a violinist. "He expects and gets the fullest amount of concentration at every rehearsal. He knows we are young and he doesn't fail to remind us that we are. 'You are young, play it from your heart,' he tells us, beating his hand over his heart."

Students respect Koussevitzky not only as a musician and conductor, but as a person. His attitude is paternalistic in the sincere sense of the word, and he seems to have a friendly interest in all the students whether in or outside the concert Shed. They feel that his ability as a teacher is on a par with his genius as a director.

Lukas Foss, now an internationally acclaimed composer and conductor, was in 1940 another spectacularly gifted student studying in the school that first summer.

He is very enlightening on the subject of Koussevitzky as a conductor. In my interview with him, he homed in on what is probably the essence of the Koussevitzky magic. "Koussevitzky was able to do the Tchaikovsky Fifth for the hundredth time as if it were the first. He was never jaded—never!"

He was a father figure to me. Lenny and I were like his children. It was a very privileged position to be in, and I was very grateful and felt a great deal of love for him. He was really wonderful. He was so giving, so generous in every respect—silly little things like when he had worn one of his suits five times and had had enough of it, he would give it to me. And he would have me try it on, like a tailor, and then he would say, "Good! Do you feel rich now?" We were his *kinder.*

My first impression of him was wonderful. I remember auditioning—we had to do a bit of *Till Eulenspiegel*, and before I started to conduct for the audition, Koussevitzky said, "You know, I see you right for Hindemith composition and for me conducting. You can't have both. That's too much. Why don't you do Hindemith this year, and next year you can study with me." And I said, "Oh, I prepared myself for this audition." "Well, you can always do the audition." So I did the audition, and when I got through he said, "If you vish, you will have." I will never forget that statement. "If you vish, you will have." So I had both.

Everything was very important to Koussevitzky. If we didn't do our work, he would say things like, "Tanglewood—4,000 people, that means 8,000 eyes are on you. And you have to look right as a conductor. You have to portray the music correctly." I had never thought of the way I look when I conduct.

Hindemith and I had a little problem at first. He went into Koussevitzky and said, "I cannot teach Lukas Foss. He wants to know, but he doesn't want to follow." Koussevitzky showed me his letter. He said, "That's wonderful. That's what I want my students to do—want to know and not to follow. I'll make him take you back." He was very daunting. But you know, young people can be very arrogant. I was more arrogant then than I am now.

This Koussevitzky speech, "On the Art of Conducting," given to the conducting students at Tanglewood in 1940, exemplifies why Bernstein, Foss, and the students found him so inspiring. Today we might even say he was quite the "New Age guy."

The art of conducting is very much like the art of a violinist, a pianist, or any virtuoso. To a conductor, the orchestra is as much an instrument as the violin is to a violinist, the piano to a pianist—with the difference that the orchestra is an instrument infinitely more complete and complex.

The conductor must possess a far greater willpower to be able to convey his artistic will to a living instrument.

Too little is known about the technique of conducting. Therefore, we often observe the method of using a great deal of energy, waving of arms, sweeping gesticulation; whereas an imperceptible beat, the slightest motion of the hand, have a reflection upon the sensitive chords of the orchestral instrument and prove far more effective.

Today, I shall not discuss that particular subject. We shall return to the significance of the technique of conducting later, during the course of our work.

When I began to think of a system for the art of conducting, or more exactly, the art of interpretation, I naturally began to recollect the experiments in this field by old masters of interpretation. Also, I began to recall my own experiments during almost my whole life—first as a soloist, then as a conductor. I realized that I had accumulated an enormous amount of material as a result of my artistic experience. On the basis of this material, I felt it was now possible to create a system of advanced technique of interpretation.

In the work and life of an artist, each separate experience should be examined, appraised, and laid in his soul as a foundation for his creative work.

In my observation of great artists, I have noticed that bodily freedom, the absence of muscular strain and a complete subjugation of the physical apparatus to the will of the performer play a great role. When this freedom is attained, the result is a splendidly organized creative labor, enabling the artist to freely reveal that which his soul feels. I myself have felt this state of creative ability on the stage; and when this happened, I experienced a feeling of liberation and was able to live on the stage by my creative work.

This is why it is essential for a conductor to possess an external technique—that is, a technique of the hands as well as an inner technique. Freedom of external technique—that is, muscular freedom—gives a tremendous possibility of concentration. The creative faculty is above all a complete concentration of the whole nature, spiritual and physical. It takes possession not only of the vision and hearing, but also of the mind, body, will, emotions, memory, and imagination. The whole spiritual and physical nature must be concentrated on that which is taking place in the soul during the transmission of a musical composition.

First of all, a musician must feel a composition and that which he himself is doing. One must always be feeling the truth, be finding it. It is essential to develop within us artistic sensitiveness to the truth of feeling and emotions, to the truth of the creative impulse struggling to manifest itself.

Truth outside us is not important, but what is important is truth within us: the truth of what we are doing.

It appears that the feeling of truth, just like the faculty of concentration and muscular control, is subject to development and exercise.

The calmer and more restrained the emotions on the stage, the greater appears the demand to restrain gesticulation.

It is necessary to work at rehearsals so that the inner essence of a composition is revealed. Standing on the platform, the hardest thing of all is to have faith in what has to be done. Without faith it is impossible to perform any composition. The most important thing is to believe sincerely, to be excited sincerely. Moments occur occasionally when, by chance, comes the gift from heaven. Sometimes the face of a musician, a movement, will instantly change the mood. How to explain this incomprehensible creative evolution? How is emotion to be forced out of its secret hiding place and forced to assume the creative initiative? It must be won in an interesting, creative, imaginative way.

Artistic values must not be understood in their outer aspect. But sometimes a young artist, in understanding the outer truth, approaches the inner one. And the inner truth begins to provoke that true emotion which arouses creative intuition. The value of such work for an artist consists in the finding of a secondary way to the artistic soul: from outer to inner; from body to soul; from incarnation to spiritual experience; from the form to the content. Of course, even a secondary artist can grasp a score outwardly. But only true talent can grasp the soul of a score and transmit the spiritual meaning of a composition.

Among the large number of pieces in an artist's repertoire are certain ones that become a part of his nature. And he has only to touch such a piece to bring it to life, without creative pains, without searching, and almost without technical work. This is because, due to chance or coincidence, the spiritual material and its forming processes are prepared by life itself. The sounds come to life, like an organic part of nature. And these sounds flow as they should. They cannot do otherwise. It is as difficult to analyze them as it is difficult to analyze our own soul.

I am convinced that, in time, we shall reach and we shall find technical means to penetrate into the artistic sanctuary which is truth, not by mere chance of our own will.

The line of intuition and emotion is always suggested by the composer. But in order to discover the innermost essence of a composition, it is imperative to make a penetrating analysis of its spiritual depths. An artist must discern the high refinement of the spirit; he must know how to grieve over the immortal soul, or to conceive the sorrow of this soul; he must understand that immortal domain which cannot be approached without emotion. . . . There are no other ways in art!

In our creative work there exists the difficult problem of safeguarding a composition from spiritual decay. Due to the great number of performances of one and the same piece, habits are formed. Therefore a spiritual preparation is necessary before the actual performance—every time, and at every repetition of it. Before re-creating a work, we should know how to enter into that spiritual atmosphere in which alone the creative sacrament is possible.

An interpreter must recognize that he is working not only on a score but also on himself. An artist must strive for perfection of the ideal—that is, for the simple, strong, deep, exalted, and beautiful expression of a live emotion.

As Koussevitzky indicated in his "Vision of a Music Center," the Berkshire Music Center would have the "greatest living composers" as teachers. With that in mind, he recruited Aaron Copland, America's leading composer, and Paul Hindemith, one of Europe's most established composers, for the school's first season.

Hindemith, with his wife, Gertrud, had recently fled Germany for Switzerland. Hitler had banned the playing of his music, and the future looked ominous. In February 1940, Hindemith left Switzerland to investigate professional and financial possibilities in the United States. Gertrud stayed behind in Switzerland until her husband could assure her that they could make a go of it in the New World. They corresponded as often as the war allowed.

Lenox, Massachusetts

July 14, 1940

Most beloved Pushulein, distant and devoutly longed-for good companion, three letters from you arrived together today to my delighted surprise, two (of June 12 and 19) that must have traveled on some mysterious ship, and a Clipper letter that took only twelve days to get here. . . .

Well, the little letter from your dear lion's paws has shown that you are being patient and calm, and that comforts me a little. I am hoping that the longed-for telegram with news of a travel opportunity will come soon. . . .

Alas, it was all so nicely planned! Here a little house beside the lake had been reserved for us; one of the Boston players had been instructed very early to look for something on my behalf. In Yale two agents were already looking around for a nice home for us, and I was slowly beginning to inspect cars! If one reaps rewards for all one has to go through, we should soon, in spite of everything, be in a position to enjoy these splendors! Let's hope so. . . .

It is lovely here; the countryside is gentle, like northern Switzerland; there are dense woods everywhere, mountains trace a softly flowing line all along the horizon, and there is also a lake. The little town is named Lenox. The school and the music festival grounds are half an hour's walk away in Tanglewood, a former manor house splendidly situated in a large and pleasant park. I am staying with Mr. Driscoll, a Congregational church preacher, have two nice, very quiet rooms with trees outside the windows, but make hardly any use of the family. My meals are at Mrs. Hageman's; I found them too costly in the hotel. I arrived here two weeks before classes start and so had time and leisure to explore the countryside undisturbed. I went for many walks and saw so many pretty spots in the woods, and particularly in a nearby national park, that for the first time I felt something like love for this country. Besides this I did some vigorous writing and almost completed a cello concerto—I hope to be able to finish the score next week.

The school started a week ago. The whole thing is a mixture of Donaueschingen, Ankara, and the Hochschule, and I am profiting greatly from all my experiences in those places. Here I am of course a very "famous" teacher, and the pupils have already spread rumors of the many unexpected things I make them do. The company is unfortunately not outstanding, except for one small and very good emigrant boy from Germany [Lukas Foss]. During the first lessons there was some resistance, partly because of the unaccustomed work I was demanding, partly in consequence of the absolute lack of attention I paid to existing scores of my patients. With suitable treatment, however, even the most obstinate began to soften, and yesterday, after I had ground them down by the well-tried method of a three-hour exercise in strict counterpoint on the blackboard, they are now all extraordinarily well-behaved, modest, and grateful. The main class—seven so-called composers—is dealt with four times a week in four morning lessons, each of four hours; then there are two other classes, each with three lessons a week; and finally on two evenings I give two more entertaining courses in the so-called academy (the section of the institute that caters more to amateurs). In these I make the participants (around one hundred each) "compose" a mixed chorus and a fugue. It is quite amusing, and everyone *enjoys* it. My boys were quite appalled when they suddenly found themselves forced to sing what they had written, and even more so when required to take lessons in playing an instrument. The most surprised was my colleague Copland, who wants to do things very differently with his six composers and to perform their stuff for them, and who talks always of mature composers, instead of considering them, as I do, utter tyros and obliging them to submit to the appropriate treatment. Koussevitzky is completely on my side and happily agreed to my proposal that members of the teaching staff be forbidden to accept for performance anything written by the composition pupils. Put like this, it all sounds a bit comical, but it is absolutely necessary if one wants to get rid of all that more than monstrous sloppiness and ignorance prevailing in this country in matters of composition and music theory. There is still a great deal to do in the next five weeks. . . .

Next week I shall be conducting my Concert Music for String Orchestra and Brass Instruments in one of the internal institute concerts; the academy choir is studying the choruses from *Das Unaufhörliche*; in five other places within the school pieces of mine are also in the program, and before long Sanromá [pianist of the Boston Symphony Orchestra and Hindemith's sometimes accompanist] will be playing all the new sonatas with their respective wind instrument players. This afternoon the trumpeter played his piece for me. It is many times finer and very powerful, and I ardently longed for my dear colleague to have been here—he would have thoroughly enjoyed it! August will be terrible—there will be three concerts each week with Koussevitzky and his orchestra (which is of course here and giving classes in the school), then thousands of cars will arrive and peace and quiet will be gone—but that will pass too. The Mathis Symphony will be played in the penultimate concert on the 17th. Perhaps by then you will already be here, or at least on your way!!! . . .

The prospects here are good. I am slowly growing used to land and people, and find that neither are worse than anywhere else; on the contrary, they offer great advantages. And when the good old fellow is at last here, we shall be in paradise, and I really cannot see what would induce me to give it up. . . .

But in this place I think much more about how you will like it here, and whether you too will slowly come to discover much that is fine behind all that seems comical and unfamiliar. Further west it would certainly be hard, but here in New England one can easily feel at home. . . . And, in addition, boundless forests, lakes, New York within reach . . . it could be the ideal spot for us both! Can you find it on your atlas? Lenox will not be shown, of course, but if with one claw you trace a line from New Haven due northwards to the Canadian border, you'll find the place about a third of the way along and a bit to the left. To here from New York is a rail journey of almost five hours. But should you arrive unexpectedly soon, you'll find me waiting at the ship.

Hindemith's composition pupils that summer were Lukas Foss, John Coleman, Norman Dello Joio, John Klein, Robert Strassburg, Charles Naginski, and Harold Shapero. Shapero gave an extensive interview to Vivian Perlis's project Oral History American Music—Yale University's invaluable source of information about this country's contributions to contemporary music. I will be drawing on these interviews liberally in this and subsequent chapters.

What Shapero said sheds a good deal of light on the dark and the light side of studying with Hindemith.

Well, my first encounter with Hindemith at Tanglewood was sort of devastating. There were two sections—this was at Tanglewood in 1940, the first year of Tanglewood, and the composers who were teaching were Hindemith and Aaron Copland. I felt more affinity with Copland but I wanted to study with Hindemith because I was always getting stuck in composition. I'd get stuck for weeks at a time in a section. Hindemith could write fast. I was ambitious. I figured if you could write fast, you could get ahead faster. So I thought that if I studied with Hindemith, some of the fastness would rub off. I'd learn how to do it quick and easy. Of course, I didn't.

I had five roommates at Tanglewood. Tanglewood didn't have very good housing the first year and my roommates turned out to be quite eminent people later. Lenny Bernstein was a roommate, and Arthur Winograd, who conducts the Hartford Symphony and was a cellist with the Juilliard Quartet, and Raphael Hillyer, who became the violist for the Juilliard Quartet, and a bass player who became the first bass player of the Boston Symphony, and a fabulous clarinet player who was the most magnificent sounding clarinetist I have ever heard, but was completely stupid and couldn't count.

The noise in this room was devastating, and I was supposed to compose and there was no place to compose. There was no place to sit down, there were no pianos, there were no practice rooms, just a roomful of jumping musicians and I was trying to compose in this mess.

So I complained to Hindemith, saying there was no place to compose with all that racket and Hindemith said, "Go to the woods" (like a real German). And I said, like a true bourgeois, "The bugs get on your music paper," which is literally what happens if you go into the woods and try to compose. Your papers get covered with insects and pine tar and all that. And he though that was a very flip answer—disrespectful—and he went to Copland, who was head of the composition department.

Years later Copland always remembered the story of how Hindemith came running into him and said, "That young man Shapero is impossible. Get him out of my class. I cannot stand him." And then two seconds later Shapero came in saying, "That Hindemith, he's a monster." In quick sequence we both came in and complained. Well, that's how it started, but I went on to study with him and it finished up a lot better.

He had all kind of fixed ideas about how to teach composition. What composers should do and what they must do. And one of them was, you must not write for instruments you can't play yourself because then you write notes that are sort of out of control. So you were supposed to study other instruments. If you played the piano, go study another instrument. He made the Boston Symphony players teach the composers extra instruments.

I picked the trumpet. I tried in six weeks to learn how to play a trumpet. I have thick lips and so could never get any embouchure. I could never get above middle C on the trumpet. But I poked away a little bit.

I brought a piece in. We all wrote for different combinations. He'd say, "You write a brass piece, you write for the harp, you write for this and such." So we wrote little practice pieces, and I came in with a little brass quartet.

The lesson that I learned on this occasion was powerful. He took the piece that you brought and put an empty piece of music paper next to it on the piano. He had a very early version of a push-button pencil so that when he wanted to go fast, he didn't even have to bother to turn the pencil. He could just squeeze it—bang, bang, bang. It was like a human musical typewriter. And then he'd rewrite your piece on the right at tremendous speed while you waited. He'd say, "Well, that's a pretty good idea, but how about changing that note? These fifths are clear but why don't we change this or move it? And his mind worked like lightning. He wrote out a whole new piece out of yours while you waited, just like having your pants pressed.

When you compared, whatever you fed into his mill came out like pure Hindemith. And his piece was always better, of course. It was more technically strong than yours. It was a sort of a composition by example. What was very impressive though was his speed and sureness. It was a tremendous show.

You realized you were being dominated, but the process of watching him write at that speed with that technical strength and coherence was awesome to me. And I said I was impressed and he said, "Well, you know, it's taken me a long time to come to the point where there is no time lost between my head and arm"—and he pointed. There wasn't any time lost, for better or for worse.

We hadn't been prepared for the degree to which Hindemith was going to push us around technically. He came right in the first day and wrote a big strict counterpoint *cantus firmus* on the board and said, "Five minutes and I'll be back. I want this finished. Okay?" Everybody's back bristled, every one of the six. We were unanimous in it. He had a heavy, Germanic, pompous air to him.

Of course we didn't finish the thing in five minutes. And he came back and said, "Oh, you're all terrible technically, too. You have no technique." We didn't have that much, but we weren't absolute zeros either.

Then he wrote another one, as fast as the chalk could fly, and he quickly added his own part to it as if to say, "See! Here's how you should be able to do it—fluent and quick." So he went out of the room for another five minutes. Meanwhile we found a couple of parallel fifths in his composition, which we marked up with yellow chalk or something like that. When he came back, that was the first time we sort of broke the ice. It was possible that he could make a mistake. He sort of mellowed a little bit from that day.

All the young composers thought, "Wow! Tanglewood. We're going to get our works played." But Hindemith immediately said, "None of this music can be played." That was for openers. And this got everybody's back up. He was on a fiercely moral kick. The idea was that he felt that if your work wasn't good, that you should have a moral obligation to keep it from being heard. And he was firm about it, and mean, too. Students are not in a position to really know whether what they have done is worth much.

But Copland was more lenient and knew our problems. He got some of the players together from the Tanglewood student orchestra and got them into an old barn and said, "Don't tell Hindemith." That way we could run through some of our things and we heard a few fragments of what we had written for the summer.

The [Charles] Naginsky episode was really a part of the class. This fellow Naginsky was older than the rest of us. I think we were in our early twenties and he was maybe in his early thirties. He had had a good deal of success and he had published some pieces. He wasn't an absolute beginner. My impression of Naginsky was that he was a rather lovable but weak character, and the power of Hindemith's ego had just completely annihilated him from the beginning.

Hindemith was really martinetlike and Naginsky was more floored than the rest of us. He'd had another ten years to get a little neurotic by that time. And it's not clear what actually happened. I think Naginsky's death came in the middle of the summer, about the third week in.

The class lasted five hours every morning, from nine to one. Around eleven o'clock we did what Hindemith really liked to do, swim. For that reason the class was held in a boathouse near the lake. It was a pleasant place, a big room in the boathouse with a piano and a blackboard. And we would come in our bathing suits, or pack a bathing suit, and then jump into the lake and come back.

Hindemith loved swimming. He'd go out there absolutely like an outboard motor. He swam sort of dog paddle, a fast dog paddle. He'd swim out to the raft, go up and dive in and out and in and out. Just watching it wore you down.

Naginsky never went swimming. He'd just pull up his trousers and sort of wade around in the lake. It was known that he couldn't swim. Now when he was found, his pants were rolled up. It was as if he went wading and then tripped on a rock and stumbled and drowned by accident. It was not quite clear that it was a suicide ever, from what I remember. And it happened at night. That was the strange part of it, because the swimming had always been at day. Anyway, Naginsky did drown in that lake, right near the place where we went swimming.

The next morning the class was held, the atmosphere was absolutely deadly, stone dead. After about two hours went by, the tension got extreme. And I remember that Hindemith suddenly burst out and said, "They said I killed him." How could you reply to that? He was so depressed. He just tried to figure out what he'd done and if it could have been his fault. He wasn't unsympathetic, you know. He did talk about it. And then we let it lie, that was the end of it. There was nothing you could do.

A very important part came out of a postseason teaching session. He took a shine to Lukas Foss and myself and he secretly told us that if we wanted to come up after Tanglewood stopped, he would be willing to give us some extra lessons. Of course, you don't neglect that opportunity. So I came up. I remember he got up very early, with the birds, and wrote. He got up with the sun, like the old composers used to do.

He gave me some manuscript paper and said, "Okay, here, go out in Lenox, out on the park bench there, and write melodies. Okay?" So I was going to write melodies.

I didn't know what he wanted and I tried to please the teacher. So I wrote Hindemith-style melodies. I wrote all kinds of melodies. He came out after an hour or two and took a quick scan at the page I had and said, "No, that's not it. Keep writing."

He kept this up for about two or three days until I was really out of my wits. And maybe the second or third day, I remember taking a little theme that I liked from my "Three Pieces for Three Pieces," a little woodwind trio. It was a little simple French sort of tune, symmetrical phrases that were sort of catchy.

He spotted that among all the others. I'd probably written 150 melodies by that time. "That's it," he said. "What do you mean, that's it?" I said. He said, "That is a sort of a source." What he meant really is that that is the source of your spontaneous melody and you should go back to that place and build on it for your music.

I knew what he was talking about, but the whole message didn't dawn on me until about two or three years later when I developed a little more. That was the most enduring thing that I retained from Hindemith.

He had a great many qualities which are extremely valuable that young composers lack. There is an awful lot of mechanical gesturing now by the youth, and if you ask them what a spontaneous melody is, I don't think that they even know. Hindemith stressed that, and he had the gift of spontaneous melody himself. His pieces are sometimes square. They are stodgy. They very often have a rather poor orchestral sound. They're not in a sonic sense particularly adventurous, but he could put together a few notes that would give you a tune, and that's a rare gift.

Composer Norman Dello Joio took a more sanguine view of Hindemith in his Yale interview.

While I was at Juilliard the announcement was made that Hindemith was going to be teaching up at Tanglewood. And I got a scholarship to go up there.

In the eight weeks I was with him there, I really felt that this was a man that I wanted to study with. Because, aside from his own technical knowledge and the technical advancement I felt I was making very rapidly with him, he had a very firm ethical and aesthetic point of view as to what the role of the composer was. I found these three aspects of the influence he had on me had a very good effect in terms of straightening myself out. At the end of that summer, he asked me to go to Yale and continue with him, which I gladly did. And then I continued with him again the next summer at Tanglewood. And that was the way I was sort of launched onto a career as a composer, with a firm conviction about what I was doing.

The "small and very good emigrant boy from Germany" who was also in Hindemith's composing class—Lukas Foss—was another Yale interviewee.

At Tanglewood, I felt like a refugee at first. But a refugee learns to call anything his home, wherever he is, so America very quickly became my home. (I was born in Germany and studied music in Paris before coming to the States at age fifteen.)

For about five years, before the neoclassicism of Stravinsky took over, my music was American. Aaron was slightly disapproving of my studying with Hindemith at Tanglewood. I remember he said, "Isn't that like bringing coals to Newcastle?" but I didn't agree with him until later. I would probably have been better advised to have studied with Aaron, but in a way I did study with him, because once I got to know him and his music, I asked him for advice and criticism. Aaron's stamp was even stronger than Hindemith's for me during those years. I had fallen in love with America because of people like Aaron.

One of Aaron Copland's most promising students at the Berkshire Music Center in 1941 was Robert Ward, whose opera The Crucible *would win a Pulitzer Prize in 1962. In a 1998 interview, he talked to me of Copland's deep impact on him, both as a teacher and as a friend.*

You had to submit some compositions to get in but, in my case, I had already known Copland and he had heard some work of mine. I applied and got in.

It was well known in the late thirties that Copland was very interested in keeping tabs on young composers coming up; so, if you came to New York, as I did when I was still a student at Eastman, you could call Aaron and you would go to see him and take some of your work along, which he was interested in. I went sometime in my third or fourth year at Eastman, which would have been in 1938 or '39.

I remember that experience of meeting Copland very well, because after we had talked a while, I asked him what he was writing at that time. He had just finished his piano sonata and I said, "Goodness, I wish I were going to be in New York to hear it." He said, "Well, would you like to hear it now?" and I said, "Sure." So he sat down and played it. And there was something about the way Aaron played the piece, particularly the second movement, the Scherzo, that was absolutely magical. And I've never heard anyone else who got quite that quality in it. It had the same kind of profound but fleeting quality that is in Emily Dickinson's poetry. It was just marvelous.

I chose to work with Copland at Tanglewood because by that time I knew quite a bit of his music, which I certainly loved and was influenced by. Plus the fact that I had come to know him.

There were other reasons, too. He was very interested in politically liberal or left causes, as I was. So there was just a whole general bond there.

Interestingly enough, that summer, when I studied with him, the work that we analyzed very seriously was Shostakovich's Fifth Symphony. Now many people at that time in the sophisticated circles in New York sort of looked down their nose a bit at Shostakovich. Partially, I think this was jealousy because he had developed this world reputation so early. But Aaron did not. He saw in this a carrying out of the ideals he had arrived at independently. So those were the things that attracted me in studying with Aaron.

We had individual lessons with him, but then he had several afternoons a week with the whole group together where we analyzed works and Aaron talked about more general issues.

I think the most important thing Aaron did for me happened when I was working on a symphony—my first symphony, if I'm not mistaken. I'm no great pianist, although I was composing at the piano all the time. Aaron thought a minute and said, "You know, I think you should get away from the piano. It's a handicap for you. You don't get around on the piano well. Your ear is fine and your orchestral sense is good. You should just be working away from the piano."

As it turned out, this was not only very good for me, but also turned out to be very practical. At Tanglewood, in order to get away from the sounds of music, you had to find some very remote place. In the boys' school, where we all stayed, there was a porch that looked over the Berkshire Mountains. It was a beautiful view and it was the one place I could go to get away from hearing other music. So I used to go out there and sit and sketch.

Another thing he mentioned to me at that time, which I have passed on to many students, was the Beethoven sketch books, which are wonderful. Aaron knew them and talked about the kind of shorthand Beethoven developed. The value of the Beethoven sketch books is that when you are composing and in the heat of inspiration, you actually are hearing the music at the same speed that it would be played in performance. Now you can't possibly write it down that fast with all the details that are there. What Beethoven wrote in those sketchbooks was the main line, which is the thing that the audience remembers. If someone says to you, Sing me the Schubert C Major Symphony, the main line is what you would sing.

Now Beethoven would sketch the main line very rapidly with only a few indications of where the harmony was or the rhythmic patterns. What he was able to do that way was to catch, to the maximum extent, what one was hearing while one was composing. Then he could go back to that and revise it. Some of his seemingly most spontaneous melodies you can find in ten versions in the sketchbooks. So that was a great revelation, and one that no one had ever spoken about to me before.

Aaron never talked systems, though he certainly knew about them. He was interested in what you were trying to communicate expressively and how you could get at that. He didn't say a great deal. He didn't go into long discussions, but what he said was very clear. It was like his writing, I mean his literary writing. It was always precise and to the point. He used words very well.

There was some partying. Leonard Bernstein, Harold Shapero, and I had come to know each other in New York, mainly on account of Aaron and the League of Composers. Both Lenny and Harold were marvelous jazz pianists, and we used to go to a bar in Lenox after concerts or in the evenings, and pretty soon Lenny or Harold were sitting down at the piano instead of whoever was being paid to be there and knocking out some of the best jazz I've ever heard. That was fun.

Beyond that, we were all very politically conscious. Margaret Grant, the woman who was the administrative head of the school, was very tolerant. We used to march into the main office at Tanglewood singing the "Internationale." She'd laugh at this.

And also, at that time we all had this sense of the war hanging over our heads, and there we were in those idyllic surroundings, not knowing when we might get back to anything like that, if ever.

For many years, Gregor Piatigorsky, one of the twentieth century's greatest cellists, headed up the chamber music department at the Berkshire Music Center. In this interview from The Music Makers *by Deena Rosenberg and Bernard Rosenberg, you can see why Koussevitzky regarded his Russian compatriot as the ideal performing artist and man to teach his* kinder.

Of all the titles applied to me I like "teacher" best of all. Though I believe one remains a student of music as long as one lives, I like to teach very much. I like young people; I like to share my experiences and, if possible, to help them. I was one of the few concert artists in this country to do a lot of teaching as well. . . .

Many of my friends, men like Rachmaninoff and Kreisler, never gave a lesson to anybody. Such people were astonished at my teaching, and they asked me, "How can you do it?" To many of them, teaching is somehow a lesser activity—only concerts matter. Certainly the world looks at it in that light. Therefore, an artist gets thousands of dollars for one concert, and only a few dollars for one lesson. Furthermore, being a teacher seems to reduce his rank. Now, I find that deplorable. Money, large audiences, standing ovations—they're all false and ridiculous criteria to a true servant of music.

I have been teaching for a very long time. I started when I was sixteen or so; there's been no respite since. One thing I would never do anywhere was to take money for giving private lessons. Not even in Russia. Because, look, nobody made me pay for lessons when I was a kid. I teach for pay at a conservator or university.

On the whole, teaching has been a positive experience, but unfortunately I never had beginning students. I'd like to have them one day. I want to start someone, to make it good from the beginning. Most of the time when students come to me they have already played many concerts, studied with many people, and developed many bad habits. It takes a long time just to help them get rid of those habits, which sometimes are purely physical. A student holds the bow in a peculiar way, or places fingers in the wrong way, by which I mean in a way that's not natural. There are many things in life that people do naturally: walking, gesturing, holding a fork. Actually, many people do everything well that they have not studied. Well, the moment they learn something about string instruments, they encounter *methods*, according to which you must use a certain finger here, you must stretch there, you *must* do this or that. All that is unnecessary and should be unlearned if possible. The point is to be natural. Technique is nothing more than the capacity to express whatever you want to express.

As the first season of the Berkshire Music Center drew to a close, it came time to do a little stock taking. BSO trustee Jerome D. Greene had this to report to Raymond B. Fosdick at the Rockefeller Foundation:

I am here in Lenox attending the first week's series of concerts by the Boston Symphony Orchestra, in the Berkshire Symphonic Festival. But my chief interest is in observing the work of the Berkshire Music Center for which the RF [Rockefeller Foundation] has provided support for two years. The manager tells me that no observers have come from the RF, and this is a great disappointment to me. Invitations were sent to the trustees and staff long ago.

This is to serve notice on you that unless you have a report made to you by one of your staff, you will have to accept mine, for I shall surely write you one when it is all over! The fact is that Koussevitzky's dream of a six weeks' session attracting the best talent from all over the country has apparently been more than realized. The activity of the place, the hard work and the happiness of the young people in that work, the amount and variety of it are simply amazing. Nothing like this has ever been done before, anywhere. Practice conducting, the playing of the best music by orchestras of different grades of proficiency and by chamber groups, classes in operatic stage technique, etc., etc., etc. It is simply glorious.

The Festival proper coincides with the last three weeks of the music center and not only gives a rich treat to the 6,000 music lovers from all over the country, but also gives the more than 300 students of the institute and academy an inspiring reward for their summer's labor. In the last week 200 of them will sing Bach's B Minor Mass with the Boston Symphony. This is the end of my rhapsody!

The president of the Rockefeller Foundation replied:

About the Berkshire Music Festival, I understand Stevens expects to be there very shortly. I notice your threat that unless we have a report made by one of our staff you will make one yourself. Please do it. We would deeply appreciate it, and I am quite sure you would be as detached and objective as any member of our staff could possibly be.

In an informal speech made at a luncheon given for the trustees, another benefactor, Mrs. Gorham Brooks, who had donated Tanglewood to the Boston Symphony, had this to say about the first season.

At the Opening Exercises of the music school at Tanglewood, while "America" was being sung, two or three rather unwashed young men students tittered and nudged each other, then sang loudly, with mock fervor.

This made me furious at the time, until I realized that to many persons, who have had no privileges except the freedom to starve physically and spiritually, the words of that anthem can have no meaning.

After spending days watching the activities of the teachers and pupils, I have been profoundly moved by the spirit with which they are imbued. The teachers have given themselves with an enthusiasm and generosity that are marvelous.

At noon, students, teachers, visitors, workmen, and famous musicians stood in line with tin trays and got their lunch from the "dog wagon," then sat peacefully in the shade of the pines eating and talking. Surely this is democracy in miniature!

Let those of us who have influence with the press persuade them to keep their social editors from stressing the so-called society angle, with lists of box owners and their guests and what they wore. The Festival must not become fashionable in that sense, or its purpose will be defeated and the people whom we want most will keep away.

The whole venture is of a magnitude and importance away beyond its musical opportunities. It is in fact a way of life, possible only in America. At this tragic time in the history of the world, to see a community of persons of many nations, creeds, and types living and working together in harmony, is a proof that democracy works.

Serge Koussevitzky, who has created this school and carried on the Festival, is not only one of the world's greatest musicians, but one whose perceptions, understanding, vision, and creative power are those of a man of genius in spiritual leadership. This spirit calls forth in all with whom he comes in contact an impulse to create beauty in some form. The future peace and freedom of America is dependent on the spiritual as well as physical nourishment given to its people.

The strength of Nazism lies in unity, but unity now used largely for destruction. Cannot democracy be unified in its need and desire for creative beauty and peace?

Would it be possible next summer for Mr. Koussevitzky, Mr. Olin Downes, and others of personality and vision to inject some such ideas into their students, who could thus be made to realize what they owe to this country?

It is for their generation to choose whether the United States shall become a totalitarian machine or a land of creative democracy. It would be interesting to know if these young men who scoffed at the singing of "America" have, after six weeks in the music school at Tanglewood, perhaps changed their attitude.

A rumor is spreading here that the Boston Symphony Orchestra board has refused to carry on the Festival and the activities of the Boston Symphony Orchestra at Tanglewood [during the war]. . . . If this rumor is correct, I consider it an act of vandalism on the part of the new president of the Boston Symphony Orchestra.

—Statement by Serge Koussevitzky to BSO trustees
April 30, 1942

CHAPTER 3

Tanglewood Goes to War

A Great Responsibility Toward the Agonized European World

When the United States declared war on Germany and Japan, another battle was soon to be fought in the Berkshires over the advisability of proceeding with the 1942 Berkshire Symphonic Festival season. Koussevitzky accused the trustees of "profound misunderstanding of the fundamental duties and aims of a musical institution" and even threatened to hand in his resignation if they canceled the Festival concerts, a drastic measure for a man for whom music was the essence of life.

He expressed his very heartfelt opinion in a message to the BSO trustees on June 4.

. . . Let me repeat here the words of a young friend, a navy officer who came to see me while on leave for two days.

When I told him that the activities at Tanglewood were about to be given up, he exclaimed: "How can this be done! We die to protect America, our people, and our civilization, and we expect those who remain in the rear to protect the cultural values of our nation. We are willing to die to conquer peace for the future. But what will *peace* and the *future* be if our culture is not preserved. We do not need to keep mediocre, sensible, superfluous things, not even our present mode of living, but we must all fight to save real values. . . "

This is also my comprehension and my credo.

The Berkshire community, fearing the loss of the tourist revenue if the Festival were canceled, produced a petition signed by 300 residents asserting that they stood unequivocally behind the concerts. Buttressed by their support, Gertrude Robinson Smith—for once in her life—sided with Koussevitzky to go full steam ahead with the plans for the summer season.

The federal government had not yet made a formal decision about whether or not to ration gasoline. It had given its blessing to the baseball season, since the games took place in urban areas where public transportation was readily available, but was more dubious about holding cultural events in the faraway countryside, with the automobile being the principal mode of transportation.

The BSO trustees had both patriotic and financial concerns about the summer season in the Berkshires. Trustee president Jerome Greene, the great champion of the Berkshire Music Center, conveyed their point of view in a letter to Miss Robinson Smith, dated April 20.

In the opinion of the trustees of the Boston Symphony Orchestra, ample reasons now exist for giving up the Festival. If the saving to national resources is *material*, we feel that we must make it. There are surely a thousand ways in which petty sacrifices as well as large ones are being imposed upon us, not of supply, but also by the purely voluntary action of millions of individuals as a matter of patriotic duty. . . .

Apart from the [opinion] which I have stressed above is another important one, namely, fairness to those artists and others who are expecting to be employed at the Festival and who if they are not to be so employed deserve the longest possible notice in order that they may make alternative plans. . . . As was indicated in the memorandum I left with you on Saturday, the trustees of the Boston Symphony Orchestra feel under the strongest moral obligations to protect the players of the orchestra from a material loss of income during the summer. Alternative methods of providing that income demand immediate attention. . . .

We earnestly hope that when your board meets this week, it will give the same weight that we do to the considerations mentioned in this letter.

Nothing daunted, the redoubtable Miss Robinson Smith was already busy exploring every possible avenue to hold the concerts in the Berkshires. She wrote to Ralph K. Davies, the deputy petroleum coordinator for the Department of the Interior, on May 6.

. . . As the Boston Symphony Orchestra has raised the question of canceling the concerts, our trustees are holding a meeting this week to discuss the situation, and it would be of great value and encouragement to us, since you have already said that the fuel supply situation might change for the better from month to month, if we could be assured of local bus transportation for the nine days of these concerts, not only increasing the service on the present lines, but also extending the lines to the Tanglewood grounds from the surrounding towns, as has been done in past years. I know that there are a great many buses available, owned by the Berkshire Street Railway Company and by various local and private individuals.

A large proportion of our audience comes from the local and summer residents who will be saving their rationed allotments of gasoline in order to attend the concerts. All of these people know that their gasoline will be rationed, but they are uniformly prepared to make substantial sacrifices in order to reach the concerts by whatever means may be available. . . .

For these reasons we are asking you, if necessary, to make a special ruling assuring us of the use of our adequate bus facilities for the nine days in question.

After many months of bickering, wartime exigencies prevailed, and the Festival was indeed canceled. Koussevitzky, who had lived through the chaos of both World War I and the Russian Revolution where he had experienced firsthand the devastating effects of war on art, could forgo the concerts but could not bear to lose his precious school.

Without consulting the Boston Symphony trustees, whom he no longer trusted, Koussevitzky decided to take matters into his own hands. With funds from the Koussevitzky Foundation, which he had set up in honor of his wife, who had died the previous winter, he was able to cover all the costs of the Music Center for the coming summer himself.

The proud new recipient of American citizenship wrote a June 4 follow-up message to the BSO trustees in which his patriotic spirit is palpable.

. . . America has a great responsibility toward the agonized European world.

America holds her traditions and culture from the Old World and now has been given the flaming torch of all the suffering and suppressed peoples to carry, to keep burning until the time of peace. And then, America will be able to restore the cultural wealth which was entrusted to her, and which she alone can save from destruction. . . .

We shall resume our work uninterrupted, undisturbed, with a strong sense of duty and responsibility toward one another and the country which is giving us this unique possibility.

Rhetoric aside, the hard realities of running an institution during wartime had begun to set in. One of the first war-related problems was how to supply the students with practice pianos.

In the first two years before the war, Lucien Wulsin, a friend of Dr. Koussevitzky and, conveniently, the president of Baldwin Pianos, had generously arranged for free pianos to be delivered to the Berkshire Music Center, a practice that continued until the company was sold.

But with war preparations in full gear, the supplying of pianos was becoming problematic. Wulsin wrote Dr. Koussevitzky.

Thanks ever so much for your wonderful letter of May 23.

I know how close to your heart the success and continued operation of the Tanglewood School is. You know that we heartily agree with you in all your ideals and plans in this direction. . . .

As you no doubt know, under present governmental restrictions there will be no more pianos made after May 31. We have been working on war contracts. In fact, I have been devoting my entire time to this problem, but getting the contracts, and next, what is more important, getting manufacturing under way and war materials in production is a long, slow process. It is not as simple as it seems to change completely from what you have done all your life to something entirely new, especially when it means training a thousand men. As yet, we do not know when we shall start delivery of the war materials. As a result of all this, all of our resources, energy, and thoughts are devoted to try to get our production moving.

I would so like to have the chance to see you again, but I don't know when that can be. However, please do keep me informed on what goes on at Tanglewood. We do want to help in every way possible, but under present conditions the possible is the big question mark.

With kindest regards to you and Miss Naoumoff [Koussevitzky's niece and personal secretary], in which Peggy [his wife] joins me most heartily.

Koussevitzky responded.

I have not thanked you yet for your good letter of May 27. Since then, as you may have noted from the announcements in the press (a copy of which I enclose herewith), I have been able to form the Koussevitzky Music Foundation, Inc., and assumed full responsibility and sponsorship of the Berkshire Music Center from June 20 to August 20.

As a result of this announcement, applications from students wishing to attend the school are steadily pouring in, and our funds are increasing through checks from our paying pupils, and through such far-reaching response and such deep understanding of the need of saving a cultural undertaking in these dark times.

I feel infinitely grateful to you for your willingness to cooperate by giving your moral support to a cause that must not die and to help me with funds which are especially needed for the school. This gives me new strength and inspiration and I thank you from my heart.

It would make me so happy if Mrs. Wulsin and you could come and stay at Seranak while the school is at work. We are planning student concerts during the last three weeks. While they will not be of the scope of the Festival concerts, and the orchestra will not have the perfection of a Boston Symphony, I can promise you that our concerts will be full of life, youth, and enthusiasm.

I shall look forward to seeing you and Mrs. Wulsin in our audience, and if our auditorium is crowded, you may rest assured that seats will be reserved for you as our special guests.

With grateful thoughts and affection.

At the Opening Exercises that year, Koussevitzky spoke passionately to the students of the threat to Western culture and what their role must be.

. . . The old world is shaken. The fundamental principles of civilization have received a severe blow. Not only culture and art, but life itself has been put in question.

. . . .We, your elders, have that responsibility toward art and toward you who are the future of America. You, and others like you, should be fully conscious of the importance of your work, not only to yourselves, but also to one another and to the art of your election.

In fulfilling each our duty, we are fulfilling our mission in life. . . .

The future of America is in your hands. We pass on to you our knowledge and our ideals. It is for you to carry them further, to persevere, to develop within yourselves the acquired atoms of a living art. I have faith in you, as I have faith in the future of mankind.

Soon after the opening student concerts had been given, "Uncle Dudley," a pseudonym used in those days by the editorials writer at the Boston Globe, *put an interesting gloss on Dr. Koussevitzky's text in his August 4 column.*

Is an index of high civilization what you want? Then here is one: to what extent can a people maintain their cultural institutions without dilution in wartime? It is a shrewd test. In the first World War an English audience in the Convent [*sic*] Garden Opera House was listening to a performance of a German opera, Wagner's *Tristan und Isolde*, during a German air raid; in ancient Athens during a thirty years' war against Sparta (for that time and place, a world war) the dramatist Aristophanes could, on the public stage, argue the case for Sparta and denounce a scoundrelly premier—which for freedom of speech is almost without parallel in history. But yesterday evening at Tanglewood two masterworks were performed by the youth orchestra and chorus, Bach's *Magnificat* and Beethoven's Ninth Symphony, whose text is Schiller's "Ode to Joy." All three works, two in music and one in verse, are by Germans. The text of the *Magnificat* is a revolutionary hymn in church Latin, and Beethoven's music to Schiller's ode is a human-to-human brotherhood.

To set these sounding gloriously from the hands and throats of talented American youths in wartime is an act of faith. Had Bach, Beethoven, and Schiller lived in the Germany of today they would probably have perished in concentration camps. The appeal is from Caesar drunk to Caesar sober. The nobler spirits of Germany a century and two centuries ago voiced aspirations of the human spirit which now, from the lips of Germany's antagonists, confound the baser elements that have misled that people. Even today, across an ocean and beyond more than one century, these aspirations toward mercy and justice uttered in supreme works of art by Germany's own men of genius, and ringing out in our embattled land, mean even more than meets the ear. The paradox is prophetic.

Many have spoken reverently of the summer of 1942 at Tanglewood as the most inspiring season of them all. Aaron Copland set the scene in a remembrance found in the BSO archives.

A large student orchestra, divided into "first" and "second" groups, worked daily with Koussevitzky and his assistants. To the amazement of all, a series of public concerts was announced in place of the BSO Festival concerts. (Lenny Bernstein and Lukas Foss worked with the second orchestra along with three other specially chosen conducting students, Frederick Fennell, Walter Hendl, and Robert Zeller.) There were many chamber music concerts, Olin Downes' lectures, and a production of [Otto] Nicolai's *Merry Wives of Windsor* by the opera department. I taught a course in twentieth-century music, and the composers' forums were initiated at the Lenox Library and patterned on the popular Town Hall Forums of the Air. We discussed topics such as "What About Opera?," "Government Support of the Arts," "Music Education for Nonprofessionals," "Nationalism," and so forth. The subjects seemed new and fresh then, and we even thought they were solvable. But I have seen the same topics up for discussion year after year, right up to the present day.

The student concerts were so successful and unique for their time that they soon began receiving nationwide publicity. The Associated Press filed a report on August 2.

NEW TRIUMPH FOR KOUSSEVITZKY
DOWAGERS THUMB RIDE TO SYMPHONIC CONCERT

LENOX, MASS. (AP)—Arriving on bicycles, on foot, in trucks, and in packed motor cars,—at least two dowagers were reported to have thumbed rides—some 3,000 persons Saturday night attended the first concert of Serge Koussevitzky's music festival at Tanglewood.

This year's program, taking the place of the world famous Berkshire Symphonic Festival, which was canceled because of war restrictions, proved to be music for its own sake.

Gone were the elaborate refreshment tents, the segregated parking area for box holders, the hundreds of shining chauffeured cars, the long lists of celebrities, and the inevitable parking jam. In place of the measured pomp and circumstance the audience heard an orchestra of 105 young musicians—recruited from Dr. Koussevitzky's Berkshire

Music Center—give remarkable performances of Hayden's Symphony no. 88, the third Leonore Overture of Beethoven, and Dmitri Shostakovich's Fifth Symphony. . . .

War conditions were reflected on the grounds by an elaborate war stamp organization of fifty girls, by many men in uniform, and by a brief address from Roy Dickinson Welch, of Washington, on the Treasury's bond campaign.

Jay Rosenfeld, then music critic of the Berkshire Eagle*, continues the description of the first two concerts in the August 2 paper.*

. . . There were less control and supervision of the mechanics of parking and ushering than in the previous big years, but withal there was no confusion, so evident was the cooperative spirit. The section in front of the boxes filled quickly, steadily, and compactly, like an expert packer laying choice morsels in a package for a boy in the service. The reserved seats formed an enclosing border for the milling crowds who gradually untangled into the far-spreading row of blue chairs.

The orchestra members, betraying their excitement and inexperience only by the eagerness of their expressions and possibly an overzealous instant of final intense blowing or bowing, spread out over the huge stage a full hundred strong, one third, it seemed, young ladies.

The entrance of Koussevitzky was the signal for a demonstration as it had been on Saturday night for a greeting in which vociferousness surpassed record and remembrance. The devotion of those on the Center school roster who were not in the orchestra, accounted possibly for the nucleus of the cordiality of the greeting, and for the applause and recalls after every performance, lacking in discrimination after a while. But the audience, in larger proportions of Berkshire than in previous summers, acquainted with the vicissitudes and vagaries preceding this year's session, took a willing hand and audible voice in the show of approval and appreciation of the Herculean efforts involved in preparing and presenting these concerts.

The presence of the students in the audience made itself heard, as it had been seen, immediately when the rousing performances of "The Star-Spangled Banner" was sounded to begin both concerts. The strong, clear, able voices of the young choristers were everywhere in evidence, and in accord with the conductor's baton, as he faced the people and invited their participation, the national anthem became a moving episode in a program as unusual as it was stimulating. . . .

The program Saturday night consisted of members [probably a misprint; perhaps the writer meant "numbers"] familiar to Tanglewood audiences, chosen from the best known of the Boston Symphony's repertory, but to the student members of the Center's orchestra much of it probably was first acquaintance. What Koussevitzky had achieved, therefore, was doubly impressive. This was one of the very rare instances where a conductor of lofty eminence had worked and trained an assemblage of inexperienced orchestral players. At the first impressive bars of the introduction of the Haydn G Major Symphony, no. 88, what he had accomplished became evident. Not merely precision, but an understanding expressed by taste and finesse, a performance of zestful vigor and tender, graceful molding; an orchestra of extraordinary alertness, intent on doing its best, even to the swift vibrato by the double-bass sections; jumping the gun in their eagerness; restraining themselves in piano passages to near-vanishment; but releasing a full-throated, vivid tone on demand. . . .

In this New York Times *article, Olin Downes was quick to appreciate that something qualitatively different was taking place in professional musical training in the United States.*

KOUSSEVITZKY SHOWS SYMPHONIC STATE OF THE NATION AT STOCKBRIDGE

When Leopold Stokowsky announced the formation of his Youth Orchestra several years ago and in due course conducted brilliant concerts of that organization in principal cities of both the Americas, the concertgoing public was astonished at the results achieved and at the capacities, newly revealed, of the young generation of orchestral players being educated in this country.

Without in the least detracting from that achievement, which would have been remarkable under any circumstances, it nevertheless holds true that a considerable factor in the quality of the performances was due to the presence in the Youth Orchestra of a number of the first-desk men of the Philadelphia Orchestra, thoroughly accustomed to Mr. Stokowski's conception and methods as a conductor, and placed in key positions among their younger colleagues.

But a week ago last night, Dr. Koussevitzky conducted the first public concert by the student orchestra of his Berkshire Music Center at Stockbridge, Massachusetts, and this could be called the debut of a 100 percent American youth organization. This orchestra, in its full symphonic proportions of over one hundred players, is composed entirely of graduate students and young professional musicians, boys and girls, in the vicinity of twenty years of age, who were assembled this season and enrolled as students at the Berkshire Music Center on less than a month's notice, and there trained, in just four weeks' time, to the pitch of excellence unanimously acclaimed by reviewers who went from many places to hear them.

There were no first-desk men from a parent orchestra to stabilize the situation or confer upon the ensemble the character of the highest professional finish in every solo part. There are twenty or twenty-one of the first-desk men of the Boston Symphony Orchestra on the faculty of Dr. Koussevitzky's school. They assiduously train their pupils in the technique of the routine and musicianly treatment of orchestral music. But that is the place where their connection with the concerts stops. It was a body of the best young American orchestral players available after the demands of the military draft had been fulfilled who made the ranks of the new organization. It was their first experience in concerts of such a nature, under a conductor of Dr. Koussevitzky's rank. He had been certain in advance of the occasion that first-desk men from an older orchestra would not be needed for representative performances—even if he had been able to get them, which was not possible. He could not have had them, since it was part of the agreement, when the trustees of the Boston Symphony Orchestra permitted Dr. Koussevitzky the use of the grounds and the administration buildings at Tanglewood for his music school, that no member of the Boston Symphony could play in the orchestra of the Berkshire Music Center.

Thus the young orchestra was on its own. Its performance was not only testimony to the capacities of the players and the repeatedly proved ability of their leader in orchestra building, but thrilling evidence of the development of orchestral training in this country, which Dr. Koussevitzky enthusiastically acknowledges as one of the more significant aspects of American culture.

Graduates of leading institutions of musical education in many states contribute to his ensemble. Back of their accomplishment is to be realized the remarkable work done in the course of the last quarter-century by the most progressive of the American high schools in the education of musically disposed students in ensemble playing and in the body of the symphonic repertory. . . . The development is nationwide, a growth that is putting an end to the conception of music in America as an importation. In the orchestra field, especially, the contrary is the fact. . . .

Great symphonic performances and public enthusiasm for them do not necessarily rest upon the presence of crack orchestras. They rest on something else; upon the spirit of music, particularly native to talented youth, and sound training, and masterful leadership. If this spirit, which fizzed from the Koussevitzky performances like champagne—this "élan"—is present, we have an essence which in the highest degree is creative. And such was the case at Tanglewood. The technical capacity, the spirit, the leadership were all there. The young musicians had utter faith in their leader, as he had in them. Those who know Dr. Koussevitzky for an extremely hard worker and indefatigable drillmaster saw him train his boys and girls with an energy and care that even he had hardly brought to another musical situation.

The unanimous pronouncements of the reviewers who reported the concerts need not be repeated or summarized here. None pretended that the orchestra has the silken sheen, brilliancy, luminosity of tone, sheer technical virtuosity of the incomparable orchestra that Dr. Koussevitzky conducts in the wintertime. But in point of sensitiveness, a superb ensemble, and a pervading spirit that carried everything before it, these were performances to remember. . . .

Dr. Koussevitzky's accomplishment is one that will have repercussions in the whole musical future of this country.

One of Koussevitzky's chief concerns was to bring music to an ever-wider audience—"to the masses," as he often put it. One of the divisions of the Music Center, the academy, consisted of advanced training for the layman music lover. They studied music appreciation, went to all the orchestral rehearsals, attended lectures, and sang in the choral works presented in concerts. Tanglewood Revisited, a remembrance written by Meredith Brown Alden, one of the academy participants, gave a vivid portrait of how the academy functioned and what it meant to these dedicated students.

It was one of the happiest summers of my life, although the year was 1942, the summer after Pearl Harbor. I had just graduated from the Dana Hall School in Wellesley, Massachusetts. My graduation present from my father was a summer as a music student at the Berkshire Music School at Tanglewood. . . . I didn't know a soul there except Stanley Chapple, the British conductor who was to be assistant to Serge Koussevitzky. Mr. Chapple, former conductor of the BBC Orchestra in London, had been our choral director at Dana Hall. It was he who suggested that I apply for the summer session at Tanglewood, and I have no doubt he saw to it that my application was accepted. . . .

We women students stayed at the Lenox boys' school for the summer, a mile and a half from Tanglewood, the site of the summer school. We hitchhiked every morning to Tanglewood. It was easy to pick up a ride, for all the local people knew we were Berkshire Music School students. With gas rationing, everyone was sharing rides. . . .

We were completely in awe of Serge Koussevitzky. Whenever we were not rehearsing or performing ourselves, we loved going to his rehearsals of the student orchestra. We would sit in the last rows of the Shed, and whenever Koussevitzky entered and walked on the stage, we would stand. He couldn't possibly have noticed, we were so far away, but we all felt a deep respect for him. . . .

I remembered a particular night when we all gathered in the public library in Lenox for the Tuesday night lecture. . . . That evening we had to wait in the darkened hall until the air raid alert "all clear" sounded. There was a piano in the room, and young Leonard Bernstein sat down to play, grinning and improvising jazz with the same creative imagination he brought to everything he did. We students all crowded around the piano. He was handsome and cocky, and enormously talented. I'm sure I wasn't the only girl who had a crush on him.

I saw Stanley Chapple and his wife and their Scottie only occasionally—usually when everyone stopped for lunch at the cafeteria bus, which arrived around noon. We took our trays of sandwiches, fruit, and drinks and sat on the grass overlooking the lake. The weather that summer was glorious, and I often slipped off my shoes to walk barefoot in the thick grass. Mr. Chapple, a proper Englishman, seemed to find this astonishing and commented on it whenever he caught me. Of course it may have been envy, for the dear man had bunions on both feet and wore shoes with slits cut out on the sides to relieve the pain. . . .

The summer ended on a high degree of excitement with the gala Russian War Relief Benefit. . . . I often ushered at the weekend concerts, but this was special—and the last time. Of course, just as I was marveling at how tiny Madame Lily Pons was, and chic, as I ushered her into her box, Stanley Chapple and his wife appeared just behind her. "Meredith, (rolling the *r*), you have your shoes on," said he!

As early as 1940, even though the United States was still a neutral party in the war, Koussevitzky felt an obligation to aid the Allies in their battle against the Nazis. He initiated the idea of putting on war relief benefits, or "manifestations," as he called them, at Tanglewood. The first was the Allied Relief Concert for British Aid on Friday, August 16.

Koussevitzky immediately appealed to the trustees of the Berkshire Symphonic Festival to pitch in and help. One such encounter was described in the Festival's board minutes of July 24.

Dr. Koussevitzky reminded the meeting that there was a central committee to help the Allies, and that now the Allies means only England. He said that this committee had asked him if we can help them to organize a concert or something to show our sympathy to England. "I think," he said, "it is for us and for New England particularly to express our sympathy to England—to help as much as possible. Such is my feeling, and for my part I am ready to do everything that I can—to conduct, to ask everybody in Tanglewood, and I have chorus, orchestra, and singers—to organize a great evening, even a grandiose manifestation.

"I will not be," he continued "a speaker to make an extraordinary speech for England. England doesn't need that. But we must show our sympathy to England because if we have a democracy, if we have a feeling for liberty, even if England wins or loses, we must express our sympathy.

"And I ask you to help me, and I will help you to organize a great manifestation. That is important because it will be the first manifestation in America for England."

Dr. Koussevitzky then said that this "manifestation" must be something absolutely apart from our concerts. "First," he said, "I think we must ask all the governors from New England to make a propaganda in all the states. Then in Tanglewood we will organize something like a fair. We will have corteges, we will have singers, we will have chorus, orchestra, fireworks. I cannot tell you all the details that can be done, but I have people in Tanglewood who will help me organize, and we will attract many more people because of this manifestation.". . .

Mr. Edman said, "I wonder if we should think so much of meeting our budget. Under natural circumstances we should strain to make every dollar we can, but these are unusual times. . . . If there are the people to promote it and operate it, if they are available and willing, then let's go ahead."

Mr. Spalding [Albert Spalding, the leading American violin soloist, a resident of the Berkshires who also sat on the board of the BSF] said: "I would like to say that I feel unqualifiedly in support of Dr. Koussevitzky's suggestion. We cannot afford not to do it. I think this will probably be the greatest manifestation or festival in an artistic and financial way, and it takes place in the heart of a country that has been so unqualifying in its disapproval of the totalitarian forms of government. . . . I think it is going to add one more laurel wreath not only to the Boston Symphony Orchestra but to the Festival. I will be only too happy to say that if I can add anything for the concert, I should be glad to give my services."

Mr. Brown said, "I am profoundly alarmed over the international situation. If England goes under, we are in a desperate situation, and symphony concerts won't amount to very much. I agree with Mr. Spalding. We cannot afford not to do it."

"There isn't any question," said Mr. Wheeler, "but that we should go ahead. I am sure that everyone will work to the last inch."

These lavish concerts were the precursor of what is now Tanglewood on Parade, the annual all-day concert presentations by the Tanglewood Music Center, culminating in a joint concert in the Shed combining the Boston Symphony with the student orchestra.

On August 17, Carl E. Lindstrom covered the British War Relief Benefit for his newspaper, the Hartford Times.

Everywhere over the grounds flew the Stars and Stripes with the Union Jack. The supporting pillars of the auditorium were draped in bunting and the capitals medallioned with wreaths. Overhead flew a solitary airplane as if in reminder that thousands were at that moment swarming over Britain with deadly cargoes. There was a sinister note too in the pair of policemen who paced back and forth over the roof of the outside rim of the huge Shed.

A New England supper was provided for thousands in gaily decorated tents. English Morris dances were presented in the gardens. Late in the evening there was a fireworks display. . . .

The main concert was devoted to works by Englishmen, Elgar's "Pomp and Circumstance," an excerpt from Holst's *Planets*, and Germans too. Handel's "Hallelujah" chorus and the beautiful Incarnatus, Crucifixus, and Resurrexit from Bach's *Mass in B minor,* which had been given complete Thursday night.

The gala occasion was further brightened by solo appearances of the artists Albert Spalding in Saint-Saëns' *Rondo Capriccioso*, Alexander Kipnis in *I Attained the Power* and Hallucination Scene from *Boris Godounov*, and Gregor Piatagorsky in the Adagio and Rondo from a Boccherini cello concerto.

For such a serious event, Lydia, the dot-dot-dot-mad writer of the "Among Us Girls" column, provided a very amusing description in her August 22 piece in the Bristol, Connecticut, Herald.

One afternoon last week we wrapped ourselves in a cultural mood, filled up the car with gas, and set out for Stockbridge to enjoy a midsummer's night dream in the Koussevitzky way. . . .

Most distinctive feature of the occasion was the audience, some 7,000 strong . . . quite different from a baseball crowd, a circus crowd, or the gathering of hopeful politicos at Elwood, Indiana, for the average age was well past the middle mark of life, indicating that there is truth in the statement that music is more necessary and more appreciated by the old than by the young. . . .

Outstanding were the numerous austere dowagers, who looked like fine old ocean liners, luxurious, expensive, but a little dated, with hats worn at Queen Mary angles. . . . Ancient sable tippets protected their necks from drafts. . . .

You could picture them riding around in well-kept, ancient Rolls-Royces or Packards, driven by cross chauffeurs. . . .

There were courtly old men, too, with flowers in their buttonholes, neat moustaches, and trimmed beards . . . also a gleam in their eye as if their Bach or Beethoven meant almost as much to them as clipping bonds. . . .

Musicians and genuine music lovers were everywhere apparent. . . . You could tell them by their look of rapt attention, the way in which they settled back in their seats contentedly as the opening strains of "Pomp and Circumstance" were played. . . .

Always accompanying great music and deep feeling is dignity, but the atmosphere was at the same time delightfully informal . . . far removed from the glitter of a Bushnell winter night. . . . There was, for instance, a democratic individuality in dress, no place more in evidence than on the platform. . . . Presiding officer Archibald MacLeish wore an almost Yale blue shirt (lucky for his reputation that it wasn't red). . . . [New York] Governor [Herbert] Lehman and the British representative were conventional in black tuxedos with stiff collars. . . . Later, while listening to the orchestra, the governor relaxed behind a pipe. . . . Dorothy Thompson was intense in a long gown and had a life-begins-at-forty-ish look. . . . Koussevitzky himself was brisk in a white coat with black trousers. . . .

The theme of the evening was Great Britain and America's need for a British victory . . . and there was no denying the audience sympathy as speaker after speaker stressed the urgency of the present European situation. . . . It was interesting to see how these outstanding figures in music, in literature, and in affairs, went straight to the point without equivocation. . . . Imaginative, sensitive, still they are able to see no glory in the world if England loses. . . .

Such persons as these have always been the prophets to whom the rest of us, a little less perceptive, a little less far-sighted, have in the long run had to listen. . . .

Meanwhile, author Owen Johnson engineered an auction, the proceeds of which were to provide a surgical unit for Britain. . . . The bidding started at fifty dollars, which left us out in the cold from the start. . . . Still, it was fascinating to hear the things go . . . an autographed copy of Edna St. Vincent Millay's *There Are No Islands*, annotated with notes for musical adaptation, for $225 . . . choice of twin registered heifers, with pedigrees worthy of Burke's peerage, for $100 . . . a 1765 Georgian tray for $375 . . . and so on, until $1,200 was raised in a little over one half hour. . . .

By now the moon was riding high . . . swiftly making its way through beautiful scattered clouds. . . . From the theater in the distance came the strains of a Strauss waltz. . . . People lingered to drink soda pop, orangeade, and watch the magnificent fireworks that went off with the full force of a blitzkrieg. . . .

And if we had not had a dreary two-hour drive ahead, we never would have dragged ourselves away from a festival that lived up to the term in every sense of the word . . . with Great Britain and the great Koussevitzky dividing the honors as the evening's hero. . . .

Many speeches were given that night. Governor Lehman urged the audience to support the American government in supplying Britain with as much war matériel as could be spared. The audience rose to its feet as Sir Louis Beals, representing the British ambassador, declared, "We think only of victory. Victory is the only condition, the only terms. In this grave and solemn hour, we are confident and unafraid."

Poet Archibald MacLeish said that musicians have always given their services generously for war sufferers out of humane instincts, but that this war was different. "The pier heads of Bordeaux and Marseilles were crowded with painters, poets, musicians, and writers driven out by the scourge of a new ideology. Hitler's was a war against artists-musicians."

The keynote speech was given by the syndicated columnist Dorothy Thompson, one of America's most respected writers on foreign affairs. MacLeish introduced her as "the American who has most clearly seen the crisis of our time." The isolationists in the audience must have raised a collective eyebrow.

This manifestation is held for the benefit of all the countries of the English-speaking world except our own, who are fighting today the Battle of Great Britain against the most ruthless tyranny of centuries. In appealing for relief for Great Britain, our near and trusted neighbor, Canada, and Australia and New Zealand, whose interests are one with ours in the Far East, we are not attempting to excite your humane or charitable impulses. We feel far too seriously for that. Our impulse to aid Great Britain and her empire and commonwealth arises from something far more primitive. It issues from a sense of sheer self-preservation. I do not think that I need to prove this to you. If tomorrow we should turn on the radio, or catch up our newspaper and hear that Great Britain had brought down the Nazi air force; if we should read that, disappointed by the failure of the attack, the Nazi government in Germany had fallen, and the war was at an end, with Britain victorious, every church bell in Christendom would ring; and here in the United States, men and women who say that they are neutral would rush into the streets, and strangers would embrace each other, and weep and laugh for joy. You know that this is true; and I know that you know that it is true. And therefore, we can speak with one another, not as politicians do, but as friends do, openly, and candidly, and simply. . . .

Just now an island in the sea, a little island, the capital of 200 million English-speaking, freedom-loving men, is keeping that rendezvous. Alone and isolated, supported only by the commonwealth of nations that long ago became as free as we, and by an empire which has been moving slowly but inexorably toward independence and freedom, Great Britain fights the battle of Western civilization. And, suddenly, seeing her imminent peril, we realize the truth. If Britain falls, a structure topples to which we, for over a hundred years, have been most intimately tied. Because of that island, because of the mighty fleet of that island, because of the tradition and way of life of that island, we the people of the United States have managed for over a hundred years to maintain the way of life that we have had. . . .

We have been proud of our independence, and rightly so. But let me tell you a secret, that soon will be no secret, no, not even to the members of Congress. No individual on this earth, and no nation on this earth, is independent. We are citizens of a great country, yes. But we are also citizens of a great planet. Space and time and size, however, are all relative.

With the wings that man has made for himself he can fly around this earth in a few days' time. It is bound together by seas—not isolated by them—and over all of it is the same sky. We move through space together—American, and Asiatics, and Africans, and Europeans. And we are all members one of another. . . .

This, therefore, is a most intimate war. It goes on in ourselves, and in our society. I had a letter the other day from an unknown Englishman, who wrote me because of a broadcast I happened to make in Canada, which was heard in England. He said: "I write this letter in the room with my wife and my little son. Hitler wants to destroy all that his parents have tried to bring out in this son. Therefore, this is a war between Hitler and me."

This war is between Hitlerism and each of us. It will be won or lost, eventually, in human minds and human souls all over the world. But meanwhile, while we sit here tonight bombs rain on the tiny island, greatest, perhaps now in their most anguished hour, as they fight as one man against the darkness which is in all our hearts. We shall win against the darkness in the end. But if England falls, we shall have to fight much, much longer. And so we, in New England, gathered to send our help—I hope very great and substantial help of planes and destroyers—and to pool our love and our faith. And we shall be aided in doing so by listening to the music of a German—the music of

Handel, a man of German blood, who lived and worked in England. It has been so in the past and it will be so again—that the vision, like music, will be the common possession of all men everywhere.

More manifestations were to follow. Nineteen forty-two was the year of the Russian War Relief Benefit, probably the most noteworthy of all the manifestations and possibly the one closest to Koussevitzky's heart. This announcement was sent out by the Berkshire Symphonic Festival on August 10.

For fifteen months, we have watched the heroic struggle of the Russian people against our common foe. We have seen these people destroy their homes, defend their cities, give their lives—for their freedom and *ours*. The blood of Russia has been spilt to give us time to prepare our country for war. But the struggle along the Don has been part of the battle we must win if we mean to stay free.

Through Russian War Relief we can convey to this fighting host of brave men, women, and children the knowledge that we Americans are determined to sacrifice and fight with them to a victory that will guarantee all of us justice and decency.

Let us in Berkshire County add our voice to that of the rest of American in saying to the Russian people, "America's heart and riches fight with you."

Help Russia TODAY. Buy several tickets to the great Russian War Relief Concert to be given at Tanglewood on next Friday, August 14.

This concert generated great excitement, as it was to feature the American concert premiere of the Shostakovich "Leningrad" Symphony, which everyone was eager to hear. Toscanini had recently given the radio premiere with the NBC Symphony of the Air, and Shostakovich himself had recently been on the cover of Time *magazine.*

In Copland: 1900 Through 1942, *the American composer described the blowout event of that summer.*

But it was the concert of August 14 that caused a sensation. The entire day was billed as a Russian War Relief Benefit. Lukas [Foss] conducted the "second" orchestra in *Billy the Kid* in the afternoon. A supper intermission followed, and in the evening, Koussevitzky conducted the "first" orchestra in the American premiere of Shostakovich's Seventh Symphony. This work, composed during the siege of Leningrad, had elicited enormous public interest and much advance speculation in the press as to who would be given permission to conduct the first American performance. Toscanini was granted the first radio broadcast, and Koussevitzky was given permission for the premier public performance. It was Koussevitzky's courage and skill in proceeding with his student orchestra instead of with the BSO that amazed everyone. But he knew just what he was doing—Koussevitzky was out to show his board of trustees and the world of music what could be accomplished at the Music Center. What better way than by presenting this much-discussed new symphony by the controversial Dmitri Shostakovich? Excitement grew as dignitaries, ambassadors, and newspaper critics arrived in Lenox. We all invited guests—mine were Marc Blitzstein, Robert Palmer, and David Diamond. The reviews for Koussevitzky and the orchestra were unanimous in praise, but divided on Shostakovich—the composer Koussevitzky considered as great as Beethoven.

Before the concert came the traditional playing of the national anthems. Theodore Podnos, a violinist in the student orchestra, recounted an amusing anecdote in the Tanglewood Music Center's fiftieth anniversary reunion scrapbook, Tanglewood Remembered: The Music Center, *assembled by Barbara Mandell.*

The beginning of the [Russian War Relief] concert was embarrassing. Both the Russian anthem, the "Internationale," and the United States' "Star-Spangled Banner" had been rehearsed the preceding day. However, at the concert Dr. Koussevitzky forgot to tell the orchestra which anthem to play first. With Maxim Litvinoff [the Russian ambassador] and Crown Princess Juliana of the Netherlands sitting in the audience, the Tanglewood [Berkshire Music Center] Orchestra commenced playing both anthems simultaneously. Fortunately, both anthems were written in the key of B flat and—for a few measures— it sounded as though the violins were playing an obbligato to "The Star-Spangled Banner." In the third measure, however, the harmonies clashed. Koussevitzky stopped and screamed, "'Internationale.'" All went smoothly after that.

Shostakovich himself wrote a newspaper article, reprinted in the Berkshire Eagle, *on how he came to write this symphony. Hitler had invaded the Soviet Union.*

In the first hot July days I started work on my seventh symphony, conceived as a broad musical embodiment of majestic ideas of the patriotic war.

The work engrossed me wholly. Nothing could hinder the flow of ideas, neither savage raids, German planes, nor the grim atmosphere of a beleaguered city. I worked with an inhuman intensity I have never reached before. I could stop to compose small pieces, marches, film pieces, and songs; attend to my organizational duties as chairman of the Leningrad Composers Association, and return to my symphony as though I had never before left it. . . .

My work is wholly at the service of my country and everything I conceive now is inspired by the magnificent spirit of our people in this war. I could no more separate it from myself than I could stop composing. I am working daily and fruitfully on a new work but it is too soon to speak of it. I can only say my plans are extensive and serious.

The performance itself was brilliant, and a crowd of more than 3,000 stood and cheered for fifteen minutes afterwards. Frederick Fennell, one of the conducting fellows that year, also played in the orchestra. He, too, vividly remembered the performance in the TMC reunion scrapbook.

The orchestra's rehearsals with him [Koussevitzky] were the great dimension including among much music Beethoven's Ninth and the first concert performance of Shostakovich's Seventh Symphony in the U.S. All of the conductor class was in the chorus for the Beethoven and were in the percussion section to build that great crescendo in the first movement of the Shostakovich. Bernstein became a bass drummer while I was beating a field drum at max! I remember that both of us had the mouth open at the performance to compensate somehow for all the great sound coming at the ears from all sections as Koussevitzky—forehead vein at the full—kept imploring us for more!! It was an unforgettable musical and highly emotional World War II experience.

Olin Downes's review in the New York Times *of August 16 drew a distinction between the occasion and the symphony itself.*

. . . The setting was ideal for the symphony which has caused the still-young Mr. Shostakovich—the same who only six years ago was in a state of political and musical eclipse in Russia after Stalin's disapproval of his opera, *Lady Macbeth of Mtsensk*—to be elevated back in the twinkling of an eye to the position of the composer of the most sought-after symphony in the world, in the instance of this score, which he created as a composer in and defender of besieged Leningrad, and completed in several months as his testimonial to the bravery of his fellow countrymen and soldiers and the heroism of the struggle, of which they are bearing the brunt today, in defense of homeland and humanity.

Dr. Koussevitzky's conception of the opening of the first movement is thus far unmatched for power and breadth in this American concertgoers' experience. No conductor could easily fail in the great crescendo, which forms a theatrical feature of the opening movement, and from which the last iota of effect was squeezed, from its beginning, with an almost inaudible rattle of the snare drum and the announcement by the strings of the ostinato theme, to the screaming climax of the passage.

In fact, the very clarity and intrepidity of the performance served to emphasize its obvious faults and its equally obvious virtues. The virtues lie in the composer's admirable facility and mastery of orchestral combinations that usually work; his brilliant counterpoint; the lyrical gift which, when it is not distorted by extra-musical considerations, is that of a true musician; and his sense of the big line and his dramatic temperament.

Cheek by jowl with these merits is the plain presence, in the score, of many poorly assimilated influences of other composers and inclusion of musical elements, some great, and some decidedly cheap, in a way that is not organic or characteristic of the close and sustained musical thinking that the symphonic form demands. Here is a passage of marked rhetorical effect; there a lyrical oasis of a feeling and poetry that points to other things. Also, there are great stretches of comparative emptiness, with patent banalities that no amount of patriotism or puffery will cause to endure.

Although the Daily Worker, *the Communist newspaper in the United States, did not regularly review Tanglewood concerts, in this case it did. Their music critic, O. V. Clyde, had this to say.*

The critical dispute over Shostakovich's Seventh Symphony still rages. But outside the confinements of the aesthetic boxing ring, the music of this young Soviet musician carries everything before it. It makes its way among the people who hear expressed in it the emotions that now stir them, emotions of combat, courage, and resolution.

I heard Toscanini unleash it at the radio studio, and on Friday night at the Tanglewood Music Festival I heard Koussevitzky deliver it. The Toscanini version, as might be expected, is more taut. Koussevitzky revealed that the score contains, in addition to the explicit tension of the battle-program, passages of beautiful tenderness and feeling.

The essential thing is to grasp what Shostakovich is trying to do. He is not writing any contemplative philosophy of life. He is not worried as to how closely he can approximate the symphonies of the nineteenth century. He writes in the midst of battle. He desires to express the emotions of a people at war, to depict and inspire. And he does it wonderfully well. He gets results and the results are not superficial, but concern the most significant emotions possible at this hour of human history.

The first movement is dramatic in the extreme. It is launched by a sweeping figure in the strings. This leads to an interlude depicting peaceful labor. Then begins the relentless advance of the now-famous ostinato (or obstinately repeated) theme accompanied by the drums.

At this point, critics have broken out into a violent quarrel; they do not like the device of the steadily repeated theme, which mounts to a furious height above the percussion. They knowingly refer to Ravel's *Boléro* where the same device is used for another effect. But this is formalistic absurdity! The device is not new with Ravel. Rossini knew all about it a hundred years ago. Shostakovich's deliberate choice of this musical method is the opposite of imitative; it is creative in the highest degree, getting its effect not only by the accumulation of the sound as such, but also by the increased density of the musical substance. This is what most of the hostile critics seem to have missed.

In her speech at the British War Relief Concert, Dorothy Thompson described the war against Germany as "intimate." Perhaps this most touching document, written by Ann Vera Elmquist in Tanglewood Remembered, brings the effects of war down to its most basic component—the value of one human life.

My brother, Hale Very, was a pianist. He had attended Tanglewood before me. Hale became a casualty of World War II when a British troop transport carrying American soldiers was torpedoed and sank in the Mediterranean on November 26, 1943. His death ended what promised to be a long and distinguished career. How many times this story was repeated during those years!

It was Hale who made it possible for me to qualify for the Tanglewood Orchestra in the wartime year of 1942 by playing with me for the Symphony Hall audition that spring. At that time I was twenty-five years old. He was a pupil of Leonard Shure and was also gaining recognition as an outstanding accompanist. Hale and I as well as our sister, Elizabeth, and our parents, frequently played together. Sunday afternoons were frequently given to chamber music. Also, Hale was always generous with his time in playing for our solos. Now I appreciate how much this experience of playing frequently with piano has enhanced my own playing.

Hale was on the faculty of St. Mark's School in Southborough and was responsible for inviting the Trapp Family Singers to present a program at that school soon after their momentous departure from the Nazi threat in Austria, as later told in *The Sound of Music.*

Hale collaborated with the cellist Paul Tortelier in several recitals. It was not long, however, before M. Tortelier was obliged to return to France because of the war. Also, at this time, Hale was invited to tour with the Metropolitan Opera bass singer Alexander Kipnis. When we played together for the Tanglewood committee in 1942, Hale was already known to some of the committee as an outstanding musician.

In 1940 Hale was called up for induction into the army. In the years that followed, Hale wrote many letters describing his impatience with military life, always longing for what he loved the most, playing music. Yet in the pictures we have of him he is always smiling, and he often told humorous stories and made amusing observations about life on military bases with its contradictions. And so he served without complaint but not without great apprehension.

For the first time since the war, Tanglewood reopened like a great flower in June of 1946 with a vigorous sense of liberation and fertility rife in all the arts. I have never ever felt such a collective purposefulness and camaraderie as was displayed during those six weeks on that handsome campus.

—Ned Rorem
Knowing When to Stop

CHAPTER 4

The Happiest Summer of My Life

Tanglewood in the Postwar Era

*T*hose three summers during the war with only the occasional token concert at Tanglewood must have seemed an eternity to Koussevitzky. But when the Festival did resume, in 1946, it was with expanded vigor on all fronts.

The Berkshire Eagle *reported that "when Serge Koussevitzky stepped to the Tanglewood podium last night to lead his huge, full Boston Symphony Orchestra in the first concert of the ninth season of the Berkshire Festival, the entire audience, which overflowed the immense Shed, rose to greet him in cordial and respectful homage." After Beethoven's* Eroica, *came the main event, the first American performance of Dimitri Shostakovich's Ninth Symphony, eagerly anticipated after the spectacular student performance of his Seventh in the Shed during the war.*

Even the great Broadway lyricist Oscar Hammerstein II came and enthused that Tanglewood "would make a wonderful background for a musical production." Unfortunately, nothing seems to have come of this idea.

The Berkshire Music Center was filled with returning war veterans, many of their scholarships paid for by the newly enacted GI Bill of Rights. Aaron Copland brought many young South American composers, whom he had met on his 1941 four-month governmental "cultural mission" to that area, to study at Tanglewood, invigorating the season with a new kind of foreign presence.

The Koussevitzky-commissioned opera Peter Grimes, *by Benjamin Britten, would have its American premiere that summer, performed by the students of the Berkshire Music Center.*

Tanglewood had definitively become "the place to be."

That Koussevitzky had survived the war with his idealism and innate optimism intact was obvious in his first Berkshire Music Center Opening Exercises speech. He told his young students that "in the light of music, the soul beholds the good and the beautiful; the heart awakens to faith in man and in his better future. If you deprive men of music—just as they were deprived of honor, dignity, human rights, conscience, faith, and freedom—you will witness the decline of the world to a state of brutality and barbarism. Music alone can still tame the beast in man—it is our comfort and hope."

It was not only the students who received Koussevitzky's comfort and hope.

According to his book Old Friends and New Music, *composer Nicolas Nabokov also got encouragement from his Russian compatriot after, for him, a musically fallow period during the war.*

The clerk at the desk of the New York hotel rolled his prechewed cigar to the other side of his mouth and mumbled through his teeth: "No, Mr. Thomson's not in. . . . He's out of town until Monday. . . ." "But didn't Mr. Thomson reserve a room for me?" I asked. Grudgingly he picked up the reservation book. "Ah, yes . . . ," he remembered, "he *did* reserve a room. . . . Let me see . . . here's the name of the party. . . ." And glancing above his spectacles at my unshaven face and my crumpled uniform he asked: "Are you Mr. . . ." He hesitated and followed up the "Mr." with an Irish-sounding deformation of my name: "Are you Mr. Nab O'Cough?"

The only "available" room was dark and tenant-beaten. It had the same smell of old food and older dust that had struck my nostrils in the lobby of the hotel. But I did not care; I was glad to have its bed, its bath, its privacy. I was glad to be out of airport waiting rooms, shabby army hotel lobbies and messes, communal washrooms and iron-clad bucket seats. "I will sleep," I thought, "I will sleep for the first time in five days, since the Azores, since Paris. I will get the drone of the motors out of my ears and the bucket-seat bend out of my back, and no one will wake me at 4 a.m. shouting: 'Flight number eighty-four will depart at 4:20 a.m., all passengers . . . ' or 'All flights canceled until tomorrow.'"

I tipped the porter, undid my bulging Valpack, ran the bath and . . . the telephone rang . . . once . . . twice. . . I picked up the receiver and was about to utter one of the juicier cusswords that had singed my ears during my eight days of army-sponsored journey, but the voice on the other end forestalled me. Familiar, calm, and business-mannered it said: "This is Western Union. We have a telegram for Nicolas Nabokov from Lenox, Massachusetts. Are you he?" "Yes, I *am* he," I replied and asked her to read it to me. I turned off the bath, found a pencil and wrote: "Welcome back. Hope you can come this weekend. Must see you at once. Call Lenox. Best regards. Serge Koussevitzky." "Will you take a reply?" I asked, when she had finished reading. No, she could not. I had to give it to the hotel operator. Could she at least tell me what time and what day of the week it was? The Western Union manners disappeared and she answered in an irritated, high-pitched bark. "Friday, May 9 . . . 1:35 a.m.," she said and hung up. I called the hotel operator and gave her my wire: "Sorry, cannot come today. Must sleep. Will call Saturday morning. Regards."

The Berkshire Express is, as everybody knows who has ever been bounced by it, a slow and sulky train. It sulks for a long while at every one of its many stops and each time I take it, it seems to have added a new one. Between stops, it crawls, shakes, and rattles.

But I did not mind its slowness and shakiness when I boarded it on Sunday morning, May 11, 1947. I was free from the pleasures of the army, I was on leave, I was going to the country, and I was eager to see Serge Alexandrovich Koussevitzky, to visit him at his "musical fun grounds," as someone in the *Stars and Stripes* had termed the Berkshire Music Festival. I had never been in Lenox or seen its famous "Shed," its open door auditorium, the opera workshop and other buildings of the Music Center, except in publicity folders or in magazines. Now I would see it all and spend a quiet two or three days with the creator of this extraordinary musical project.

Besides, it was May, the weather was balmy, the windows were open, and as the train passed Danbury and began winding along narrow valleys, the smell of young leaves, of pine, and of honeysuckle filled the car and gave me the taste of the springy countryside. Though shaken and dandled about, I felt happy as I began to think about the man I was going to visit, about his life, his work, his achievements, and his fantastic, unique success. I had never visited Koussevitzky before, nor had I seen much of him since I had come to America in 1933. Even before 1933, in Europe, despite the fact that I was one of "his" composers (my music was published by the publishing house for Russian music that he had owned until 1948) and that Koussevitzky was the first important conductor to perform my music in America, I had seen him only on rare occasions, when, after his American season, he came to Paris and spent a month or two in his comfortable home on the edge of the Bois de Boulogne.

Nabokov had spent the war years teaching music in an isolated college in upstate New York, "far away from the active center of music." But immediately after the war . . .

. . . I received an unexpected assignment to go overseas as an employee of the War Department. Once in Germany a chain of accidents moved me into the position of a deputy chief of the American military government's control of German music. Although I occupied this venerable post for only a very short time and soon drifted into more important bureaucratic occupations and acquired a more imposing nomenclature, I was able during this short interval to do something in the line of duty which seemed at the time of vital importance to the Koussevitzky publishing house.

The center of the publishing house since its foundation had been Berlin. During the bombing, the building in which the publishing house had its offices and where the main records (such as contracts with composers, manuscripts, and other documents) were kept had been reduced to rubble. Moreover, the Berlin director of the house had lost contact with the main director of the firm, who lived in Paris. In short, the latter asked me to find the former, give him food and help, and also find out whether the scores, parts, and documents were intact in Germany. I did all of those things, and even arranged a two-week-long digging expedition at the desolate site of the destroyed publishing house in order to unearth, or rather unrubble, a steel safe in which the contracts were kept. We did not find the *Schrank*, as the German diggers called it, but my "activities" were duly reported to S. A. K., and several weeks later I received a very gracious letter from him thanking me for my trouble and asking me to visit him in Boston as soon as I returned home.

Yet I knew at least one person in the Koussevitzky household, his niece, who soon was to become his wife, Olga Naoumov. Before coming to America she had lived with her parents in the south of France, in Nice, where the Naoumovs owned a villa surrounded by a large garden on one of the lovely hillside streets. My mother's apartment was only a fifteen-minute walk from there. We used to go there for tea or lunch when I came home from Paris to visit my mother. Olga and I became friends during one of my Easter visits, in 1924 or 1925. I liked her at once. She was so different from the usual uneducated girls of the wealthy Russian upper classes. She looked slight and fragile and spoke in a thoughtful subdued tone of voice of earnest matters. We used to find a bench in the lovely garden of their villa and there, in the mild afternoon sun, we would sit until dinnertime, having endless Russian talks. We talked of Russia, of her future, of the great Russian writers and poets, of philosophy and religion (Olga belonged to a devout Greek Orthodox family and was herself deeply religious), of Russian music, and of her uncle Serge.

I was therefore happy to see Olga waiting for me at the Lenox station, greeting me in the subdued voice I remembered, and, as we drove past the gates of Tanglewood, telling me how busy Serge Alexandrovich was, how much work had to be done in preparation for the festival, how little time he had to rest, and how exhausting was the Boston season with its four concerts a week and its harrowing tours. A moment later we drove past a sign marked SERANAK—PRIVATE and stopped under a wooden canopy in front of a rambling white house.

"Sh . . . sh . . . ," said a white-haired lady in a mauve silk dress, trying to quiet the bark of an old black cocker spaniel: "Beema! Be quiet!" It was Henrietta Leopoldovna Hirschmann, a close friend of the Koussevitzkys, who, during the summer months, stayed at Seranak and worked for him as a secretary, a confidential assistant, and an all-round helper. "Serge Alexandrovich is still in conference," she said, and pointed to the drawn curtain which hung across the bright broad corridor of the lobby. "Why didn't you come yesterday?" she continued in a hushed tone. "The weather was wonderful yesterday, and now, you see, it's raining."

We went out on the covered porch to see the view. The rain had stopped for an instant. Heavy cumulus clouds covered the skyline and hung low above the landscape. Between them, here and there, were patches of deep blue. The distant hills, bathed by a shadow of the rain, were barely visible. The earth was warm and damp, and in the stillness the odor of the grasses, flowers, and fruit trees smelled intensely of an abundant spring.

The house, Seranak (an anagram made up of *Ser* from Serge and *Na* from Natalya, Koussevitzky's late wife and forty-year-long companion, and *K* for Koussevitzky), stands on a terraced hillside, about a mile to the west, and high above the festival grounds. It is a large two-story house dominating an extraordinarily broad and panoramic view. From its terrace one can see a vast horizon filled with the blue rolling pattern of the Berkshires and, at its feet, encased between these hills, like a huge oval mirror, lies Lake Mahkeenac, the Stockbridge Bowl. The back of the house is protected from the north winds by a high-forested hill. In front of the house, the hillside descends in a sharp incline to the Lenox-Stockbridge Highway, planted with large old apple and plum trees. The whole gives the impression of great serenity, a peaceful detachment from the busy life down in the valley, near the lake. And as one learns the mode of life of the inhabitants of the house, the feeling is pervasive, infinitely restful for visitors. Everything in Seranak is unhurried, calm, subdued repose. Even during the hectic days of the festival season this atmosphere of serenity and peace remains unchanged.

Inside the house the rooms are large and airy, softly carpeted and softly furnished. Decorated in a neat and well-mannered way, it resembles the somewhat bulky style in which the wealthy St. Petersburg merchants of the early nineteenth century furnished the interiors of their large Finnish *dachas* (the suburban villas) or the style in which the industrial magnates of the Rhineland adorned their comfortable houses near Düsseldorf or Cologne. But Seranak has its own style, very personal and very Russian. Russian not only because its inhabitants, with the exception of one or two maids, are all Russian and constantly speak Russian, but because the mode of life, the habits, of its master and both of its successive mistresses have molded the environment around them and given it a distinct flavor of an old Russian *Oussadba*, the country home of a wealthy squire, with all of its charm and quiet simplicity.

The curtains opened and Koussevitzky came toward me with a broad smile on his face, his eyes shining with pleasure and friendliness. In his broad Russian he explained: "Where *were* you all these years, where were you hiding?" in the tone of a stage father scolding his disobedient child. "We looked and looked for you *everywhere* until we finally tracked you down in Germany." And he looked me over as if he was appraising me. "*Noo, poydem, oydem, oydem,*" he said. "It's late and you must be hungry. Olya, Guenia, where's lunch?" The meal was long and relaxed. Koussevitzky bombarded me with questions about Germany, about our relations with the Russians, about my experiences with the army and the military government, and listened with avid interest to my detailed account of the new music I had seen or heard in France, in Austria, in Berlin, and in particular the music at the closed concerts of the Soviet military authorities, to which I had been occasionally invited. He wanted to know whether I had news from Prokofiev, and whether it was true that Prokofiev had been so terribly ill that he couldn't compose for more than a year.

At the end of the meal, as we were getting up from the table, he turned to me with a glint in his eye and said: "And now I have to talk to you privately about something which may be quite interesting to you." He led me ceremoniously to the living room as if he had prepared there a surprise for me. "What I want to talk to you about," he began as we sat down, "is"—he paused—"a commission. Yes, we were looking for you all over the place last winter to . . . give you a commission. But we couldn't find you!" And he threw his arms in the air. I apologized for having been such a needle in the haystack and explained that I had been overseas and thus of necessity completely divorced from music and musical life in America. "No, no," he exclaimed, "I do not mean now, I do not mean these last years since the war . . . I mean before. Where were you before the war? Why did you hide from me? What did you do? What did you write?"

I hesitated, not knowing whether I should answer. Somehow I felt that he really did not care for answers, but that these questions were rhetorical, giving weight and impact to his Maecenaic proposal. "Well, anyhow," he continued after a moment's silence, "what would you like to write for us, for the Koussevitzky Foundation? We have put money aside to commission you to write a piece."

I had suspected when I received Koussevitzky's wire that something in the nature of a commission might be on his mind. At least, I hoped that this was the meaning of the phrase "must see you at once." I had thought about it on the train and decided that if he offered me a commission I would suggest writing the piece that, at moments of relative leisure between bureaucratic routine and official parties, I had begun sketching at the blond piano of my Berlin billet. I thanked Koussevitzky for his offer and began explaining. "Yes," I said, "I have a piece in mind, Serge Alexandrovich. I even started working on it while I was in Berlin. It has to do with a long poem of Pushkin, and I don't know yet whether I should write it for orchestra alone or set the text of the poem to music for tenor voice."

At the mention of the name of Pushkin his face beamed. But he did not approve of a solo tenor voice. "The public does not like long solo pieces for tenor," he explained. "They are hard to place because there are few good tenors nowadays. Here in Tanglewood we have a marvelous young tenor, David Lloyd, but elsewhere I know of almost no one . . . like an elephant." He paused for a moment and, as if a splendid idea had just struck him, he began speaking excitedly, his face growing crimson and the veins on his forehead swelling: "I tell you what you do. You write a concerto for soprano and orchestra. No one has ever tried it and I always wanted someone to write one. It will be a real novelty. And you should treat the voice as if it were an instrument; like an oboe . . . or a . . . flute." And getting more excited at his proposal he exclaimed: "Write me a good concerto for this combination, and I will find you an excellent singer and play it everywhere. As for the text . . . it does not matter what kind of a text you use, you can take a poem of Pushkin in Russian . . . you can take a poem in . . Burmese, or anything you want. For a piece like this the text doesn't matter. It would be like the words of a . . . Handel aria. What is important is that it should show off the voice and be interesting musically."

He paused again and added in a quieter tone: "You know who should sing it? The little Marina . . . do you know her? Marina Koshetz, Nina Koshetz's daughter. She has a wonderful voice and her mother's schooling." I answered that I never had heard Marina but that I knew that her voice was very good, nearly as good as her mother's had been.

"But . . . but . . Serge Alexandrovich, my idea is different from yours," I tried to explain. "To me the meaning of Pushkin's poem is paramount. The words express something very intimate, something terribly close to my heart. In fact it is a kind of personal confession . . . a very grave and important thing to me." At first I was afraid that he would be annoyed but, on the contrary, as I went on his expression changed and he because visibly more interested. Finally he interrupted me.

"But what poem of Pushkin is it?" he said. "Can you recite it?"

"Yes, of course I can," I answered, "but before reciting to you I must tell you how I came about choosing this particular poem so that you know what it really means to me . . . but it will take a long time and you probably should go and have your afternoon nap." He looked at me with a gentle, friendly smile and said:

"Go ahead, Kolyenka, tell me your story. Never mind the siesta. I can rest later. Go ahead."

Because of Koussevitzky's abiding interest in championing new music—especially American music—young composers, as they had before the war, continued to flock to Tanglewood to study and work. Ned Rorem was there in the summer of 1946, the first of two summers he would spend at the Berkshire Music Center. He infused that time with a golden glow in his memoir, Knowing When to Stop.

In the summer of '46 I got a scholarship to Tanglewood and became one of Aaron [Copland]'s six protégés. The protégés were billeted in one huge stable in a Great Barrington girls' school (now a golf club), along with [Bohuslav] Martinů's six protégés, and Martinů himself. . . . The twelve student composers had two lessons a week with their respective maestros, plus two group sessions, plus access to all kinds of rehearsal, notably of *Peter Grimes*, which received its American premiere there. It was the happiest summer of my life.

I gleaned less from the one-on-one meetings at Tanglewood than from the classes. The class in orchestration was most canny. Aaron had us all score the same passage— five or six measures—from a piece of his. We did this, each in our own corner for an hour, then regathered to compare the results against the original. Very instructive.

Appalachian Spring had just been published, and we all carried our own little score around like holy writ, the way the Latin-Americans carried around the Falla Harpsichord Concerto and the French students *Pelléas*. (This, please note, was five years before the [Pierre] Boulez backlash.) But Aaron, sly fox, had us orchestrating sections of *Statements*, which we couldn't possibly have known beforehand. Sometimes he would invite outsiders. For example, Britten came to talk about *Peter Grimes*, and Harold Shapero analyzed his Classical Symphony. We had a class in movie music, and one in modern vocal music. Aaron had yet to write the Dickinson songs, and didn't yet feel of himself as a song composer.

He was more interested in other composers than any composer I've known. That was the season he imported youngish geniuses from all over South America: [Hector] Tosar from Uruguay, [Julián] Orbon from Cuba, [Juan] Orrego-Salas from Chile, [Alberto] Ginastera from Argentina. . . . Aaron listened patiently to every note of every one, then commented in a very general way. He was less a pedagogue than an advisor—a sort of musical protocol expert. Exhilarating on the spot, but I recall the details less accurately than with my Virgilan contact [Virgil Thomson]. Virgil was more naturally verbal. Also Aaron, although in theory unbiased as to your style, was in fact disposed to praise music that most sounded like his own. . . .

Networking has always been a well-practiced skill for the Tanglewood students, and many a career has been furthered through a summer's stay at the Music Center. Ned Rorem is no exception.

Aaron lived in Pittsfield and invited me to dine once or twice, and to see *Señorita Toreador*, an Esther Williams movie that used *El Salón México* as background music. He also offered me scotch and sodas (he was never a drinker, but I was), which quite went to my head: Aaron was my teacher, after all. "Don't tell anyone," said he, "because one can't make a habit of inviting students out." But what did he really think of me?

A bus took us each morning after breakfast (pancakes), via Stockbridge, to Tanglewood near Lenox, about thirty minutes away, and returned us in the evening, unless there was a concert, which there usually was. In our dorm I recall Howard Shanet, Earl George, Vladimir Ussachevsky, Louis Lane, and Danny Pinkham (all students of Martinů's) bunking demurely in a row, and of the girls Sarah Cunningham plus two auditors—Grace Cohen and Paula Graham, a singer. Also the morbidly seductive—both his music and his person—Heitor Tosar.

Bohuslav Martinů was staying alone in the mansion too. His terrible accident happened during that first week. I had visited his small New York apartment on Fifty-ninth Street the previous winter when David Diamond was subletting, but had never met the man. Aaron now admonished me to be nice to Martinů ("Those Europeans are always at loose ends without their wives, you know"), and when I asked Aaron what the Czech's music was like, he answered: "Like a Chinese nightclub under water." One evening, when Paula and I were savoring lemon meringues at a Barrington bakery, in wandered Martinů, at loose ends without his wife. We invited him to our table, chatted amiably for an hour as darkness fell, then returned down the avenue to the jasmine-scented gardens of our communal school, and said good night. Five minutes later, a crash, a yelp, a groan. Martinů had fallen from a fifteen-foot parapet leading from the mansion to the nearby golf course. Ambulance, hospital. (Nikolai Lopatnikoff was quickly called to substitute for the remainder of the season.) We never saw Martinů again, but he lived in continual pain until his death thirteen years later [a point disputed by Martinů's wife].

The Czech composer Bohuslav Martinů was the first international composer in residence at the Berkshire Music Center after the war. It was his second tour of duty, having taught there in 1942, replacing Igor Stravinsky, who had canceled at the last minute. Martinů's wife, Charlotte, recalls the events of the summer of 1946 there in her book, My Life with Bohuslav Martinů.

But man proposes, God disposes. In May 1946, we were just about to leave for Europe when Serge Koussevitzky asked Bohuš to take up again his teaching post at the Berkshire school. Bohuš was working on his Fifth Symphony, but without much hesitation he accepted the offer and our plans for the journey to Europe came to naught. However, since I ardently desired to return to France to see my relatives, I decided in June to make the plane trip alone. My husband was to follow as soon as his teaching job at the school ended. . . .

My first month of vacation in Vieux Moulin was happy and almost idyllic. After the noise and bustle of New York, it was a true pastorale of beautiful weather, of place, and of tranquility. Bohuš wrote regularly; he was very satisfied with his work at the Barrington School of Music at Great Barrington [she means the Berkshire Music Center in Lenox], Massachusetts. He lived there in a circular room that he had inherited from his predecessor, Robert Casadesus. His students, six men and two women, all chosen by Aaron Copland, were pleasant, especially one of them, George Earl, who was particularly gifted, and Bohuš predicted a great future for him. "He listens to me as if I were the Holy Scripture," he wrote of Earl; they had become good friends.

His life at Great Barrington passed like that at a college. The school was housed in a large manor house. Bohuš cleaned his own room, and the dining room had a self-service system. There was no wine, only water and milk, but Bohuš compensated for this lack by going to a restaurant, to which he often invited his students.

He had a piano in his room, and at that time he was composing the *Toccata e due Canzoni* for Paul Sacher. He only taught in the morning, while the afternoons and weekends were free.

At Great Barrington, the day started with breakfast at seven-thirty. Bohuš then gave lessons in his room and he noted with satisfaction that his difficulties with the English language had diminished considerably since 1942, and that he expressed himself nearly always correctly. In the afternoon, silence reigned at the college. The students had taken the bus to go to concerts at Tanglewood. In the evening, other concerts given by the students took place in the study hall, during which they played quartets or only the piano. The students proposed to play one of Bohuš's string quartets, which pleased him. But it was Misha Elman who gave him particular joy when he decided to play Bohuš's

Violin Concerto at the next Tanglewood concert. At Great Barrington everything went admirably; even the nights, which had first been disagreeably cold, became warm. Bohuš went only twice a week to the Tanglewood concerts, as he did not like the travel or the crowds, and he preferred to stay very quietly by himself.

Late in the evening of July 17, 1946, Bohuš came out on the terrace to relax; it was not lighted and there was no railing. He stayed there a long time, and when he wanted to go back in, he noticed that the French doors had been locked from the inside. Bohuš then wanted to go down the staircase of the terrace but his first step was one into emptiness: there were no stairs! He fell down onto the concrete, ten feet below. By chance, the cook was not yet asleep and she heard the fall. She found Bohuš unconscious and covered with blood. In the hospital they diagnosed several broken ribs and a serious injury to the cranial bone, and the principal central nerve had been injured.

Rudolf Firkušny, called by Serge Koussevitzky, wrote me immediately. I was terrified. Rudolf assured me that there was no reason to be alarmed, as Koussevitzky had engaged the best doctors, and that they were optimistic. Two days after the fall, Bohuš even added several reassuring words to Firkušny's letter.

The kindness shown Bohuš by everyone raised his morale again. His pupils assured him of their devotion and affection and, as always, Rudolf Firkušny once again gave proof of his friendship by arranging everything possible, without hesitation. Koussevitzky sent over yet another specialist. Louise Dushkin came also, as did Luboschutz, Jan Lõwenbach, and many others. When Frank Rybka leaned of the accident, he took his car and drove 300 miles to personally find out about Bohuš's condition.

As for me, I tried to get back to the United States, but boats and airplanes were reserved immediately after the war for the families of American soldiers. They had priority and I had no chance to get a reservation. Bohuš, of course, wrote me regularly and his convalescence proceeded satisfactorily. But I was terribly restless and every time I was refused a seat on a boat or plane, I went back sadly to Vieux Moulin. I made numerous trips to Paris, but without success. I waited in front of different doors, entered all sorts of offices, and asked competent authorities to make my departure possible. The wonderful time of my first days in Vieux Moulin was gone and it was my sole desire to leave as soon as possible the France that I had so wanted to see again, to be near my husband in the United States.

It is possible that Bohuslav Martinů had the toughness of a Bohemian peasant, since the condition of his health improved day by day. He would have loved to be present at Misha Elman's concert at Tanglewood, but his doctor dissuaded him from going. The enthusiasm of the 9,000 listeners testified to the success of the work, which pleased him enormously.

Ned Rorem had more to say about his two summers at Tanglewood.

Along with running the whole show at Tanglewood and giving his six pupils two private lessons a week, Aaron Copland in his classes gave lectures on instrumentation (for one of these he took us to the Shed and had each first-desk man of the Boston Symphony demonstrate his instrument), on other composers' methods, and on how to write movie music. During the war Aaron had been the only "serious" composer to go to Hollywood, first to score *Of Mice and Men,* [then] *Our Town,* and then Samuel Goldwyn's *North Star.* He introduced a new aesthetic—"the Copland sound"—to films, which dominated sound tracks until the late 1950s, when all cinema, here and abroad, stopped using anything but pop. In off hours Aaron mingled with the Hollywood intelligentsia, mainly European refugees, and heard his chamber music played on special recitals. At one of these he performed his own brittle Piano Sonata, after which who should come backstage but Groucho Marx. "Groucho, what are you doing at this kind of concert?

I have a split personality, so don't tell Mr. Goldwyn." "Oh, he doesn't mind," said Groucho, "as long as you split it with him."

Oh, the fragrance of those giant elms, especially in the rain, when sounds like odors carry pugnaciously and the last movement of Sibelius's Third spreads through the winds, conducted first in the morning by Seymour Lipkin, and in the afternoon by Gerald Samuel, Koussevitzky's chief new pets. Koussy (as he was called)'s chief regular pet was, of course, Lukas Foss, who, because the eminent Russian conductor couldn't read scores, acted as a literate assistant, playing all music, new and old, submitted to the maestro.

Lukas, about my age, was more flamboyantly facile and versed than me. A German refugee—and retaining even today a crusty accent—his music was virulently non-European, meaning lean, angular, muscular, diatonic, unromantic, and using folklike tunes and jazzy rhythms, either foursquare or in 5/8 meters. Lukas and Lenny were intimates, vying amiably for their simultaneous reputations as triple threats. Lukas was surely as good a pianist as Lenny, a thoroughly trained conductor, and a composer (at twenty-two) of large-scope works that were conspicuously performed by major orchestras.

That he was at this time more American than the pope (Aaron) reflects the yearnings of the naturalized citizen—yearnings to be accepted, to be in the swim. In the ensuing years Lukas has leapt onto so many bandwagons (the wide-open spaces vehicle, the twelve-tone vehicle, "chance," "happenings," the "masterpiece" syndrome, neoromaticism, minimalism, always using the "right" poets if vocalism was called for—in sum, so up to date that his music grew dated with each fashion change) that if all the art of our century were wiped off the earth save that of Lukas, the next century could reconstitute our musical history through his scores alone. Those who criticize this bent *chez lui* miss the point—that cultural promiscuity *is* Lukas, even as spreading-himself-thin is Lenny.

He was socially promiscuous too, and, being heterosexual, for all practical purposes, made passes at various girls including my friend, the beauteous Grace Cohen, whose

Nefertiti features, long lilac hair, and plangent torso of a modern dancer pleaded for defilement, even as her Bronxy voice pleaded for mercy.

Lenny brought Lukas and a guest, Marc Blitzstein, to a party one night in the great hall of our Barrington school. We all sat on the floor while Lukas played and sang—or rather, bleated as composers do—a spacious *Parable* he was composing for Todd Duncan and orchestra. I was jealous not only of his inspired technique for manipulating so large a canvas, which I'd have been incapable of despite my narcissistic act of self-assurance, but of his cool ability to show his cards so expertly in front of everyone. I resented my own reticence, my lack of exhibitionism on the grand scale, and rationalized that, well, I wasn't Jewish.

Blitzstein was even more of a performer. Drenched in the gold dust of reputation, he was part of American history with his leftist operas of yore, his army stint in Europe from whence he'd just returned, and his recent huge piece of patriotic gore, which Lenny had just conducted in New York, called the *Airborne* Symphony. Now here he was in the flesh, about to show *his* cards.

It is a truth universally acknowledged that inside every composer lurks a singer longing to get out. What is known in the trade as "the composer's voice"—that squeaky, unpitched organ with which composers audition their vocal wares to baffled sopranos or uninterested opera producers—may explain their becoming composers in the first place, out of frustrated vengeance. The human voice is, after all, both the primal and the ultimate expression, the instrument all others seek to emulate. I have known only two American exceptions to the rule that the composer-as-singer sabotages his own work. One was Samuel Barber, who had a true, gentle baritone of professional class, albeit with the rolled *r*'s of upper-crust Philadelphia. The other was Marc Blitzstein, who, true, had a "composer's voice," but who composed specifically for such a voice. With his wheezy larynx he could put over his own songs because of a fearless, horny conviction that I've never heard elsewhere. Indeed, during the long run of *Threepenny Opera*, all of the regularly changing cast seemed to be hired according to how much they sounded like Blitzstein.

Now here he was in Barrington, cajoling, whispering, rapping his new song, which Lenny was calling a masterpiece, and which in fact was called "Zipper Fly." We could not then know the dancer from the dance, for with Marc at play, his song (to his own text) seemed irresistibly witty. In retrospect, heard through "real" voices, one realized that his left-wing ditties are lessened by standard beauty.

I wanted to know Marc Blitzstein, and would, but not then.

The fellow student composer I came to know best and longest was Daniel Pinkham, he of the eternally even temper, ingratiating smile, roving eye, biggish ears that were maximally experienced for church music. Like me, Danny wrote songs—indeed, specialized in songs, although choral music and little operas were very much in his catalogue too since in Cambridge, where he lived and had a church job, he had access to all sorts of professional singers. We weren't quite aware at the time that all composers didn't write songs: the icy truth is that songwriters are as rare among composers as composers are rare among football players, and this specialty within a specialty proved a bond between Danny and me. By *song* I mean a lyric poem of moderate length set to music for single voice with piano. (A lyric poem is an expression of its author's feelings rather than a narrative of events. A moderate length is up to five minutes. Single voice means the instrument of one singer. A piano is a piano.)

Danny, protégé of Piston and Boulanger, grandson of Lydia Pinkham, and a proper Bostonian with long *a*'s and soft *r*'s, did not show feelings other than optimistic ones. One can't picture him weeping. Blazingly intelligent, his culture was—is—nonetheless restricted to music. He *is* music. Reading matter, no matter how abstruse, seems cogent only insofar as it serves his muse. His conversation, though clever, is nondevelopmental, almost strictly anecdotal, as though he feared where an evolving *entretien* might lead. He remains a major American harpsichordist and organist, and a confector of—at its best—delicious and sometimes touching *Gebrauchsmusik*. He has never shown envy, and attributes his smallish reputation to his not being in the swim. He has always lived in Massachusetts.

Danny had a station wagon, the better to cart around his ever-present harpsichord. He was always going somewhere or coming back, saying good-bye or saying hello, transferring hitchhikers, unloading students at the nearby lake where we swam at noon, sometimes tearing off a piece in the backseat. Our relationship was platonic. We remain faithful colleagues and mutual champions.

Composer Jacob Druckman studied twice at the Berkshire Music Center. His experience, as recounted in his interview with the Yale Oral History American Music archives, underlines the singular importance of Aaron Copland to several generations of American composers.

I had always thought of myself as a composer, but in my late teens I thought I would make my living as a violinist playing in symphony orchestras to support the composing habit. I spent the summer of 1948 at Tanglewood as an orchestral violinist and ended up hating it. I also felt that nobody was paying any attention to the music I was writing. After that first summer at Tanglewood, I turned my back on music and spent most of the year working as a commercial artist. Then, just on a fluke, as a kind of last chance, I sent some scores to Aaron [Copland], and he accepted me as a student and gave me a scholarship to study composition at Tanglewood. (Aaron had heard my first string quartet during the summer of 1948.) The whole path of events changed after that.

Aaron was a huge presence at Tanglewood. It was, in those years, one of the most glamorous places ever. In the middle of it was Aaron, not only as the important American composer at the time but also as the person reaching out to other composers. When I first went to study with him, I thought of Copland as representing a kind of neoclassic Americana. My own natural inclinations had very little to do with Americana, and I worried that he would be unsympathetic to other kinds of music. I remember in an early lesson my bristling when he said, "How come you always use intervals like minor thirds and major sevenths? Why don't you ever use a perfect fifth?" And I thought, "This is the Americana bit rising up." But that was not the case at all. He was very erudite and his tastes were catholic. He could criticize twelve-tone composers and had a genuine interest in composers of all kinds of music, as well as those working closer to his own style. Aaron had a wonderful eye and ear for the shape of a piece. He could very quickly recognize the original premise of a work and just as quickly put his finger on spots that didn't live up to the promise of the opening. Copland was really the most amazing teacher.

Composer Howard Shanet, another Yale interviewee, felt the same way.

My presence at Tanglewood came about through Copland. I telephoned him at a mutual friend's suggestion, and I went on at length about how much I wanted to go to Tanglewood. It suddenly occurred to me that I hadn't made it clear to Aaron that I meant in *conducting*! Here I was talking to America's best-known composer, and I couldn't make myself say that I didn't mean to study with him at all! When Aaron said, "My class is filled, but you may get into Martinů's group," I thought I had better go along. I dug out whatever scores I had and sent them along with an application. To my surprise, I was accepted as a composer to study with Martinů and returned the next year in [Arthur] Honegger's class.

One of my jobs was to organize the student composers' concerts. On one occasion, I had to conduct a quintet because no one else would take it on. Afterward, Aaron came up and said, "Why didn't you tell me you were a conductor?" I said, "That's what I have been trying to do all this time!" Aaron offered to tell Koussevitzky about me.

Alberto Ginastera, probably the leading South American composer of his generation, was influenced in a different way by Copland. Again from the Yale interviews:

Copland obtained the scholarship for me to go to Tanglewood. My main reason was to study the problems of education and music institutions, and this was very useful for me, because in Argentina I created the first music school of professional level and the first chair of musicology. Copland instructed me where to go to investigate. He told me that one very great experience would be Tanglewood. Just that year of 1946 was a very remarkable year, because there were Latin American composers who became well known, and there was also Bernstein and Lukas Foss. It was one of the years you never forget. And then I attended Copland's classes, because I was very much interested in the teaching of composition. It can be said I was a pupil of Copland. His spirit is very open and generous. Every time he could help us in trying to open a certain door, he always did it. These powerful communications were due also to the fact that he spoke Spanish.

In my country, I have been the equivalent of what Copland is in this country. There is a parallel: our love for humanity and for our countries. What Copland did could be bigger because it is a much bigger country. I always say that I am a composer thanks to the United States.

One student, Yehudi Wyner, who later was to become a longtime faculty member at the Music Center, wrote Aaron Copland on May 21, 1947, about a problem he was anticipating. Ah, the wisdom of youth!

May 21, 1947

Dear Mr. Copland:

In the light of your recent telephone conversation with my father, Lazar Weiner [*sic*], I decided to write to you to explain more fully what was discussed then. As he probably told you, I graduated Juilliard last year and am now at Yale University working for an A.B. with a major in composition. My intentions for this summer are to go to Tanglewood—and to work, not to mess around. I feel that a great part of this last year has been a waste of time from a musical standpoint, and feel great remorse and guilt over it. I've got a few ideas for a composition or two flitting about and must get a chance to work them out. Tanglewood seems like a good place at which to accomplish that. However—from friends who have been there I've heard a lot about the situation in Department 5 (into which I've been placed) and due to the fantastic amount of distraction which prevails, I'd hardly say that it sounds promising to one who doesn't want to spend a six-week "vacation" in the usual (happy-go-lucky, haphazard, and amusementative) way. It boils down to this—I would like to have a place where I can practice and compose in peace for a few hours each day. If I don't accomplish anything with that time, then the blame will be entirely on myself; if I do turn out something worthwhile, then so much the better—it will be a summer well spent.

Surely you have had similar difficulties and can understand how I feel.

Do you have any suggestions? Can you help me find a place at Tanglewood (other than the woods themselves) where "peace and tranquility reign supreme" and where" the imagination can fly unbounded and exist undistracted??!"

All this had become a moot point because Wyner, at seventeen, was too young to be admitted.

According to what he wrote in the Tanglewood Remembered collection, Robert Starer was one of the few composers whose memories of Tanglewood were not so rosy.

My recollections of Tanglewood—I was there the summer of 1948—are not entirely pleasant. I remember it as a highly political place, in which many music students were trying to curry favor with influential musicians or simply to impress them. I don't suppose it has changed much in the past forty years—I have not been back.

On the positive side I remember advice Darius Milhaud gave—I quoted him in my book *Continuo* [" . . . if you cannot use an idea immediately, you should throw it away. 'If you don't have another idea soon,' he said, 'you're not a composer'"]—and the bright spot of my summer was Koussevitzky saying to me after looking at a score of mine: "There are many people who write notes on paper. You are a *real* composer."

I also remember a rather amusing debate about women composers (this was forty years ago), which Copland moderated. Leonard Bernstein represented the faculty; Lukas Foss and I spoke for the students.

Olga Gratch Gorelli from the TMC reunion remembrances:

I remember when I participated in Aaron Copland's forum discussion on the place of women in music. One of my fellow students prepared me by making me drink apricot brandy (to lower my voice). I was asked to talk about women composers and I created a bit of controversy by describing the antifeminist position I was holding at the time, under the influence of Madame Milhaud [Ms. Gorelli had been a pupil of Madame's husband, Darius]. She had convinced me that women cannot think abstractly and therefore could never be great composers (or mathematicians). So I said that women cannot do great things, but they can do "nice things." Years later, when I was studying with Milhaud in Santa Barbara, I saw Lukas Foss again, and he still remembered that phrase of mine and teased me quite a bit.

From the very beginning of the Music Center, women had always been active participants. Often they comprised around half of the student orchestra. One of Koussevitzky's favorite soloists in the Shed was violinist Ruth Posselt. Dr. Margaret Grant was the first executive secretary (later called administrator) of the Music Center. Koussevitzky gave anyone with talent a chance. And it wasn't just musical talent that attracted his interest.

Photographs of Tanglewood abound, but few are more memorable than those taken by Ruth Orkin. In 1946, she was a twentysomething girl whose main claim to fame was that she had just photographed Leonard Bernstein at Lewisohn Stadium on assignment for the New York Times.

In the future she would make her mark as a photojournalist in the golden age of picture magazines with such pictures as the flirtatious "American Girl in Italy" for Life *magazine. Her memorable series of pictures of Central Park, taken from her apartment window while dying of cancer, are her most famous, but in 1946 all she wanted to do was combine her*

The redoubtable Miss Gertrude Robinson Smith, founder and moving force of the Berkshire Symphonic Festival. (Boston Symphony Orchestra)

The Berkshire Symphonic Board of Trustees, in front of Gertrude Robinson Smith's home in Glendale. She presented this picture to the Selectmen of Stockbridge. From left to right: Milton Warner, Mrs. Carlos M. de Heredia, Mrs. Owen Johnson, Miss Robinson Smith, Mrs. Henry Francis, John C. Lynch, Owen Johnson, Mrs. Charles C. Griswold, William L. Bull, and George W. Edman. (Boston Symphony Orchestra)

Dan Hanna's horse ring becomes the first Berkshire Music Festival concert venue on the afternoon of August 25, 1934. (Boston Symphony Orchestra; David Milton Jones)

The sight lines at the Hanna farm concert site must have left something to be desired. (Boston Symphony Orchestra)

The box office is open for business the afternoon of the first concert. In the foreground are three members of the BSF board: John C. Lynch, Henry W. Dwight, and George W. Edman, with his back to the camera. (Boston Symphony Orchestra; David Milton Jones)

Holmwood tent.

The BSF group convenes before the tent of the 1936 concert series at Holmwood. Standing, top left, is the hardworking clerk George Edman, here with his sleeves rolled up. Also standing: Sheriff Bruce McIntyre; Granville Willis, engineer. Seated: John C. Lynch, treasurer; Joseph Franz; Gertrude Robinson Smith, president; unknown; Elizabeth Downing, secretary to Gertrude Robinson Smith. Ground: Willard Sistare, chief usher; unknown.

The Shed under construction. (Boston Symphony Orchestra; David Milton Jones)

The always impeccably tailored Serge Koussevitzky steps out of his limousine before a concert. (Boston Symphony Orchestra)

The rainstorm that launched the fundraising effort to build the Shed. Think of how many white shoes were ruined that evening! (*Berkshire Eagle*)

The Tanglewood parking lot, circa late 1930s. (Boston Symphony Orchestra)

The 1937 box holders dressed a little more formally than today's Tanglewood audiences. (*Berkshire Eagle*)

The "Berkshire Cottage" on the grounds of Tanglewood is transformed into the Main House, headquarters of the Berkshire Music Center. (Boston Symphony Orchestra)

The Berkshire Symphonic Festival board members were never slackers when it came to publicity. This 1939 banner, if nothing else, is bold. (Boston Symphony Orchestra)

The elegant new Tanglewood grounds shortly after the Shed was inaugurated, as seen from the air. (*Berkshire Eagle*)

Ever aware of new and emerging talent, Koussevitzky presents his latest "find," Dorothy Maynor. (Boston Symphony Orchestra)

Early Shed audience, undated. (*Berkshire Eagle*)

Serge Koussevitzky and his protégé Leonard Bernstein in this memorable Heinz Weissenstein photograph. (Whitestone Photo)

Koussevitzky with Lukas Foss taking a bow after a concert. Doesn't the maestro seem proud of his other protégé? Concertmaster Richard Burgin joins in the appreciation. (Boston Symphony Orchestra)

Composer Paul Hindemith, looking avuncular—not the way his students saw him. (Boston Symphony Orchestra; Ellsworth Ford)

Composer Aaron Copland, looking reflective—definitely the way his students saw him. (Boston Symphony Orchestra)

Aaron Copland teaching a composing class in the 1940s. (Boston Symphony Orchestra; Howard S. Babbitt Jr.)

A little time off for good behavior: The Music Center beach on the Stockbridge Bowl, with Lukas Foss standing on the dock. (Boston Symphony Orchestra; John Brook)

A crowd enjoying a concert at the Theatre-Concert Hall. Thanks to a gift from Mary Louise Curtis Bok, the hall was opened in 1941. Even though architects Eliel Saarinen and his son Eero were put out by the changes made in the Shed, Koussevitzky convinced them to design this new building, as well as the nearby Chamber Music Hall, where Phyllis Curtin now gives her master classes. (*Berkshire Eagle*; Joe Petrovec)

Serge Koussevitzky's birthdays, on July 26, were always important Tanglewood occasions—particularly for the Music Center students. Here, in 1940, he is flanked by Leonard Bernstein (left) and Lukas Foss (right). They often wrote celebratory pieces to be performed in Koussevitzky's honor. Foss produced a birthday ode for chorus and piano, and Bernstein composed the infamous "Koussevitzky Blues," followed by "Also sprach Koussevitzky." (Boston Symphony Orchestra)

Miss Elizabeth Cabot shows off a poster for the British Aid concert. (Boston Symphony Orchestra)

Serge Koussevitzky seated at a Baldwin piano. His great friend Lucien Wulsin, president of Baldwin Piano Co., provided free pianos for the Music Center for many years, until the company went out of business. (*Berkshire Eagle*)

Here at the raffle booth, a pair of nylon stockings takes precedence over the Bobby Jones golf clubs. (*Berkshire Eagle*)

The Allied Relief Concert for British Aid, which Koussevitzky called a "Manifestation," went on for most of the day. On the lawn, people listen to the concert while raffle tickets are sold and donations contributed. (*Berkshire Eagle*)

And the winner is . . . : Socialite Else Maxwell, violinist and BSF board member Albert Spalding, and Mrs. J. Frederic Schenct Jr. draw for the prizes. (Boston Symphony Orchestra)

Dorothy Thompson, the leading foreign correspondent of her day, urges everyone to support the British in their great war effort. (*Berkshire Eagle*)

Dorothy Thompson being congratulated by Serge Koussevitzky (left) and Maxim Litvinov, Soviet ambassador to Great Britain (right). (*Berkshire Eagle*)

Arthur Honegger, Berkshire Music Center composer in residence, 1947. Unfortunately, two weeks after he arrived at Tanglewood, he suffered a heart attack, from which he recovered. He was replaced by Samuel Barber. (Boston Symphony Orchestra; Howard S. Babbitt Jr.)

The distinguished faculty of the Berkshire Music Center, 1948.

Front row: Unknown, Irving Fine, Lukas Foss, James Stagliano, Catherine Wolf, Frederick Fennell, Irwin Hoffman, Seymour Lipkin, Howard Shanet, Willem Walkenier, Edith Gomberg.

Row 2: Richard Burgin, Gregor Piatigorsky, Jacob Raichman, Georges Moleux, Darius Milhaud, Ralph Berkowitz, Aaron Copland, Leonard Bernstein, Serge Koussevitzky, Eleazar de Carvalho, George Laurent, Bernard Zighers, unknown (2).

Row 3: Einar Hansen, Roman Szulc, Louis Speyer, Hugh Ross, Wolfus (first name unknown), Boris Goldovsky, Rosario Mazzeo, Georges Mager, Victor Polatschek, Raymond Allard, unknown (4).

Ruth Orkin's camera captured a lighter mood at the same time the official 1948 BMC picture was taken. Seated on ground: Frederick Fennell. Row 1, on bench, left to right: BMC administrator Ralph Berkowitz, Aaron Copland, Serge Koussevitzky, Eleazar de Carvalho, and George Laurent. (Ruth Orkin)

World-renowned cellist Gregor Piatigorsky and violinist Jascha Heifetz taking time off for a cigarette break outside the Shed in 1949. (Boston Symphony Orchestra)

A Tanglewood jam session with Leonard Bernstein (no doubt at the piano) next to the trombone player. (Ruth Orkin)

Leonard Bernstein, at the piano, analyzes his "Age of Anxiety" for the conducting auditors in 1949. (Boston Symphony Orchestra; Howard S. Babbitt Jr.)

Serge Koussevitzky on the terrace of his house, Seranak, overlooking the Stockbridge Bowl. (Boston Symphony Orchestra; William Whitaker)

Benjamin Britten and Serge Koussevitzky backstage at a *Peter Grimes* production. As Koussevitzky said, "There is *Carmen*. And there is *Peter Grimes*." (Boston Symphony Orchestra; Howard S. Babbitt Jr.)

Benjamin Britten, director Eric Crozier (front row on left), and conductor Leonard Bernstein (in white jacket in middle of front row) take their curtain calls for *Peter Grimes*. (*Berkshire Eagle*)

Ruth Orkin (left) takes her own picture on the Tanglewood lawn with (left to right) unknown, Marc Blitzstein, and Leonard Bernstein. (Ruth Orkin)

One of the most famous pictures of Lenny and Koussy. (Ruth Orkin)

Assembled for the annual group picture in the hot July sun are (center row, left to right) Leonard Bernstein; Aaron Copland; Serge Koussevitzky, with his own solution to avoiding heat prostration; Stanley Chapple; and Richard Burgin. (Ruth Orkin)

BMC fellow on the move in front of the Music Store. (Ruth Orkin)

A beautiful day on the lawn in front of the Shed. (Ruth Orkin)

Two musicians on their way to work. (Ruth Orkin)

Boris Goldovsky conducts the Berkshire Music Center orchestra in a production of Rossini's *Il Turco in Italia*. (Boston Symphony Orchestra)

Boris Goldovsky (far right) rehearsing *Eugene Onegin* with singers (from left to right) Ilona Strasser, Ellen Faull, and Phyllis Curtin—Koussevitzky's Tatiana. (Boston Symphony Orchestra; Howard S. Babbitt Jr.)

A 1948 Goldovsky student production of *Pelléas et Mélisande*, which was presented in the Tanglewood garden, as was *Acis & Galatea*. (Boston Symphony Orchestra; Howard S. Babbitt Jr.)

passion for music and photography by spending the summer at Tanglewood. She told the story in her book A Photo Journal.

The Tanglewood Music Festival in 1946 was my best school of all. In response to a note that I had sent to the Boston Symphony Orchestra, I received a curt reply that said in closing "freelancing would be very limited." But I went up anyway, with all my dark-room equipment and my cello. I set up all my darkroom equipment in the basement of the Lenox Hotel; the cello was insurance in the event that I needed to masquerade as a student.

As it turned out, I had no trouble getting on the grounds, and before long the Boston Symphony publicity man was out of necessity sending over many of the newspaper and magazine reporters who needed one-of-a-kind photographs to go along with their articles. It was Tanglewood's first year of operation since the beginning of the war, and the orchestra had underestimated the interest of the press.

Tanglewood was a dream come true. It was like the Hollywood Bowl, the Peter Meremblum Orchestra, a summer camp, a holiday resort, and a working and money-making experience all rolled into one. I couldn't have been more stimulated, prolific, or happy. However, I still had only the Rolleiflex to work with. Since it was so difficult for me to shoot candid shots with the ground glass (partly because of my nearsightedness), I would set up corny pictorial shots such as string players rehearsing on the lawn.

The money that I made during that summer, plus a loan, enabled me to buy my first 35-mm camera, a Contax . . . at long last!

Over the following winter, Orkin put together a charming little souvenir book, which she hoped to sell on the Tanglewood grounds the following summer. But there were stumbling blocks in her way, as you can tell from this quite cheeky letter to Dr. Koussevitzky she wrote.

April 28, 1947

Dear Dr. Koussevitzky:

I'm still eager to publish that little Tanglewood souvenir book (which I showed you last Thurs. after your rehearsal), but now another problem has come up. First it was the money I had to raise because Mr. Judd said there could be no advertising. Remember, you said, "You will find it." Well, I found it . . . and now Mr. Burk has written that Mr. Judd said "I cannot promise to sell any publications at Tanglewood, except in the shop."

Well, now I can understand why there's never been any souvenir book of Tanglewood published before. Only a rich man's daughter could afford to take a chance under conditions like that. The money I've raised is not mine, and I would be a fool to invest it under the present setup. If the books were only sold in the Music Shop, you couldn't sell more than four or five hundred (or in other words I'd get back about one third of this investment, and lose the other $650).

Dr. Koussevitzky . . . do you know that 90 percent of the Festival audience never comes *near* the Music Shop? They simply don't know it exists. Last summer I even met members of the Boston Symphony who never heard of it. Is it any wonder that it loses money?

I can understand the BSO not wanting to make Tanglewood commercialized (I'm not advocating neon lights) . . . but I honestly feel Mr. Judd is leaning over backwards in this case. He says the Music Shop is only there as a service. However, if a visitor merely wants to buy a nickel postcard to send home, he's forced to set out on an exploration in order to find one. There isn't even a sign in front of the bushes directing people to it.

And after they get there, there isn't anything in the way of a pictorial souvenir . . . combination guidebook-and–information pamphlet (like mine, if it ever gets published) for them to buy.

And that's how I got the idea for the souvenir book in the first place . . . from hanging around the Music Shop, and getting the feeling that a lot of visitors were disappointed because they felt they were leaving Tanglewood empty-handed. . . .that they had nothing really representative to show the people back home. (If they can't carry the music in their hearts, there are records to buy. But if they can't describe Tanglewood like a raconteur, there should at least be pictures to take away.)

All I am asking—and this is the reason for this whole letter—is that the souvenir book can be *sold on little tables placed around the Shed* . . . just as Mr. [M. A. DeWolfe] Howe's book *Tale of Tanglewood* was sold last summer. When I spoke to you I was under the impression that it would be . . . since Mr. Perry said he could see no reason why not (and I can't for the life of me see why not either). But since Mr. Judd has the last word over Mr. Perry, and you have the last word over Mr. Judd, there is no one for me to go to but you—altho I hate to bother you with things like this when I know you have more important things on your mind.

Getting over the advertising obstacle and being forced to raise all the money myself is hard enough (even the Boston Symphony program is allowed to take advertising—there were fifteen pages of it last summer) . . . but going ahead now would be like pouring money down a drain.

I'm so anxious about this whole thing mainly because I'm the photographer. . . . I've never seen all my pictures in one book before. Besides, I've taken time out from work to spend more than a month on it . . . preparing it with the layout artist, writing the copy, doing research. I don't mind admitting it's going to be awfully disappointing not to see it come to life. And another thing, it took *six weeks* last summer to even *take* the pictures. At the present time there isn't another photographer who could put such a book together.

Mr. Burk says he admires my "courage" for wanting to take the risk even after Mr. Judd said there could be no advertising. However, unless your word bolsters me up and the book can be sold on tables along with Mr. Howe's book, I'll have to sorrowfully admit defeat.

The only courage I have is based on the fact that I feel confident that Tanglewood visitors think enough of the place to want to buy a souvenir of it. But unless the souvenir is placed where they can see it, even I don't believe they're going to *hunt* for something they don't even know exists.

Last Wednesday when I saw Mr. Burk, Mr. Perry, and Mr. Judd, they all tried to discourage me . . . saying that I would lose money. Well, I just want to say for the record that last year in this same month I wrote Mr. Judd asking if I could come to Tanglewood as a freelance photographer. He wrote back saying that their photographs were all taken care of in advance . . . that the opportunities for a freelancer were extremely limited . . . and in short, he was *very* discouraging.

Well, I came up anyway (complete with darkroom) and here's what happened: Mr. Burk bought $100 worth of pictures for the BSO files . . . the students and visitors bought 400-odd pictures through the Music Shop . . . and every newspaper and magazine writer in the press booth came to me asking for pictures. In the end (except for two exceptions), every picture published about the 1946 season were ones I took that six weeks. My conclusion is, *I* have confidence in the souvenir book. I wish somebody would remember what happened last summer and have confidence in me.

Sincerely yours,
Ruth Orkin

I suspect that Koussevitzky admired Orkin's pluck and saw something of himself in her. In any event, she did publish a charming souvenir book in 1948, which offered the following description of the Berkshire Music Center to the visitor:

On the first day a symphonic potpourri begins. The hubbub doesn't cease for six weeks. Music fills the air from every direction. The twenty-five little practice studios in the Main House are in constant use. The clamor of rehearsing orchestras and choruses drift across the lawns from every building.

That first night Lenox drugstores are cluttered with tired students. "My dorm is a madhouse. After I found two trombonists in the bathroom I couldn't stand it any longer. You even have to reserve the closets two weeks in advance!"

But an alma mater spirit has already begun. Everyone's one-word description of Tanglewood is: "Terrific!" . . .

Clothes that set the style are sweatshirts, plain shirts, peasant blouses, dirndls, braids, bow ties, and corduroy jackets. But at student concerts orchestra members "dress up" in white jackets and dresses. Koussevitzky sits up front with his entourage. The proud teacher passing judgment on his pupils.

In summer of 1998, the Boston Symphony mounted an exhibition of Ruth Orkin's Tanglewood photographs in the Main House gallery. The spirit of her pictures was well expressed in this handout given to visitors.

The photos in this exhibit reflect the joy and energy of those postwar years at Tanglewood. Musicians smile into the camera, students move briskly, audiences seem animated or sensuously at rest. Ms. Orkin's camera is a welcome guest. She is there when Koussevitzky celebrates his seventy-second birthday. She captures Leonard Bernstein singing from the steps of this house [the Main House], Koussevitzky cutting his cake, and the merry creators of a birthday card. At a large gathering at the Music Center the musicians, including Aaron Copland, Koussevitzky, and Eleazar de Carvalho burst into laughter. One can sense the photographer's youth and delight.

Tod Perry summed up the 1947 season in the Tanglewood Alumni Bulletin:

The amount of music to be heard at Tanglewood is almost unbelievable, especially when one sits down and tots up the score. In the forty-two days of the session, there were sixty-one concerts. Ten of these were the big Festival concerts by the Boston Symphony Orchestra (Dr. Koussevitzky conducted seven of them, Leonard Bernstein two, and Robert Shaw one), two Bach and two Mozart concerts conducted by Dr. Koussevitzky, and one super show, with the eager help of RCA Victor, for the benefit of the Music Center, reminiscent of the gala benefits during the war. There were three Coolidge Chamber Music Concerts—the Gordon String Quartet, the Albeneri Trio, and the Berkshire Woodwind Ensemble. The Juilliard Quartet played modern American chamber music, and Leonard Bernstein conducted a group of the BSO players in an all-Stravinsky chamber music program. That leaves forty-one concerts that were prepared and performed by the students, including the three performances of *Idomeneo*. And the performances were excellent. Where else could a school orchestra attract as many as 2,500 people, as the Friday night advanced-orchestra concerts did? Where else could you draw six or seven hundred people out for chamber music at ten-thirty [on] Sunday morning? *Idomeneo*, of course, was on an SRO basis for over a month before the performances. And all the guests at these concerts, except the students, were people who had made contributions to the support of the school through the Friends of the Berkshire Music Center—in short, who came because they believed in what they saw.

Let's give the last word to Ned Rorem.

The next summer I went back to recapture Paradise. You never quite can, can you? And yet I did. In 1947 the guest composer-teacher was Honegger. Like Martinů before him, Honegger was stricken during his first week and spent the rest of the time in the hospital. So Samuel Barber, who just happened to be on campus, agreed to replace him. I was still in Copland's class, but Barber's chief pupil was Bill Flanagan, who thereupon, until his death in 1969, became my best friend (platonic) in the music world. By then I had already published a few songs and had a firmer ego than the year before. Aaron seemed to repeat himself with the new class, even as I doubtless do today at Curtis, hoping no one will notice.

I returned to Tanglewood for a few days in 1948 when Hugh Ross introduced my Sappho madrigals. Then I stayed away until 1959, when I stopped by for lunch with Aaron and Harold Clurman. In the shade of the Shed I shed a tear and haven't been back since.

Throughout that time [the 1940s and '50s] Tanglewood was the foremost laboratory for operatic experimentation in the United States, and perhaps even in the world.

The carte blanche we were given during those many summers at Tanglewood changed the nature of opera in the United States. For the methods we developed have since permeated the length and breadth of the country and will eventually, I am convinced, change the attitude toward opera throughout the world.

—Boris Goldovsky
My Road to Opera

Boris Goldovsky
and the
Opera Department

Carte Blanche to Treat Opera Singers Like Full-fledged Artists

Although opera workshops are now to be found all over the country, until 1940 there was almost no place in the United States where apprentice singers could practice their craft after finishing their formal studies. Then, Europe was their only proving ground.

However, with the Berkshire Music Center Opera Department, Koussevitzky was to change all of that. As an indication of how successful the department would become, within a few short years an impressive number of world-class American opera singers had began their careers at Tanglewood. Consider the names Adele Addison, Phyllis Curtin, Justino Diaz, Rosalind Elias, Sherrill Milnes, Leontyne Price, Robert Rounseville, Marni Nixon, Richard Cassilly, Shirley Verrett, and George Shirley. And they are only the tip of the Tanglewood vocal iceberg.

The opera department seems to have originally been the brainchild of Metropolitan Opera stage director Herbert Graf. Boris Goldovsky, the man who would eventually really put opera on the map at Tanglewood, described Graf as "a short, intense-looking Austrian, with thin lips, blue black hair, and black eyes." Goldovsky admitted that "there was no denying the technical competence of a man whose father had been a famous music critic and who had spent most of his life working on the opera stage," but Goldovsky found his acting instruction "too casual for my dramatic taste"—all of which would come into play later on.

But for now, Graf sets the scene in his book, Opera for the People.

One of the first of these school opera groups developed at Koussevitzky's Berkshire Music Center at Tanglewood in Massachusetts, from a suggestion I made in 1939. With World War II threatening to break out in Europe, I decided to spend the summer in America trying to make myself familiar with the summertime operatic activities in this country. Olin Downes advised me to visit the Music Festival at Tanglewood and there introduced me to Dr. Koussevitzky after the last concert of the season.

The next morning, at Artur Rodzinski's home, where Dr. Koussevitzky was staying at the time, I heard him outline his ideas and dreams for the school of the Berkshire Music Center, which was to open the next summer (1940). He talked, too, about his plans for festive musical plays to be given along the lines of Greek musical dramas and scenic oratorios, and about his hope of building a huge open-air theater on the meadow that slopes down from the concert "Shed" to the lake.

I was enthusiastic about this prospect and immediately suggested the addition of an opera department to the program of the new school as a first step toward making opera a part of the Tanglewood festival. At Dr. Koussevitzky's request I put this suggestion into writing, assuring him that all that would be needed for a beginning, in addition to my work as a dramatic teacher, would be a music instructor, a room sufficiently large to permit the acting of a group of singers, a piano, and the help of his office staff. The expenses would therefore be modest.

This proposal was accepted by Dr. Koussevitzky and his board and opera became part of the Music Center's curriculum in time for the school's opening.

I asked Boris Goldovsky, then in Cleveland, to assist me, and we held auditions and began rehearsing opera scenes, working in the garage adjacent to the small temporary stage which at that time served all the various activities of the school. As soon as we saw the excellent qualifications our singers had for certain roles, we wanted to give a performance of opera scenes, but no funds for such a purpose had been provided in the budget.

Fortunately, [Ward] Gaston, the superintendent of the Tanglewood grounds, who lived in a little house near the garage, enjoyed the enthusiasm of the young singers—and perhaps also the good looks of some of the would-be prima donnas. He gave us permission to browse through his house and take along a stove, a couch, a table, two chairs, a water glass and two bottles, house key and two candles. And there we were, all set to go into production with the scene between Rudolph and Mimi in act 1 of *La Bohème*.

In a similar manner, we got together the necessary properties for some other scenes, and our first performance of opera excerpts took place.

Its success increased our appetite. Now we wanted to perform an entire opera. There was a fine student orchestra at Tanglewood, but there was no money to pay for the renting of the necessary scenery and lighting equipment. Dr. Koussevitzky, always with an open heart for young artists, counseled patience; we would find a way out. And we did.

The prop master for this first opera effort was a young man by the name of Thomas D. Perry—Tod to his many friends and colleagues. At that time he was a member of the 1940 Berkshire Music Center class, although he would subsequently go on to work his way up through the BSO ranks, eventually becoming the orchestra's distinguished, longtime manager. He was a man of great style and wit, as is obvious from his description of Tanglewood's first venture into full-scale opera, written for the 1948 edition of the Tanglewood Alumni Bulletin. We will hear more from Mr. Perry in subsequent chapters.

The impressiveness and brilliance of the productions of the opera department in the last few seasons—the premiere of Benjamin Britten's *Peter Grimes* in 1946 and the first

American performance of Mozart's *Idomeneo* in 1947—the international attention they have received and the celebrity of the audiences, give rise to recollections of the first opera production at Tanglewood: Handel's *Acis & Galatea* in 1940. It was put on in the formal garden, where a temporary stage was constructed between the hedges, using the southern Berkshire Hills for a background. The use of the natural setting was lovely, indeed, but gave rise to complications from the point of view of the stage director. Since the stage stretched from hedge to hedge, the only exits had to be off the rear, where the actor had the choice of picking his way down a set of steps, disappearing gradually from the audience, or taking off into midair and surviving the six-foot drop as best he might. To reenter he could either climb the stairs, and thus gradually appear like the Cheshire Cat several seconds before he could deliver a line, or run a half block around the hedge and pant through the audience up one of two ramps on either side of the stage. The set consisted of a paper rock on which most of the action took place.

The day of the performance was clear and hot—in fact, a regular Berkshire scorcher. The orchestra was to be concealed, more or less, behind the hedges. In order to prevent melting the varnish from the instruments, since everyone was in the bright sun, the players were each provided with an umbrella, secured from heaven knows where. Mr. Goldovsky was the conductor. Since he needed both hands to conduct, he was unable to cope with an umbrella and resorted to a handkerchief on his head. The appearance to the audience, who saw only the tops of forty-odd umbrellas and Mr. Goldovsky's white-crowned pate, was little short of fascinating.

Acis, the tenor, was supposed to spend some little time dying, and dead, on the tar-paper rock. The rock became so hot in the sun that it was quite out of the question to walk on it, much less lie upon it. The problem was solved by hosing the whole stage down with water at the last possible moment. This was at best a temporary solution, since the water steamed away quickly in gentle clouds of vapor, as from a concrete pavement after a summer shower. This was picturesque and idyllic enough, but it left Don Hultgren, who sang Acis and who was dressed à la Grec in a short chiton, with some rather agonizing last moments as he lay stretched on the nearly molten rock, with Galatea singing a tender air over him.

A chorus of dancers was involved, recruited from the country dancing class. The arrangements were such that this chorus had to hide some fifty yards away in the grape arbor until the cue came. The trick was to get the cue from that distance, where the orchestra was devised, a discreet wigwag (since the wigwagger was in full view of the audience) and the dancers came bounding gaily upon the scene singing, as I recall, "Happy, happy, happy we."

The monster of the piece, Polyphemus, who was sung by Frank Capelli, in order to look truly monstrous he had to be covered from head to foot with upholsterer's hair, which was stuck on with spirit gum. The heat of the day, the hair, and the bearskin that was his costume combined to make the monster's lot probably the unhappiest of all, which was probably the librettist's idea in the first place.

With all these hardships, the performance could have been excused for being a little disjointed. It was, on the contrary, superb. The atmosphere of the setting, the charm of the opera, and the excellent work of the singers and orchestra combined to make it a memorable day.

Thus was the Berkshire Music Center Opera Department launched on its road to celebrity.

Boris Goldovsky was intimately involved in the opera department from its inception. In years to come, he would found the New England Opera Theater and the Goldovsky Opera Theater and become rather famous as a regular contributor to the Metropolitan Opera's Saturday afternoon broadcasts for over forty years. In his book My Road to Opera, *Goldovsky remembered the part he initially played in bringing new life to opera at Tanglewood.*

In September of 1939 I had received a letter from Herbert Graf informing me that Serge Koussevitzky, the conductor of the Boston Symphony Orchestra, was opening a summer music school at Lenox, Massachusetts, in July of the following year. He had asked Graf to head the new music center's opera department, but not being an opera conductor, Graf, who knew me well from our work together in Philadelphia and Cleveland, had suggested that I be chosen as his musical assistant. The proposal had apparently met with Koussevitzky's approval, for he and George Judd, the manager of the Boston Symphony Orchestra, were prepared to pay me $500 to help Dr. Graf during the Berkshire Music Festival of 1940.

Although we were both of Russian origin, this was the first time I had ever had any dealings with Serge Koussevitzky. Mother, I knew, was an old friend of his, and Uncle Pierre had often accompanied him on the piano at a time when Koussevitzky was touring Russia as a double-bass virtuoso. Pierre had also helped him later, playing orchestral scores on the piano when Koussevitzky was so laboriously learning to become a conductor, and he had even sailed down the Volga with him on one of Koussevitzky's famous pre–First World War orchestral tours. . . .

Koussevitzky began the summer course by calling in the various teachers to find out what they would like to undertake during the summer session. "Here, in Tanglewood," he said to me, "you will be able to realize your secret dreams, to experiment with ideas you could not try out elsewhere. Now tell me, have you anything of the sort in mind?"

"Some of my ideas may seem utopian," I replied, "but still, I would like to find out what would happen if we were to treat opera singers like full-fledged artists and not like unmusical and clumsy marionettes who cannot be trusted to think for themselves."

"You expect opera singers . . . to be artists who think for themselves?"—Koussevitzky's hazel eyes seemed to widen as he stared at me fixedly. "But, Good Lord," he said, as though he had just listened to some scandalous enormity, "this certainly cannot be done."

"You may be right," I said. "Perhaps it cannot be done. But would you mind if I try?"

"Oh, no," he said. "Go ahead and try. By all means, go ahead and try. I give you carte blanche."

Our main problem, however, was the absence of a theater. All that was available was an open-air platform, covered by a large circus tent. When it rained, the marquee would gradually fill with water and begin to sag, and we would have to interrupt rehearsals to shake off the water. The tent was also too small to shelter the spectators, who had to sit, beyond its protective canopy, on chairs lined up on the grass.

For all these reasons we had to limit our ambitions to short excerpts and one-act operas. The first complete work chosen, in obvious deference to its composer, Paul Hindemith, was a musical and dramatic prank entitled *Hin und Zurück*. In this curious piece—the kind one is willing to see once but never again—the music, like the action, moves forward and then begins reversing backward, like a cinematic reel, to its original point of departure. The result was clever, but that was about all one could say for it. I doubt that the performers—led by Richard Burgin, the concertmaster of the Boston Symphony Orchestra—enjoyed it any more than I, who had to play the four-hand piano part along with the composer.

Hindemith—a very opinionated gentleman from Frankfurt who had been offered a teaching post at Yale—may have sensed our lukewarmness toward his elaborate leg-pull, for he was soon complaining to Koussevitzky about the opera department, warning him that if he wasn't careful, "it will develop an insatiable appetite and devour everything else around here." Unfortunately for himself, he was so overbearing in pressing his strong feelings on every possible subject that he finally got on Koussevitzky's nerves. They had a violent argument about something, and Hindemith left Tanglewood in a huff. He was never invited back. . . .

We were repeatedly told by Koussevitzky that he expected us to "deliver 200 percent." Apparently we did, for at the end of the summer school he informed Herbert Graf and myself that he would like us back at Tanglewood next year. He had great plans for the summer school of 1941, and if all went well we would have an "opera house" to perform in when we returned.

He was as good as his word. Mrs. Curtis Bok, who had attended some of the 1940 concerts, had generously donated $10,000, and Koussevitzky had persuaded a number of other wealthy patrons to give him the money needed to build a Theatre–Concert Hall capable of seating 1,200 spectators.

In an October 6, 1941, article in Opera News, *"Sky-hooks for Opera," an anonymous Tanglewood auditor described Tanglewood's new opera theater.*

Five huge, orange trusses, known picturesquely as Sky-hooks, over the roof of the new theatre near Stockbridge, Massachusetts, focused the attention and wonder of the many thousands who last summer thronged the vast lawns and formal English gardens of Tanglewood for the Berkshire Music Festival. . . .

Four low wooden entrance doors, each in a different pastel shade of yellow, orange, green, or blue, lead to an equally informal interior: the gravel flooring sloping gently toward the stage; sun and air streaming in from slats in the ceiling. The unusual sense of lightness and airiness is credited to suspension from the roof, an idea of its Finnish architects, Eliel and Eero Saarinen.

To the professional eye, the stage proved of greatest interest. Here every modern theatrical device offered its technical facility. Movable panels permitted enlargement or contraction. A proscenium stage with entrances on both sides and steps leading to the pit, as in the Greek form of theater, intimately united performers and audience. Scene shifting was accelerated by large work spaces in the wings, from which prepared sets could be quickly rolled on casters to the stage. The plaster dome provided a perspective absent even in the Metropolitan's hug cyclorama. The orchestra platform could be lowered or raised at will. In each dressing room stood a miniature piano, serving to equip it as a backstage studio.

This is obviously a long way from sets made of broiling tar and hankies on the head as shelter from the sun. Boris Goldovsky continues the story.

The summer school's activities were once again opened with a formal "commencement" addressed, *prononced* by Koussevitzky, who, as I was beginning to discover, loved to "*prononce* a speech" on every possible occasion. He expressed gratitude to the "trusties" of the Boston Symphony Orchestra whose generosity was making it possible to bring music to the "maces" ("masses"). He was also pleased to *annonce* a special ceremony, which was to take place exactly three days hence, on Thursday, to inaugurate the new Theatre–Concert Hall.

Working at a "200 percent delivery" tempo, Herbert Graf and I managed to prepare a few scenes from Mozart's *Così fan tutte* so as to have something to put on stage when the Theatre–Concert Hall was formally inaugurated. These musical offerings were accompanied by several speeches, one of which was made by Graf, as head of the Center's opera department. This noble building, he declared, was a symbol of the dawning of a new age when, instead of importing our traditions from Europe, we would begin to cultivate our own American ways of doing things. . . .

Having begun the summer course with several extracts from Mozart's *Così fan tutte*, Herbert Graf and I decided to finish it with a full-length performance of the opera. When the time came for the dress rehearsal, Koussevitzky made a dramatic appearance, striding majestically down the aisle in his famous black cape and taking a seat in the middle of the auditorium. In accordance with the ideas that Richard Wagner had first put into practice at Bayreuth, the orchestra pit in our new Theatre–Concert Hall had been so constructed that neither the conductor nor the instrumentalists could be seen by the audience. So I was not unduly surprised, in the middle of the overture, to see Koussevitzky learning over the balustrade and observing us intently.

A short scene followed the overture, and then, while the scenery was being changed, I hopped out of the pit and made my way back to the middle of the auditorium, where Koussevitzky was seated. He was obviously upset. His forehead was clouded and the blue vein over his left eyebrow was pulsating ominously—a sure sign that he was angry.

"How was the ensemble? How was the balance?" I asked a bit nervously.

"Both the ensemble and the balance are good," he replied in a sepulchral tone.

"Please, Serge Alexandrovich," I pleaded with him, "tell me what is wrong. Something is obviously wrong. But this is only the dress rehearsal. Maybe there is still time to correct it."

He let a long moment go by before answering. "Yes," he finally said, "something is wrong, something is disgracefully wrong. And it is all your fault!" he went on, with sudden vehemence. "How can you? How could you? That baseball bat! That telephone pole! Break it into a thousand pieces, throw it away, get rid of it at once!"

I heard the blistering words in a kind of dream, while my dazed brain sought to understand what he was referring to. Suddenly I knew: it was my baton, the nice, harmless stick with the thin cork handle which I had learned to use under Fritz Reiner, but which was very different from the pencil-thin wand which Koussevitzky dangled between the middle and ring fingers of his right hand. Serge Alexandrovich was hurt, hurt at the thought that one of *his* faculty members, conducting in *his* theater, for one of *his* Tanglewood rehearsals, someone who had had ample chance to study *his* conducting technique and who could easily have procured himself *his* kind of stick, had nevertheless chosen to use a different, foreign, disgraceful utensil. After returning to the orchestra pit, I broke Reiner's "telephone pole" into two ignominious stumps. I have never used a baton since that day.

When Herbert Graf and I returned to Tanglewood in July of 1942, we were in for a surprise. One of my duties, as the person responsible for the musical side of the opera department, was to audition singers applying for admission to the Berkshire Music Center, selecting the best one for our summer program. Almost all of them had already been examined, and those accepted had been given their assignments. But among the few who still needed to be auditioned on the first Monday of the summer-school term was a young truck driver from Philadelphia who had been admitted to the Berkshire Music Center on instructions from Serge Alexandrovich himself.

Alfredo—or Mario Lanza, as he now called himself (having adopted his mother's maiden name)—had managed to attract Koussevitzky's attention in Philadelphia during one of the Boston Symphony Orchestra's periodic visits to that city. After finding where Koussevitzky was staying, he had persuaded the desk clerk to give him a room next to Serge Alexandrovich's suite, and once installed he had given full throat to bel canto tunes and snatches of operatic areas. Intrigued by the extraordinary sound he heard issuing from his neighbor's room, Koussevitzky had introduced himself and invited Cocozza-Lanza to come to Tanglewood.

When the time came, on that first Monday, to test Lanza's tenor voice, Serge Alexandrovich came in person to listen to his protégé. Lanza was paired off with a young Mexican soprano named Irma Gonzalez, and the two were asked to sing part of the duet from the third act of *La Bohème*—this being something that Lanza had learned by heart (probably by listening to phonograph recordings). The tenor sound that issued from that simple truck driver's throat was gorgeous, unforgettable, out of this world. I could hardly believe my ears. Koussevitzky, seated next to me, was so excited that the tears began rolling down his cheeks, as they had a way of doing in moments of intense emotion.

"Caruso *redivivus!* "Caruso *redivivus!"* he whispered to me ecstatically, as he wiped his cheeks. He was overjoyed at the thought that his "discovery" was genuine, a priceless addition to the world of music, and that his first, favorable impression in Philadelphia was not mistaken.

"Listen," Koussevitzky said to me after the audition, "five weeks from now we are going to do Beethoven's Ninth Symphony, and I want this boy to sing the tenor part in it."

"Very well, Serge Alexandrovich," I assured him, "I will prepare him personally."

I gave instructions to have Lanza report to me the next morning for special coaching. But once we were together in the rehearsal room I realized that I was faced with an uphill job. Lanza, to begin with, could not read a line of music. Even worse, he had never had any solfège instruction and his ear was totally untrained. I would play one note on the piano and he would sing another. I would move up the scale, and, instead of following me, his voice would move down.

After several coaching sessions, I was ready to throw in the sponge. We were getting nowhere in a great hurry. At the lunch table I confessed by predicament to Ifor Jones, one of the choral directors at Tanglewood, who was also leader of the Bach Choir in Bethlehem, Pennsylvania: "Koussy wants Lanza to sing the tenor part in the Ninth Symphony, and he asked me to prepare it. But how can I coach somebody who can't read a note of music and whose ear is totally untrained?"

"You can't," was Ifor Jones's answer. "I know Lanza. I wanted to engage him for my festival performances. No good. It can't be done. You can't teach him anything."

We finally decided to go together to break the news to Koussevitzky. To avoid a scene, I decided to broach the subject as diplomatically as possible: "Dr. Koussevitzky, I just don't know how to teach this boy. He's got a beautiful tenor voice—there's no denying it—but he's musically untrained. Neither Dr. Jones nor I know how to go about teaching him the fundamentals. So why don't you select someone else who will prepare him for you?"

Koussevitzky was no fool. He realized immediately that if the two of us could not teach Lanza to sing the tenor part, then nobody could. The idea was allowed to die a quiet death.

Finally, after putting our heads together with Herbert Graf, we decided that Lanza might after all be taught to sing Fenton in Otto Nicolai's *The Merry Wives of Windsor*. Even though we shortened this small role as much as possible, it still required a lot of work. Somehow we managed to pound the words and music into Lanza's head, and he even scored a great hit with the audience when he sang the serenade in the second act. But most of the teachers and students of the opera department developed a hearty dislike for this fat, uncouth individual, who behaved like a vulgar lecher, pawing the girls and luring them into empty practice rooms.

His voice, of course, was phenomenal, and later on in Hollywood, his musical promoters were able to splice together bits of arias and other pieces to make him sound like a great opera star. But it was a bogus star, which glittered for some years like a supernova before going out forever. Today his name is not even recorded in most operatic textbooks or encyclopedias, and this is as it should be, for someone who cannot perform a role on stage has no right to be considered an opera singer.

Years later, when he was at the pinnacle of his fame, he came back to visit Tanglewood during another summer session. When the news was brought to me that "Mario Lanza is here, don't you want to see him?" I answered, "No. I don't want to have anything to do with him. He is not the kind of singer or person I even want to shake hands with."

In 1946 the opera department was on the brink of a major leap forward. Koussevitzky had commissioned Benjamin Britten's opera Peter Grimes, *which was to be performed by the student singers and orchestra, a major risk as well as a rare opportunity.*

This production became the impetus for a power shift in the department, according to Steven Ledbetter, former head of publications for the Boston Symphony Orchestra, who referred to it in his program notes for the fiftieth-anniversary production of Peter Grimes.

Plans for the production went ahead in the spring, though with a growing unease on the part of Herbert Graf, the Metropolitan Opera stage director who had been in charge of the opera department from Tanglewood's first season, assisted by Boris Goldovsky. Part of the reason might simply have been that Goldovsky spoke Russian and could communicate with the conductor with perfect accuracy. (Kousseviztky occasionally misheard or misunderstood comments made to him in English, and once an idea had mistakenly become fixed in his mind in this way, he could rarely be persuaded to reconsider it.) Or perhaps Koussevitzky felt that Graf was not equally committed to "new stage and production techniques, new methods, and new attitudes, all leading to a more vital presentation of music dramas" (these words come from the minutes of a BMC faculty meeting held on February 17, in which Koussevitzky explained that this was why he had commissioned *Peter Grimes*). Already by this time Graf had learned that Koussevitzky had not approved of his plans for the following summer, which had included some work in the standard repertory operas as well as *Grimes*, and that Goldovsky had been put in charge of the "experimental work" of the opera department. [The stage direction of *Peter Grimes* was taken over by Eric Crozier, who had overseen the first production in London.] Graf had spoken to a number of potential students who had expressed their unwillingness to spend a summer at Tanglewood if their only opportunity to sing were in the many smaller parts in *Peter Grimes*, without other operatic experiences. After Graf had expressed this view again at the February 17 faculty meeting, Koussevitzky may have taken Graf's slight reservation as an attack on his vision. In any case, in the following months Goldovsky received more and more independence.

Ned Rorem, a student that summer, became one of the opera's most enthusiastic admirers.

Preparations for *Peter Grimes* dominated every segment of Tanglewood during that summer of 1946. Rumor had it that Britten himself would be there, and Koussevitzky had already stated: "There is *Carmen*. And there is *Peter Grimes*." Britten was only a name to me, one I assigned to the present blancmange notion of British music. England had produced some pretty good authors and painters in the past 250 years but had not, for some reason, a single composer of any weight since the death of Purcell in 1695 (except for maybe Sir Arthur Sullivan). Suddenly, issuing from every rehearsal hall on campus were the most persuasive tunes imaginable, long and inevitable and strong and mournful. Over there in Studio B was Phyllis Curtin (then Phyllis Smith) with two fellow sopranos and pianist, venerable Felix Wolfes, going through the trio that closes act 2 and, with its soaring otherworldliness, putting *Rosenkavalier* to shame. Over here in the espalier terrace were Hugh Ross and his large chorus practicing the vast a cappella ensembles which, as fully as any of the soloists, will propel the opera's tragedy. Down in the main Shed was Lenny disciplining an orchestra which, though standard in makeup, emitted, thanks to Britten's unique ear for checks and balances, noises that were more than music—that *were*, literally, chalk cliffs and waves and stifled lust and fear. So English music, like Sleeping Beauty, now with Britten's kiss, had awakened after two centuries. The odd aspect: Britten was no innovator; he was as conservative as Poulenc in pursuing the tried and true, and, like Poulenc, his every measure seemed traceable to another composer. He was *better than*, not *different from*, speaking the same language with a more singular accent. Because in the next decades Britten would become the brightest light in English music, and by extension the strongest influence on the young, those young emerged writing conservatively. England did not, like America and France and Germany and Italy, have to suffer the convulsions of serial experimentation.

A great work is one you never get used to. *Peter Grimes*, like *The Rite of Spring*, was one of my milestones. Before opening night I bought and brooded over the score and befriended as many of the cast as possible. (Though not Phyllis Curtin, whom I scarcely met and would not come to know until 1959, when she turned into, and has remained, the most important soprano of my career.) Not the least of my motives for this detailed study was the report I made to Kubly [Herbert Kubly, author and *Time* magazine music critic] (for yes, our friendship was still on) in his capacity of reporter. Since he could not attend the premiere, I sent a detailed telegram, and this was published, scarcely edited, in *Time*.

An excerpt of that review:

There has not been a first-rate and popular opera written since Richard Strauss's *Der Rosenkavalier* in 1911. Last week U.S. critics got a first look and listen to a year-old English opera, *Peter Grimes*. They almost unanimously hailed frail, thirty-two-year-old Benjamin Britten as the most promising operatic composer of the day.

Dr. Koussevitzky had commissioned *Peter Grimes* in memory of his late wife, and he proudly proclaimed it the greatest opera since *Carmen*. He did not conduct its U.S. premiere, but left it to his prize protégé, Manhattan's Leonard Bernstein. The theater got three hours of violent and raw emotion, and agreed that in plot, at least, *Peter Grimes* had much in common with Bizet's lurid tale of smuggling and murder. . . .

Two student casts alternate on different evenings in singing *Peter Grimes*. Tenors Joseph Laderoute and William Horne in the title role wrestled with the high notes, which Britten had created for his good friend tenor Peter Pears (pronounced Peers) whose coloraturalike soarings are a legend in England. The most unimpressed member of the Tanglewood audience was composer Britten himself. Said he stiffly, "There's no use pretending it was professional. . . . It was a very lively student performance."

At Tanglewood he glumly watched rehearsals wearing a pearl-gray jacket, a yellow tie, and strap sandals.

After the first two performances, Britten enplaned for England, where his new opera, *The Rape of Lucretia*, opened last month and got even better notices than *Peter Grimes*.

Benjamin Britten made a big hit with the American press after the premiere. One of the more amusing pieces about him appeared in the August issue of Musical America *in a column called "Mephisto's Musings."*

At another moment, too, I thought I was back where I belonged. Undoubtedly Benjamin Britten thought he was there as well, for the distinguished young composer of *Peter Grimes* had some harrowing experiences during his short visit. I won't even mention the agony a composer goes through at the mounting of such an ambitious work—any sensitive nature is bound to suffer unless every detail is prefect, and I am told that there were many elements of the *Grimes* student production that left something to be desired. But when you put that on top of a transatlantic plane hop, the social demands on such a personage, and then add a sleepless night between dress rehearsal and performance (his car ran out of gas on a lonely road, I'm told), you have the ingredients for a nervous crisis. All the more credit, therefore, to the traditional British calm which Britten displayed the morning after the premiere. Hounded by representatives of the magazine press who didn't know enough to quit after some rather summary brush-offs by various guardians of the celebrity's peace of mind, Britten was at last cornered in a cul-de-sac backstage in the theater. Weary to the bone but still sweet-tempered, he answered questions and posed for photographers. With cameras focused and flashguns poised they shot him over and over. And wouldn't you know it—almost the very first flashbulb exploded right in his face! A private blitz for Britten.

But if words could make him happy, he had plenty of laudatory ones. The most delicious came directly from the deity of Tanglewood, Dr. Koussevitzky himself. I wrote down most of his curtain speech at the *Grimes* premiere and herewith reproduce it as best I can—you must try to imagine the accent:

"Benjamin Britten say to me: 'This opera belongs to you.' 'No, my dear,' I say, 'this opera belongs to the world, and the world is happy.' This is history-making. The second opera who is a real music drama. I congratulate the world. After *Carmen* is *Peter Grimes.*

"I should like to remember you: this is a student performance. Dat dunt means dat I ask you to excuse—just opposite!"

Stories about this production of Peter Grimes *abound. Here are two. The first is a recollection by one of the singers, Charlie (Charles) Weintraub, who wrote it for the Tanglewood Music Center's anniversary collection,* Tanglewood Remembered.

This story is almost unbelievable:

For some reason I could never understand, because I did not possess an unusual voice, by any means, when we started rehearsing *Peter Grimes* at Tanglewood in '46, Lenny assigned to me the solo line that I believe I mentioned—the local seaman who announces, "There's been a landslide up the coast." The line was written for a bass, and I am a baritone (although I did have a wide range, close to three octaves). For some reason that I cannot think of now, except that my very low notes were quite weak, to the point of being hardly audible, I started my line a third higher than it was written. I did this for the first two performances. On the evening of our third and last performance, our rehearsal pianist grabbed me just as I was about to make my entrance and said, "Here's your note, and Lenny says if you don't sing it right this time he's 'gonna throw the baton at you!'"

So I sang it in the correct range and I don't know if anybody heard it.

Some time in about 1952 or '53 (I don't remember the date, but it was after I stopped singing with the Schola Cantorum), I and my wife were attending a concert at Carnegie Hall at which Bernstein was playing the piano and also directing the orchestra.

I suggested to my wife that we go backstage, as many people did, and say hello to Lenny, even though he probably would not remember me.

We did this, and I got on the line that was greeting Lenny, with my wife alongside me.

When we got to Lenny, I extended my hand, which he took rather gingerly while he examined my face as I was saying, "You probably don't remember me." He said, "Uh . . . ," and I sang, "There's been a landslide up the coast!"

"Weintraub," he exclaimed, and shook my hand rather warmly!

He was really "quite a guy."

Arnold Fromme remembered the second story.

I was a student there in 1946, '47, and '48 and played principal trombone in the advanced student orchestra. I'll never forget the first complete run-through of the opera *Peter Grimes* with the complete cast. Britten, Koussevitzky, and Copland were there, Bernstein conducting, and the performance was unbelievably thrilling. When the rehearsal was over, close to midnight, and everyone seemed drunk with excitement, someone yelled, "Look!" pointing to the sky. There, as if God Him/Herself were applauding, was an unbelievable display of the northern lights. I had never seen them before (nor have I since.). Many of us lay on the grass for over an hour watching. Talk about awesome!

By 1947, Graf, well aware of his diminishing standing at Tanglewood, had decamped for Los Angeles, pleasing Koussevitzky no end. The latter preferred the more open-hearted, emotional acting of the Moscow Arts Theater founded by his friend, Konstantin Stanislavsky, and had once commented to Goldovsky that Graf "talks big but the results are mediocre."

What Koussevitzky wanted was "a great laboratory where we will work out new problems connected with opera–dramatic art. There is no doubt about the need of a drastic and radical change in this direction. For, indeed, no other branch of art can so easily slip into routine provincialism and bad taste as opera."

Boris Goldovsky was his man for this job. Now it remained to be determined what direction he would take.

While doing some research before the '47 season, Goldovsky had come across a Mozart opera completely unknown to him, Idomeneo, King of Crete. *It had been commissioned and performed for the Elector of Bavaria in 1781 but, due to its altogether serious nature and extreme length, it was never again presented until the 1930s, when it was revived for two performances in England.*

Along with Don Giovanni, *Mozart considered* Idomeneo *to be his finest opera. Goldovsky agreed.*

It did not take me long to understand why he valued it so highly. *Idomeneo*, being an *opera seria,* is devoid of light comic touches. It was meant to be a mighty tragic drama in the classic Greek tradition, and this all along was Mozart's supreme ambition. He wanted to shine as a creator of serious works rather than as a purveyor of opera buffa or *dramma giocoso. . . .*

What astounded me, as I delved into the score, was the stupefying mastery which a young composer of twenty-four could display in this, for him, unfamiliar genre of serious opera. Elettra's first aria left me spellbound. In order to portray her all-consuming jealousy and psychological disarray, Mozart injected triple-time phrases into the 4/4 meter of the orchestral accompaniment. The result is an earthquakelike upheaval, in which the universe tilts and ends up out of joint. So, too, the storm which later breaks out as Idamante and Elettra are about to embark for Argos. It is a musical miracle—with sudden, startling changes of keys which no eighteenth-century composer had even begun to imagine might exist, and orchestral innovations—including the use of muted trumpets—I had never encountered in any of Mozart's other works. No less breathtaking was the chorus of lamentation in the last act, the accompaniment to which Beethoven imitated in his *Moonlight* Sonata.

So Idomeneo *became Goldovsky's first production. Erica Perl, writing for the October 6, 1947,* Opera News, *reported on its progress.*

For days the lovely Tanglewood grounds swarmed with reminders of the dim mythological past. A group of young people dressed in the flowing robes of ancient Greece flitted about, cutting green boughs from the bushes to celebrate the end of the Trojan war; a high priest stalked solemnly up and down, a score in one hand, a soft drink in the other; a group of Cretans reclined in the shade, their conversation occasionally drowned out by the hammering and sawing from the nearby scenery-shed; the aroma of the tall pines mingled with the smell of fresh paint and varnish. From the open doors of a large wooden building issued the hearty melody of a rousing chorus, stopped abruptly from tine to time by the command of a voice . . . the voice of Boris Goldovsky who, from the orchestra pit of the Theatre–Concert Hall, was conducting a dress rehearsal of Mozart's

Idomeneo. Patiently Mr. Goldovsky advised, reminded, admonished, and praised singers and chorus, changed stage directions, handed out red and blue pencils to the members of the orchestra to mark the score.

It was indeed no easy task that Mr. Goldovsky had taken upon himself when he decided to perform this opera for the first time in the United States. Composed when Mozart was only twenty-four, it was his own best-loved work, with some of the most beautiful music he ever wrote, but in its original form it is too lengthy for present-day standards. Mr. Goldovsky painstakingly edited and condensed the overlong score without actually changing a single note of the music. No amount of effort was considered too great in bringing this neglected masterpiece to the public, for Mr. Goldovsky maintained that "those who are privileged to perform Mozart have a custodian's duty to make his great music heard."

How much he succeeded can best be described by quoting Rudolph Elie Jr. of the *Boston Herald* who reported that "before audiences of the most sensitive musical people in the country Mozart's *Idomeneo*—as the composer himself must surely have conceived it—sprang to life. I think I can speak for both audiences in saying that it was one of the most effective and beautiful things that ever was . . . in what seemed to me the finest student performance I ever heard in my life was a thesaurus of everything that ever happened in music up to Mozart, and the clue to everything that has happened since."

Goldovsky was on his way to bringing new theatrical life to opera as well as discovering and presenting a whole string of then virtually unknown operas. Idomeneo *was soon to be followed by another "new" Mozart opera,* La Clemenza di Tito, *Gluck's* Iphigenia in Tauris, *Rossini's* The Turk in Italy, *Puccini's* La Rondine, *Tchaikovsky's* The Queen of Spades, *and many more. Today every one has become a staple in the modern opera house.*

One way Goldovsky made these operas fresh and alive on the stage was his ability to see the contemporary significance to be found in them.

We were rehearsing the opera at Tanglewood when it suddenly dawned on me that *Idomeneo* was anything but an old-fashioned story bequeathed to us by the bards of ancient Greece; it was a cautionary tale that had immense relevance to the present. And so, before the curtain rose on August 4, I came out and delivered a short speech, as I had been doing with all of our operatic productions. This opera, I explained, was really an allegory about what was happening in the world today. By exploding the atomic bomb, the United States had unleashed the awesome forces of nature. But the world was going to have to pay a price to keep these forces tamed and from wreaking universal havoc and destruction. The price was the sacrifice of national sovereignty, a sacrifice comparable to the one that Idomeneo had promised to make by killing his son [i.e., Jupiter's reward for giving the Greeks' victory in war].

Goldovsky held up high theatrical standards for his students in order that they might become "full-fledged artists." Every year he sent detailed instructions to the students on how to prepare for a coming Tanglewood season of study. One spring, the following communication arrived in the mail.

The chief aim of the opera workshop will be the exploration of all paths leading to operatic performance consistent with dramatic truth and believable characterization. Great stress will be laid on independent collective efforts by students, who will be divided into study groups to carry out specially selected projects, leading eventually to performances of scenes, acts, and short operas. Each study group will include the necessary number of singers, a conductor, a pianist, a stage director, and a musicologist. Although these projects will be guided and supervised by me, the final responsibility for all preparation and performance will rest with the students themselves.

This, however, does not mean that the regular study of the standard operatic material will be neglected. There will be a three-hour daily class (1:30 to 4:30) devoted to musical and dramatic realization of scenes from standard operas. At this time, each active participant will receive individual instruction in operatic dramatics, and the entire group will participate in a complete analysis and criticism of the present-day methods of operatic mise-en-scène. I will also give a series of daily lectures (11:30 to 12:30) on the technique of the stage; the principles of operatic dramaturgy; methods of study of score and text; Italian, French, German, and English diction; and other subjects dealing with the theory and practice of opera.

He then assigned them a little homework.

Study of the Music

Learn your entire role without any cuts. Do not change any notes in the vocal line. Try to memorize your entire roll, but in all events be sure to have the first few scenes ready by July 1.

Study of the Text

The performer should be able to answer in as much detail as possible the following seven questions concerning his role:

1. Who am I? (name, age, occupation, financial and social status, etc.)
2. How do I look? (clothes, makeup, hairdo, etc.)
3. What are my surrounding? (milieu of the play, geographic location, historical period, etc.)

4. With whom do I associate? (relation to the other characters in the play)
5. What do I know? (also, what do I not know!)
6. What do I want?
7. What do I discover as the plot unfolds and how does it affect me?

Do not rely on synopses of plots, but read through the entire text of the opera and also study very carefully the background texts, which are indicated below.

But, as the old saw goes, all good things must come to an end. Goldovsky was ready to form his own opera company, the Boston Symphony trustees were reluctant to continue financing an opera department when their main order of business was the performance of symphonic music, and—what else is new—funding was harder and harder to come by.

In a March 23, 1959, letter to Aaron Copland, Leonard Burkat, administrator of the Berkshire Music Center, speculated on the coming demise of the Tanglewood Opera Department.

The opera department has met with the worst. Its fate is not worse than death, but suspension is important and was not considered lightly. Mr. Cabot and Mr. Munch both went into the thing pretty thoroughly. Mr. Cabot and Tod [Perry] tried very hard for a number of individual and foundation benefactions that might have kept it going this year, but nothing worked. There was no money to be found elsewhere. . . .

We have made a public statement that the department has suspended its activities in 1959 while Boris travels abroad and writes a book that he has been planning for some time, one that will summarize and consolidate his years of accumulated knowledge and experience. He tells us that this is what he is going to do, and I do hope that time will prove it to have been no more than that.

Burkat turned out to be wrong. Goldovsky did establish his own company, and there was to be no more opera at Tanglewood until the 1960s, when Erich Leinsdorf would bring it back in an entirely different form.

Could Tanglewood exist without you?

—Gertrude Robinson Smith to Serge Koussevitzky

CHAPTER 6

Transitions

The Changing of the Guard

In the 1940s, many dissonances were to be heard concerning nonmusical matters at Tanglewood. It was becoming apparent that two symphonic boards of trustees were one too many.

Originally, Gertrude Robinson Smith and her Berkshire Symphonic Festival trustees produced and administered two summer seasons of concerts with a pickup orchestra from the New York Philharmonic under the baton of Henry Hadley, also a freelancer. When the Boston Symphony was hired, they came equipped with a professional management team and a renowned and powerful conductor in Serge Koussevitzky. Increasingly, they felt that they could manage Tanglewood with only minimal help from Miss Robinson Smith et al. To further complicate things, the Boston Symphony owned the property of Tanglewood and the Berkshire Symphonic Festival the Shed. A power struggle between the Berkshire Festival trustees and the BSO over control of Festival was becoming inevitable.

One of the more subtle signs of trouble surfaced early on in a letter dated January 20, 1940, to Miss Robinson Smith from George Edman, her hardworking board member.

May I repeat an old argument, that we are associated with the Boston Symphony Orchestra in an important project and what helps one, helps the other. The future of the Festival is undeniably associated with whatever plans the orchestra trustees have in mind. . . .

Then we come to the use of the name "Tanglewood." Whether we like it or whether we don't, the public and newspapers are not going to twist their tongues to say "the Berkshire Symphonic Festival" repeatedly. They are going to use "Tanglewood," because it is a lovely and euphonious name with traditions. It lends itself beautifully to a catch-phrase and for headlines. You'll never be able to shake it.

By August 30, 1941, Gertrude Robinson Smith was complaining about the heavy-handed tactics of the BSO in a letter to another Festival board member, Mrs. Bruce Crane.

. . . As you know, the [Boston Symphony] board of trustees at their meeting in June passed a motion requesting Mr. Dane to appoint a committee to meet with us for the purpose of discussing the elimination of the fifty-fifty division of profits [of the Festival]. . . .

You know as well as I do that the Boston board has put it all over ours. The contract we have is entirely in their favor. This coming year it expires, and when the new one is entered into we should make our position very definite. I fail to see why they should take our property away from us or treat us like their children. If only our board could realize the true situation. I think they might take a firmer stand. . . .

In this letter of August from Ernest B. Dane, the president of the BSO trustees, it is obvious that the Boston Symphony was lobbying quite adamantly to gain control of the Festival.

. . . Tanglewood presents a physical, and in some respects, a financial problem. For five years now the owner and lessor has had the responsibility of maintenance; these maintenance expenses, without reference to school items, have substantially exceeded the amounts distributed to us on account of our share of net proceeds from the concerts. . . .

The orchestra has taken, and in the nature of things, must take, the initiative in establishing and widening its musical horizons, and we are prepared so far as lies in our power to undertake the whole responsibility of ensuring the indefinite continuance of these Festival concerts. . . .

The orchestra essentially wanted to own all the Tanglewood property, manage the concerts and affiliated activities, and retain all the box office receipts. According to the BSO plan, the Berkshire Symphonic Festival's sole function was to promote the concerts locally for a fee. All other revenues were to go to the Boston Symphony to finance its activities at Tanglewood.

Serge Koussevitzky was, of course, deeply involved in the controversy. He wrote Miss Robinson Smith on September 22, stressing the primacy of the Boston Symphony over the Berkshire board in the Festival's operation.

When you asked me, "Could Tanglewood exist without you?" I took your question jokingly, and answered in the same light vein. But later my thoughts returned to your question time after time, and I wondered whether you meant it seriously. In this case, my answer to a seriously put question will be serious, too.

Could Tanglewood exist without you?—if asked in joke, the answer is, of course, no. If meant in earnest, then my answer will be thus.

In the artistic field, the part of the organizer is an ungrateful one. Only a few realize it and are really interested in the organizer. If tomorrow you decide to give up organizing the Berkshire Festival concerts, true the masses will be hardly conscious of it. With the masses, the importance lies in what takes place on the platform and what the stage can offer: if they are attracted, they will come; if not, they will stay away.

I do not intend, however, to explain what the part of the Organizer is—you are well aware of it. What I want to say is that your question becomes important if you put it seriously, because it then means that your personal part and efforts in the enterprise overshadow the aim, that is, Art, as it is created in Tanglewood. Yet you must realize that Tanglewood occupies today such an outstanding place in the world of music, that each and every one connected with it should feel a responsibility toward the nation and, particularly, toward American youth, who come to learn and to listen to great Art in the making.

For that reason, everything personal should fall back: every effort should be centered on the Aim and its development, striving to uphold as well as to constantly further the achievements of an organization which is now regarded by the entire world as a Musical Sanctuary. And anyone who, being connected with this work, introduces a feeling of contention will bear a heavy responsibility.

This is what I wanted to tell you as an afterthought and in addition to our conversation at Saratoga.

On September 24, Miss Robinson Smith wrote angrily to Stuart Montgomery, the BSF lawyer in Boston.

The enclosed from Koussy may interest you. I don't have to tell you that I did not ask him if he thought Tanglewood could exist without me but, rather, if he thought "the Festival would be as successful without our group." He can always twist things especially to my disadvantage. This particular conversation took place at the time he was telling me how the musicians backed him and that they would do whatever he wanted. And that *he* could give the Festival himself and engage the orchestra, etc., etc. I think I told you all this.

I'm surprised he didn't ask me to call a meeting of our board and propose to them that we should turn over all the profits to the school.

For the five years of World War II, there had been a very real and bitter division of opinion within the Berkshire Symphonic Festival board. Some trustees felt the urgent necessity of maintaining control of the Music Festival, while others believed the Boston Symphony would be the more appropriate manager.

Push came to shove when it became obvious that Tanglewood would reopen at the end of the war. Lacking the cohesion to continue the battle and recognizing that the Boston Symphony had far more firepower than the Berkshire Symphonic Festival, on October 4, 1945, Robinson Smith sent this gracious telegram of acquiescence to the BSO.

IT GIVES US GREAT PLEASURE TO NOTIFY YOU THAT THE BOARD OF TRUSTEES OF THE BERKSHIRE SYMPHONIC FESTIVAL AT THEIR ANNUAL MEETING HELD THIS AFTERNOON IN STOCKBRIDGE VOTED UNANIMOUSLY TO MAKE A GIFT OF THE MUSIC SHED AND ITS CONTENTS AT TANGLEWOOD TO THE BOSTON SYMPHONY ORCHESTRA THUS GIVING THEM ENTIRE CONTROL AND MANAGEMENT OF FUTURE FESTIVAL AT TANGLEWOOD STOP . . . OUR BEST WISHES TO YOUR TRUSTEES YOUR GREAT CONDUCTOR AND YOUR FINE MUSICIANS FOR MANY YEARS OF HAPPY AND SUCCESSFUL FESTIVALS

Koussevitzky responded in kind.

INFINITELY TOUCHED TO RECEIVE YOUR MESSAGE STOP YOUR DECISION IS A MAGNIFICENT AND FAR-REACHING ACTION WHICH WILL BE REMEMBERED BY THE MUSICAL WORLD STOP TO YOU AND YOUR BOARD GO MY DEEPFELT APPRECIATION AND GREETINGS. SERGE KOUSSEVITZKY

However, in 1949 a more radical change was in the wind. Koussevitzky was about to celebrate his seventy-fifth birthday as well as his twenty-fifth, "silver," anniversary as conductor of the Boston Symphony. There was nothing he wanted more than to have Leonard Bernstein succeed him when he retired. But the BSO trustees would not hear of this, so Koussevitzky threatened to quit unless they complied with his wishes.

He had occasionally threatened to resign in the past, and this technique had usually produced the results he was looking for. But much to his surprise, this time the trustees accepted his resignation.

Charles Munch, the brilliant, charismatic, and very good-looking French conductor, was appointed to succeed him in the 1949–50 season—not, as Koussevitzky wished, Leonard Bernstein. So Koussevitzky's "deal" with the orchestra was that he would give up conducting the Boston concerts in Symphony Hall but would continue conducting the concerts at Tanglewood and have complete control over the Berkshire Music Festival.

Already a reluctant retiree, he took great offense, when, without consulting him, Victor de Sabata—an Italian maestro and not *a member of the Tanglewood family—was engaged to guest conduct a pair of concerts in the Shed that summer.*

Koussevitzky let the trustees know exactly what he thought of this plan in a radio interview with James Fassett on Your Invitation to Music, *broadcast by CBS.*

This year is something happen unexpected for me. Some of the guest conductors, like my pupils, Leonard Bernstein and Eleazar de Carvalho—they are considered by myself and by the faculty the best of my pupils. Therefore I invite them to conduct the Festival concerts. And I considered always that this school is for the Americas and for America's gifted people.

But it happened this season that the trustees, without my knowledge, without to ask me, they invited themselves a guest conductor. So this year I take off any responsibility for the programs of the Festival, except those of my pupils and my own. I do not want any responsibilities apart from Tanglewood. Tanglewood, it is my child. It is my creation. It is my blood and tears. I will never give it up.

Worse things were to occur. Koussevitzky soon discovered that his name had been dropped as music director of the orchestra for the oncoming Tanglewood season. He poured his feelings out to a reporter from the Berkshire Eagle.

I have never resigned from Tanglewood. If any agreement had been signed by the president of the Boston Symphony Orchestra with anyone else as musical director at Tanglewood, it was done without consulting me and without my knowledge. I strongly believed that the institution I created and developed at Tanglewood should have a strong leadership and artistic authority and the tradition I established be carried on.

The diplomatic Charles Munch announced that if ever he were to conduct at Tanglewood, he would wait for an invitation from Koussevitzky, acknowledging indirectly that he thought it more advisable to spend the summer in Europe, taking up his official duties in Boston the following winter.

In the end, de Sabata scored a singular triumph with the Tanglewood audience, and the following spring, all this became a moot point.

On June 4, 1951, Koussevitzky died rather suddenly of a rare blood disease, with his wife and Bernstein at his bedside. Only the summer before, he had conducted a magnificent end-of-the-season concert at Tanglewood, with performances of the Prokofiev Fifth and the Brahms First that had greatly moved the enormous crowd. They applauded him and brought him back seven times to take his bows. That winter he had led the Israel Philharmonic on a tour of North America and was preparing to conduct Tchaikovsky's Pique Dame *with the Music Center students at Tanglewood.*

Koussevitzky's unexpected death came as a great shock to all musicians and the music-loving public, and particularly to Leonard Bernstein, his disciple and musical son. No finer appreciation of Koussevitzky's persona and legacy has ever been made than that of Bernstein's Opening Exercises speech the following summer at Tanglewood.

I would like to say a few personal words to you, expressly to you of the student body, to whom I feel so close both in time and in spirit.

Only eleven years ago today, I sat, exactly as you are now, at the Opening Exercises of Tanglewood's first summer. I was an old student by that time, and I [had] already sat through many opening and closing and other assorted exercises. I had become accustomed to being impressed.

But I was not prepared for what awaited me here.

A man arose to address us—a beautiful man, radiating a charge of electricity about him, setting in motion the fluids in the surrounding air. A man named Koussevitzky, a simple, single soul. Before he had even uttered a word we were caught in some sort of magic; we were already infused with his élan vital, which has never left us, nor ever can leave us. And when he began to speak, in his unique and personal way, he spoke of a "Central Line"—a line of fire and mystery, the line to be followed by dedicated people. To him we were, by our very presence on that day, automatically dedicated people; boys and girls who had found in music a center, a core, a backbone for the service of our lives.

From that moment there followed six weeks of bliss. How we accomplished all that we did in that short time I shall never know. We ate, drank, and dreamed music—all kinds of music—and always under this the aegis of a standard that knew no compromise, that tolerated no mediocrity. If we *were* mediocre, we were magnificently mediocre. If we were inadequate, we were inspired in our inadequacy. And always the Central Line stretched before us, burning with the dedication of Koussevitzky.

During that marvelous summer, I came to know him and love him; and in the ten years that followed, this knowledge deepened and expanded and crystallized. I learned, bit by bit, just what was involved in following this Central Line: the devotion, the consistency of approach, the law of being true to one's inner self, the joy of participating in one's success, and the wonder of humility before beauty and the absolute. Perhaps the greatest mystery lay in how these elements were communicated: never by speeches, never by moralizing or preaching; but by a curious osmosis which is the manner of all great teaching—a combination of personal example and dynamic contact which rammed these truths home deep in the unconscious, where they can never be lost.

Out of these truths was fashioned Tanglewood, a permanent, self-renewing embodiment of the Koussevitzky ethic. Tanglewood is not a school, in the strict sense. It does not offer courses, degrees, credits, or disciplinary action. No student is striving for grades. The goals are much higher than that. Tanglewood is a musical universe where for six weeks, a young musician is subjected to gravitational pulls, magnetic fields, electrical impulses, varying atmospheres, and a changing topography. What he emerges with after it is all over is not a report card, or the ability to play faster than the next fellow. What Tanglewood hopes—and what Koussevitzky desired—was that the student emerge from this model universe with a conception of his own true orbit; that the young planet acquire its direction, its sense of relationship to its fellow planets, and its particular function in the larger universe outside.

When all you young planets leave this hall today to take up your activities in this six-week solar system, remember that every solar system revolves about its sun, and that in this case the sun is the Koussevitzky ethic. Although he will not be making those magical appearances at the gate in his fabulous capes; although he will not be here to remind you daily that "you can do better"; although he will not be sharing with us his elegance, his strength, his singleness, his graciousness—still every note that you play will be played in tribute to him; every idea that you have will derive from his solar energy; and every moment you lose will be a tragic waste. Don't lose your chance. Drink in all you can; relax, and let yourself be affected, let your concepts grow, your ideas change, your powers increase. We of the faculty stand ready to help in every way. Most of us have been here since the beginning of the history of Tanglewood, and have had the joy and honor of working closely with Koussevitzky. We have dedicated ourselves to the continuation and development of his aims in the Berkshire Music Center. For these weeks to come we exist for no other reason than to put the services of Tanglewood at your disposition. It is for you—all for you; and if you will only grasp it, and make it your own, you will be touched by his spirit, which lives and breathes in this place; you will discover your own Central Line; and you will be paying him the supreme honor.

The summer of Koussevitzky's death, Munch came immediately to conduct the concerts in the Shed, and Bernstein took over the main responsibilities at the Music Center.

Munch was an extraordinary conductor, and for the next eleven summers gave a series of brilliant concerts—albeit often a rehash of the winter Boston season—favoring the French and German repertory, with a dash of contemporary music. His reviews were exemplary and players and audiences adored him. Even Gertrude Robinson Smith was again seen on the grounds after a few summers of self-exile in Europe.

However, Munch did not feel himself to be an educator. At the Music Center he confined himself to giving some marvelous Opening Exercises speeches and once or twice a summer conducted the student orchestra.

However, during his tenure a number of brilliant students studied conducting at Tanglewood. Among them was Zubin Mehta. In Zubin *by Martin Bookspan and Ross Yockey, we get an excellent picture of the Music Center at that time.*

There were eight young conductors, studying primarily under Eleazar de Carvalho of Brazil (later of the St. Louis Symphony). Ostensibly, they were also under the guidance of the Boston Symphony's music director, Charles Munch. However, Munch cared little for the administrative workings of the school and concentrated instead on the performances of his own orchestra, as well as on his golf fame at the Stockbridge Country Club.

[Zubin Mehta is speaking.] "I had really hoped to get to know Munch. The Boston Symphony sounded glorious under him and also under Pierre Monteux, who was there as guest conductor. But it seemed as though Munch was impossible to meet. He just never paid much attention to the students.

"He would sometimes come to rehearsals and just sit there, and every now and then he would scream at us or at the members of the orchestra. Claudio [Abbado] he ignored completely, but he did say something to me once. He yelled at me,

'Put your feet together!' That was the only instruction he ever gave me."

Much later, Zubin discovered that Charles Munch had indeed been paying very close attention to the young man from India who stood with his feet apart, but at Tanglewood Zubin's compliments came from less influential sources.

In fact, the Tanglewood crowd of 1958 was buzzing with gossip about the amazing crop of young conductors. Not the visitors, of course, who came with their picnic suppers to commune with nature and to hear the Boston Symphony under the stars. But the students, at the beach and in the dormitories, discussed the prodigious talent evident in Zubin Mehta, Claudio Abbado, and David Zinman (who would go on to conduct the Netherlands Chamber Orchestra and the Rochester Philharmonic). [He later became music director of the Baltimore Symphony, the Aspen Music Festival, and the Tonhalle Orchestra in Zurich. Gustav Meier was also in that class.] The orchestra members were particularly impressed with Zubin's handling of Richard Strauss's *Don Juan* and Schönberg's *Chamber Symphony*.

At least two members of the faculty were also impressed. One of them was conductor-pianist Seymour Lipkin, who remembers, "It was obvious that there was really somebody there, a big, big talent. And I, well, I just filed it away." The other faculty member was Lukas Foss, of the composition department at the Music Center. . . .

"I have my own definition of a conductor's job," says Foss. "First, he must be a detective, finding the trouble spots at rehearsals; then he must be a doctor, diagnosing the trouble and finally curing it. That makes a good conductor. It usually takes many years to learn, but Zubin had that from the start, which seemed incredible to me.

"On top of that he had charisma, the commanding personality it takes to work with others and get them to do their jobs. He got results. He had enthusiasm, which of course many young people have, but in him it was coupled with a natural talent and technical skill. That was rare." . . .

One of the great lessons of Tanglewood for Zubin was the value of ensemble playing in an orchestra. The string students were together virtually every moment of the day, as were the winds, the brass, and the percussionists. Communication, awareness of the other members, "team spirit"—these things came about of themselves and produced an ensemble sound that could not help but be appreciated by the audience. On the bulletin board backstage at the theater, someone had posted a sign that read, Remember, the Orchestra That Plays Together Stays Together. That sign was still there in 1976 [and still is in 2007].

At the end of the second week in August, the festival was over and prizes were awarded. In the conducting class, the first-place Koussevitzky Prize went to Claudio Abbado, while Zubin won the runner-up Gertrude Robinson Smith Prize.

Actually, Gustav Meier won second prize. He became an important conductor and conducting teacher, and returned to Tanglewood to teach conducting during the '70s and '80s

In 1960, another of Munch's "pupils"—a twenty-four-year-old Japanese student conductor—would also go on to do great things. But more about him later.

I interpret the word *festival* as meaning "the observing of something special."

—Erich Leinsdorf

CHAPTER 7

The
Leinsdorf
Era

All the Music Making Was Outdoors

A very complex man with pronounced gifts both musical and intellectual, Erich Leinsdorf was in many ways ideally suited to be Koussevitzky's successor at Tanglewood—especially at the Berkshire Music Center, where a renaissance would take place under his leadership. The Festival programming in the Shed, too, would become far more adventuresome.

During his nine-year tenure as music director, he also to ruffled many a BSO feather—including those of their very popular orchestra manager and the orchestra players who considered him overly dictatorial. "He was not a warm and fuzzy guy," as Joseph Silverstein, concertmaster under Leinsdorf, put it, but "one of the first things he said to me was that his responsibility was to realize the vision of Koussevitzky at Tanglewood."

To my mind, Mr. Leinsdorf is one of the most interesting and underappreciated characters of all in the tale of Tanglewood. In 1963 he was appointed Munch's successor as music director of the BSO. In his autobiography, Cadenza, *he described the situation at the BSO at the time of his appointment.*

A few days earlier [Tod] Perry phoned to ask me if I could arrive before the company and take lunch with him and the president of the board of trustees, Henry Cabot. This sounded pleasant enough because I had not met Cabot at all during my guest stint and looked forward to an agreeable hour. Little did I foresee that with the arrival of the main course Cabot would turn to me and say, "We would like you to come to Boston as Munch's successor as music director of the orchestra." He spoke plainly and openly of Munch's fatigue, that he would not continue beyond the summer of 1962, and that the trustees did not want the customary interim period of guest conductors, especially since they all were convinced that I was their best choice.

On the whole, Leinsdorf was not a happy camper in his dealings with the Boston Symphony Orchestra, but Tanglewood held a very special place in his heart. In Cadenza *he explained why.*

The summers in the Berkshires were the happiest times of my Boston years. They remain a glowing memory, and if there were moments of exasperation, they have evaporated and are no longer within my recall. I like the landscape, the Shed, the acoustics, the lawn with or without people, the open-car driving to and from rehearsals and concerts, the parties, the restaurants, the symposia we arranged on all sorts of related subjects, the often screwballish contemporary concerts, and even the buzzing mosquitoes. That is one place I shall not readily revisit lest one of my most cherished recollections dissolve into gray fog.

Some of the reasons why all this looks so radiant in retrospect reflect my general tastes in life. All the music making was outdoors, which I prefer to indoors.

All the concerts in the winter season were for subscribers, but none of the Tanglewood ones were. Only a performer who has experienced both types of audiences will readily appreciate the difference. The simple facilities of the Shed made contact between performers and public closer and more intimate than it could ever have been in the formal atmosphere of a concert hall. The few demarcation ropes were disregarded by one and all, the musicians talked with the audience at intermission, people gathered backstage and took pictures. The entire sequence of events resembled a real communal experience, and I wished that we could find ways of transferring the mood, informality, and lively spirit to the whole year.

Leinsdorf elaborated in a 1967 television interview with Edwin Newman of NBC News.

Also I find that music making in the open, with nature around us, adds another dimension, and so we feel very often that some pieces take on a new meaning when we do them here. Many composers had a very strong relationship to nature, to forests, to the mountains, to the lakes—think of Beethoven and all his walks, think of Brahms, Schumann, Debussy—clouds, you know. We find often pieces take on a different meaning here. For instance, the Mahler Fourth Symphony, when we played it, a lot of the musicians and a lot of the people in the audience came to me and said, you know—look here, this is an outdoor piece.

There is lots of outdoor music in [the Brahms First Symphony]. Now that opening in the Andante of the fourth movement, that horn that is deep in the woods and the answering flute—if I've ever heard a bird, this is it!

I remember here at Tanglewood a performance of Verdi's *Requiem* when in the "Dies Irae" in time for the last trumpet sounds, we had the good fortune of having a tremendous thunderstorm. The thunder and lightning were going on outside of the Shed. There the trumpets were blaring away around the last judgment. It was a very effective thing. You couldn't have duplicated this in the city except maybe with the subway rumbling under the hall.

Leinsdorf was to make many changes at Tanglewood. One of his first, again from Cadenza, *has become a Tanglewood fixture.*

Tanglewood's principal problem was the Friday night concert, which was only sparsely attended, no matter how attractive the program. Our public came mainly from New York and Boston for weekends, and not even the fastest driver made an 8 p.m. start after leaving his office at five. As the years progressed I found an answer that made some difference. I scheduled a small concert, a recital, chamber music or short choral selections, to be performed for the local residents, who were able to come at any hour, from seven to eight. There followed a one-hour dinner interval, with facilities on the grounds for those who wanted to eat. By nine, when the commuting population could comfortably be at hand, we began the regular Boston Symphony program. I saw to it that the "Prelude" (as the short hour of recital was called) had thematic relation with the entire weekend.

In his review of Leinsdorf's first Tanglewood concert, Harold Schonberg of the New York Times *commented on the new regime in action.*

The first weekend of the 1963 Berkshire Music Festival started this evening before 6,410 happy listeners. Festival officials called it a remarkable turnout, all the more because the day had been spotted with heavy showers. But the evening turned out to be beautiful, almost autumnlike, with a bracing, cool breeze and a nearly full moon as an obbligato to Mozart. . . .

Mozart was not a specialty of Serge Koussevitzky and his successor, Charles Munch. Both of them did occasionally present one of the better-known Mozart works, but their prime interests and strengths lay elsewhere.

Now that Erich Leinsdorf has taken over, however, we can expect a concentration on the German and Austrian composers, together with much more of an emphasis on the contemporary international scene. Mr. Leinsdorf has more catholic tastes than either of his predecessors. The proof is in this opening series; in the Prokofiev music to come and in the American premiere on July 27 of Benjamin Britten's *War Requiem*, a major choral work.

Leinsdorf's stated intention was to reshape the programming of the Festival. "I interpret the word festival *as meaning 'the observing of something special,'" he stated to the press. "Each year my major concern [is] to find for one or two early programs at Tanglewood enough musical 'news' to attract the New York press. Their write-ups would, in turn, create more publicity for the rest of the summer's doings."*

His Prokofiev concerts, celebrating the tenth anniversary of the composer's death, and his Mozart concerto series with Rudolf Serkin certainly got the ball rolling. But the most "special" concert was the American premiere of Benjamin Britten's War Requiem, *a fusion of the traditional Latin text with the antiwar poems of Wilfred Owen.*

In a 1963 speech in London, Leinsdorf told his audience why this performance would be special.

For a variety of reasons we found that the Britten premiere would best be given as soon as the entire orchestra was available. Also a factor in the scheduling was that I wished to put the Britten work on the traditional observance of Serge Koussevitzky's anniversary.

But more interesting than the scheduling might be the events that led me to ask for the first performance rights to this great work. In February 1962 I was in London to do some concerts with the BBC Symphony and Benjamin Britten's publisher, with whom I have had a very long acquaintance, sent me upon my request an early printing of the vocal score. I will never forget the afternoon when I had a few hours to read through the score. It was very cold—the radiator in my room at the hotel barely gave enough heat. I sat with my feet stretched toward the radiator to get the maximum warmth, but as I read through the pages of the vocal score another kind of warmth enveloped me soon, and after I finished the reading of the score, I phoned the publisher and asked then and there to have the first American performance rights for Tanglewood.

Phyllis Curtin, the soprano soloist in the American premiere, told me that the War Requiem *was the most remarkable piece she ever sang.*

I was brought up in a strongly religious family. I had a wonderful education. Nothing in my whole life made me think so seriously about war and peace and religion as that work. And it is in the music as well as in the text chosen. The brilliance in choosing the poetry in juxtaposition to the mass—it was absolutely breathtaking. I must have sung thirty-five performances of that piece and never once without being more profoundly moved than by almost anything else.

The reviews were, by and large, extremely glowing. In the New York Herald Tribune *of July 29, Paul Henry Lang proclaimed:*

This magnificent work has subtle meanings which perhaps no audience unacquainted with the tremendous past of Christian ritual music could be expected fully to discern. . . . The emotional intensity of his music, his capacity to communicate, his sense of the beauty and mystery and pathos of life are what give *War Requiem* its haunting tenderness. There may be substance in this music for those who are losing hope in the barbarous menace of today.

Choral and solo writing are magnificently idiomatic, and the musical language—a total language—acknowledging no school, no tendency, no regimentation whatsoever but proudly observing the ancient spirit of the service for the dead, is the composer's own. No higher praise could be bestowed on a composer today.

The principal dissenter was Harold Schonberg, whose review appeared in the New York Times.

On Saturday evening, the Berkshire Music Festival at Tanglewood came up with one of the two major musical events of the summer in this country—the American premiere of Benjamin Britten's *War Requiem.* (The other will be the production of Alban Berg's *Lulu* in Santa Fe next week.) In the past, Tanglewood has had its share of premieres, but certainly nothing so ambitious as the Britten work.

When the *War Requiem* had its world premiere on May 30, 1962, it was immediately accepted as one of Britten's major works, probably his masterpiece to date, and it has been hailed as one of the major choral works of the century. Britten himself is a pacifist, and in composing a score about the horrors of war he was writing something very close to his heart. The specific occasion for the long (almost an hour and a half) requiem mass was the consecration of the restored St. Michael's Cathedral in Coventry. But Britten has addressed his score to mankind.

This is not an ordinary requiem mass, and it has its unorthodox moments, though scholars will point out many precedents in pre-Bach music. What the composer has done is combine sacred and secular elements. Juxtaposed to the words of the requiem mass—the *missa pro defunctis*—are settings of poems by Wilfred Owen. . . .

For these settings, Mr. Britten has used a chamber orchestra with tenor and baritone soloists. For the requiem itself, he has scored for an unusually large orchestra, soprano solo, organ, piano (apparently not used last night), mixed chorus, and boys' choir. . . .

There can be no doubt that *A War Requiem* does live up to its reputation as an important, large-scale, and even imposing work. Whether it is all that its admirers claim for it is another question. In England it seems to be an article of faith that the *War Requiem* is worthy of standing alongside the Verdi *Requiem* and other ecclesiastical masterpieces. But one wonders.

With all of its virtues, with all of its exciting orchestration and technical mastery, with all the validity of the basic message about war, it may turn out that the *War Requiem* will not, in the long run, have staying power because of a certain obviousness. The effects are a little too heart-on-sleeve, the sorrow is a little too sorrowful, the melodic content a little too calculated. . . .

The performance from all concerned was vigorous, assertive, and well coordinated. Even the boys, on temporary bleachers along the left side of the auditorium, came in on time and sang in tune. Nearly 11,000 attended, and the applause lasted a good twenty minutes. All obviously liked Tanglewood's new ideas. Mr. Leinsdorf must have been very pleased.

The performance before an overflow crowd was later televised by public television in New York, Boston, and Washington, D.C., thus advancing Leinsdorf's publicity agenda.

Although Leinsdorf was from the very beginning of his career an opera man, when he got to Tanglewood one of the first events he presided over was the demise of the Tanglewood Opera Department that Boris Goldovsky had made so popular and successful.

It its place, he presented operas-in-concert in the Shed, beginning in 1965 with an entire weekend performance of Wagner's uncut version of Lohengrin. *One act was given each night of the final weekend of the 1965 season, and it created a virtual firestorm from the critics, with the New York critics loathing it, and everyone else brimming over with praise.*

Here is a sampling of opinions.

Harold Schonberg of the *New York Times*: "It was not a very exhilarating weekend, though. An opera has to be awfully good to survive concert treatment."

Michael Steinberg of the *Boston Globe*: "The performance seemed to me remarkably successful and certainly incomparably better than any I have seen at or heard from the Metropolitan in twenty years. . . . Lohengrin achieved a discipline and precision rarely encountered in the theater.

Warren B. Syer in *High Fidelity/Musical America*: "The fact, simply stated, is that the BSO *Lohengrin* was, by definition, the most interesting thing which has been done at Tanglewood in years."

Schonberg thought that, of all the singers, only Sandor Konya, as Lohengrin, sang with "purity, with ease, with strength and musicianship." Steinberg disliked him. Oh, well, the Berkshire Eagle *thought everything about the performance was "thrilling." Opera was off to a lively start at Tanglewood during the Leinsdorf era.*

Things got even livelier in 1968 when the Berkshire Music Center and the Fromm Music Foundation presented the premiere of Stanley Silverman and Richard Foreman's "occult opera," Elephant Steps, *the Berkshire Music Center's first foray into full-scale opera since Goldovsky. The conductor was the young Michael Tilson Thomas, then a conducting fellow at the Center, who won the Koussevitzky Prize that year and would become the BSO's assistant conductor the following year.*

This production definitely qualified as one of the "screwballish contemporary concerts" that Leinsdorf so delighted in. The New York Times *was intrigued enough that it sent two critics to pass judgment on it. Raymond Ericson described the goings on in the August 10 issue of the paper as using "all musical forms of opera, live and taped, plus speech, films, slide projections, and other apparatus becoming familiar through mixed-media happenings."*

In a fact sheet found in the archives of the BSO, composer Silverman, then thirty, gave a seemingly straightforward outline of the opera's plot.

Hartman, who is ill, is warned he must free himself from the spiritual influence of the mysterious Reinheart. Sneaking off to Reinheart's house, he faints upon finding the front door locked. Seized by his enemies, they try to broadcast his public confession over the radio. Back home, safe in his kitchen, Hartman dreams of Reinheart, as Elephant-Angels appear and lead him into the street, up a ladder to Reinheart's second-floor window. The window begins to quiver with light, and mysteriously . . . Hartman is transformed.

Theodore Strongin, the Times*'s other critic, put another spin on the plot.*

Next, does it have a plot? Well, there's this character, Reinheart . . . or are there two Reinhearts? And who is Hartman? Reinheart is in bed as the "opera" begins. He falls out of bed several times. There's a doctor in the room. A man (Hartman?) comes in the room. He goes out and is trapped in a wall with his head showing in the room. He has two large, shaggy, white hands. Everyone is preoccupied with hands.

Then there is the radio station. Does Hartman get on the air or doesn't he? It's not clear. And so on until the end when Reinheart (or was it Hartman?) climbs up a ladder and stays there.

Get it? Well, to a man the critics found this hour-long performance frustrating until they realized that the better part of valor was just to relax and accept the opera's dada premise. According to Ericson, "The composer believes that some people were put off the work because of its opening, in which by the intentional use of boring, droning sounds, which drown out the singing onstage, is a statement about the opening of many conventional operas—there's all that deadly recitative."

Strongin gave the best explanation of all.

What they have done is taken all the senses, not just hearing, and given them equal value. The have stretched the awareness. Reinheart's falling out of bed, for instance, has the same function as a musical note or accent. So does a green lightbulb that keeps going on and off, irregularly but often, and a silent film loop in which a man takes gloves out of his pocket and puts them on over and over again. In a stream-of-consciousness way, *Elephant Steps* has form.

Which brings us to the Leinsdorf era at the Berkshire Music Center, where, according to Harold Schonberg, there had been "a complete reorientation." In Cadenza*, Leinsdorf described the post-Munch state of affairs at the Center.*

He [Henry Cabot, the president of the trustees of the Boston Symphony] spoke mostly of his concern with the Berkshire Music Center, which had deteriorated since its inception. Koussevitzky, wanting to teach, had created around the outdoor concerts at Tanglewood a master class for young conductors, which led in turn to a student orchestra and gradually to other related and unrelated activities. After resigning in 1949, Koussevitzky still held on to the summer school until he died two years later [Koussevitzky actually died the year after his resignation], by which time Munch had seen enough of the task upon him to flatly refuse involvement with the Music Center. His title, director, was purely nominal by mutual agreement. Since 1951 there had been a vacuum in direction, and Cabot expected me to fill this and bring it new thinking.

Harry Kraut, then the administrator of the Center and later Leonard Bernstein's very influential manager, gave a good description of the Center at that time in Aaron Copland and Vivian Perlis's Copland: Since 1943.

Leinsdorf was deeply interested in the school [Berkshire Music Center]. The structure had remained the same all during Munch's time, and it was getting harder each year to maintain a high level of student quality. There was not the volume of good string players then, and many were going to other summer places. They were given the impression by their teachers that if they were really good, God forbid they should show interest in playing in an orchestra! There were not so many good composition students applying, either.

Leinsdorf was given a mandate by the BSO trustees to do something about the Center. My juggling the numbers persuaded them it would not cost that much more money to keep it going.

The simple change that was made between 1963 and 1964 was that Paul Fromm's money was used as the main support for the entire performance program, and all the contemporary music activities were melded into the performance program rather than being separate. Fromm approved, agreed, and increased his support. This enabled the underwriting of the new fellowship program, and attracted the best students.

This resulted in the renaissance of the Music Center, and the acceptance letters Kraut sent to the incoming students set the perimeters of the new regime.

Mr. Scott Nickrenz
347 East 85th Street
New York, N.Y.

Dear Mr. Nickrenz:

The instrumental program at the Berkshire Music Center has been radically revised. Mr. Leinsdorf has planned to move the average quality of our members to a postgraduate level. The program in 1965 begins June 27 and lasts eight weeks ending on August 22. Included in *each* instrumentalist's program will be chamber music, baroque music (under the supervision of Mr. Igor Kipnis), contemporary music (Fromm Program under the supervision of Mr. Gunther Schuller), and orchestra (conducted by Messrs. Leinsdorf, Schuller, and others).

We would like you to be a member and accept a fellowship in viola (one of eight). There is no tuition, but out of the $500 fellowship stipend, you must pay fees (registration and dormitory) totaling $300; the balance of $200 will be paid to you in cash to defray your other expenses.

Would you let me know whether you would like to return? Since we are being very selective this year, I must know as quickly as possible whether you will be able to enroll this summer. Will you let me know by March 5? A card is enclosed for your convenience.

Nickrenz accepted the fellowship and later became one of the Fromm Players.

Leinsdorf described his initial experience with the Music Center conducting students in his 1981 book The Composer's Advocate: A Radical Orthodoxy for Musicians.

When I began my first season as director of the Berkshire Music Center in 1963, I found in my conducting seminar twenty-eight candidates admitted by the previous regime's screening process. They were unknown to me. For evaluation I gave them a three-part quiz. In the first part they were to find a wrong note in a C-major triad played by the four horns in the slow introduction of Weber's *Freischütz* Overture. (There is one Breitkopf and Härtel edition of the score that contains that misprint.) Nobody spotted it, which meant that there was no connection between eye and ear, even in such an utterly simple harmonic configuration. After the unsuccessful search for a wrong note in Weber, my twenty-eight seminarists were asked, without scores for reference, in how many symphonic movements Brahms had used trombones. What followed resembled an auction rather than a seminar. Bids flew from all sides. They ranged from five to a dozen! By contrast, we had a *succès fou* with the third question, which lifted twenty-eight hands in the air. All voices answered correctly in virtual unison. What had the question been? "Where does Brahms use a percussion instrument?"

These reactions showed that my seminarists mostly had listened to recordings, on which a triangle can be heard far more clearly than the trombones playing inner voices in a mixture of lower-frequency instruments, which are not always distinguishable. To know with assurance what instruments were woven into the center of the music's fabric, these students would have needed the firsthand acquaintance achieved through reading the score. The ability to read scores accurately and fluently is the obvious first step to understanding what a composer has written and how he wishes it to sound. Yet an astonishing number of conductors have avoided taking it.

The press had begun to comment on the changes at the Center, beginning with Harold Schonberg's piece of July 14 in the Times.

As for the Music Center, Mr. Leinsdorf has a good many ideas, some of which he has already put into execution. He thinks that not enough care is taken in selecting the students; that in the past there has been too much mediocrity. This season, every applicant had to undergo an audition, and blood flowed. This did not in the least disturb Mr. Leinsdorf. In fact, this weeding-out of unqualified applicants pleased him, for he considers musical culture among professionals and would-be professionals at a low state, and he would not like the Music Center to be a forum for the unqualified.

Leinsdorf's first Opening Exercises speech in 1963, one of the longest on record and often interrupted by one of those violent thunderstorms so familiar to Berkshire residents, left no doubt of his high expectations for the students.

It is of primary interest to us not to enlarge the squads of displaced and discontented musicians. Our faculty members are determined not to encourage sluggish minds or mediocre ability. That group is unfortunately more than sufficiently represented within our profession.

This brings me to the crux of the question: what is a musician? Is it one who painstakingly deciphers a set of hieroglyphics and subsequently must practice like a beaver to motorize a number of sections into a sensible piece of music? Or is a musician one to whom a musical text speaks at first sight? I do not wish to convey the meaning that one must be able to faultlessly play on sight any given phrase of passage, but that from the very point of departure it is immediately apparent how meaningful or meaningless a score appears to the player.

The unhappy auditionist who is seemingly fluent in his sonata or concerto, only to collapse from the shock of nonrecognition when it comes to "reading" is not as much to blame as his mentors who have encouraged him to pursue musical ambitions without thorough training. Many are the dubious advisors who steer their charges toward great solo virtuoso stardom; the hope of filling the spot vacated by a [Fritz] Kreisler or a[n] [Emanuel] Feuermann is a heady enough dream to induce hundreds of hopefuls to drill themselves into a stupor of Paganini Caprices while neglecting to acquire a real musical education.

Afterwards, a faculty member was heard to remark, "For the first time in many years things are organized around here. Those kids better look out. Big Brother is watching them."

By 1969, Leinsdorf's last year with the Center, he had brought about seismic changes. The student body had grown to 160, all on full scholarships subsidized by the Boston Symphony and many new individual donors. By this time the students were tackling music far more challenging and adventurous than the musical fare usually heard in the Shed.

As his parting shot at the Music Center, Leinsdorf conducted the students in a performance of Alben Berg's opera Wozzeck, a work so difficult and complex that it had been performed infrequently since its first performance in 1925. Acknowledging the gamble he was taking, Leinsdorf informed a reporter that "when the Vienna Staatsoper did its first Wozzek many years ago, it had thirty-four orchestral rehearsals. We did it with one orchestra rehearsal and four dress rehearsals. These young people don't resist the music as the older professionals of thirty and forty years ago did, and during rehearsals they went to their more experienced colleagues in the Boston Symphony and asked how seemingly impossible passages in the score could be played. This is what the Music Center is all about."

The students concurred. A twenty-year-old oboist allowed to the same reporter that "it was especially difficult rhythmically, but it also gave me a whole new concept of tonality and showed me how much more stamina you need for something like this."

It was a critically acclaimed performance, and Koussevitzky would have been very proud.

Leinsdorf was dedicated to the across-the-board improvement of musical standards—a trait he very much shared with Koussevitzky. This applied not only to the students but equally to the professional musicians. Consequently, he organized numerous symposia devoted to all aspects of musical performance.

*One of his pet peeves, as he put it, was the need for musicians to have a greater under-
standing of musicology—specifically an awareness of eighteenth- and nineteenth-century
performance styles. This became one of the themes of his 1964 Opening Exercises address to
the students.*

Musicologists are making a life study of the conditions during specific periods in which
they specialize, and it can only benefit performers to consider these findings as an essential part of their own preparation. Thus I hope that the old cliché of the ivory-tower
bookworm who has no contact with live music may be once and for all shattered, to be
replaced by your receptivity of what the musicologists have to offer. I expect that all
our enrollment will attend the musicological symposium this summer, will listen to the
papers read, and participate in the discussions with the panelists. The symposium will
offer you a magnificent opportunity to get some of the more puzzling questions about
ornamentation, appoggiatura, and a number of traditional do's and don'ts answered
authoritatively. We do not expect that all of our participants will agree with each other,
and this in turn will make the whole affair ever so much more vital and inspiring.

*He elaborated on this while addressing the participants of the Musicological Symposium
of 1964.*

In various talks I have stressed to our young enrolled people here the need for the
modern performer to be broadly cultured, not only in music, but in all the phases of
Western civilization; and I need not convince you that with a repertoire of nearly 300
years of music, more and more awareness of past practices is indispensable if the performer wishes to be authoritative and in style.

The dire necessity for better-schooled, better-informed performers has so often been
impressed upon me, that I cannot begin to quote chapter and verse. More recently, one
special occasion stands out in my mind. A baritone auditioned for me, singing the recitative of Beethoven's Ninth Symphony. After he had finished, I asked him why he had not
made the appoggiatura, G to F, in the fifth measure of the recitative, "O Freunde, Nicht
Diese Tone." He, with a rather indulgent smile, said, "I just sang this Ninth Symphony
with A. B. (initials of a very well-known conductor), who did not take issue with the way
I sang it, and I sang it just the way I sang it for you. *After all*, this is a matter of opinion."

I said, "My dear fellow, in this case, and in some other cases, it is *not* a matter of
opinion, because if you look at the previous phrase, you will see that in the orchestra
parts the appoggiatura is spelled out. It was taken for granted that singers would do
it; and there are many such proofs in eighteenth-century scores." Well, he was totally
unconvinced.

There is a great need to distinguish between what is opinion and interpretation, and what is a must. I remember another incident, much earlier, which showed me how much a performer should know about performance practices in past eras. It was in a rehearsal of *Falstaff*, conducted by Toscanini, that a musician wonderingly asked him why he insisted that passages marked with four *p*'s in Verdi's score were played in a full-bodied, singing, piano tone, to which Toscanini replied that Verdi marked extremes to offset the indifferent dynamics of the Italian opera orchestras which he knew so well. The marking against bad habits is one of the foremost studies for performers, and I look to you, to the musicologist, to give us sufficient awareness of past performance practices.

These are the directions in which our young performers, (and sometimes our not-so-young performers) need a great deal of guidance, because the primitive view, "observe the letter of the score," will not do when one tries to master 300 years of music; for during those 300 years, I need not tell *you*, a lot has changed in the spelling of music, and the same letter meant quite different things in 1750 than it did in 1950. . . .

Leinsdorf was a very serious man, a perfectionist with a sharp tongue, steeped in the technical and intellectual side of music. Nevertheless, he knew the deep value of a true love of music and responded to it. He saved this correspondence in the archives of the Boston Symphony.

Brookfield, Illinois 60513
August 30, 1966

Dear Mr. Leinsdorf:

Since viewing your concert from Tanglewood this month, via television, I know now I must talk to you by means of this letter, to show my appreciation of your work.

Some two years ago, I hurt my elbow—the greatest thing that ever happened to me. I had to give up bowling. I then started to listen to my FM radio more in earnest. This radio was a Christmas gift from my husband, a few months previous.

Although I had always liked classical music, when I heard it, I had never been exposed to much of it, and never had opportunities to *really* hear it.

I subscribed to our two Chicago FM schedules, and I have been listening ever since, from the time I get up in the morning until I retire. My bowling money has been going for records. I have some of yours, with Arthur Rubinstein—absolute perfection—also, I have your Beethoven Symphony no. 3. I never tire of hearing it.

I had always thought I liked light classics, which I do, really, but I just didn't know the beauty and ecstasy that abound in the masters' music.

Beethoven has long since been my favorite of favorites. . . .

Occasionally, on hearing Beethoven's Sixth Symphony, I find it brings tears to my eyes—I am so moved, and touched, by the beauty. It gives me an ecstatic glow, which I have never felt from anything else, in my life.

I am so sorry I did not know of these feelings years ago—I am forty-six, with six children—two married. Possibly, I could have directed my life into something concerning music. I know I could never play an instrument—not very well, at least—if I could, I don't think I could contain the joy and pleasure I would derive from it.

I attended our local West Suburban Symphony in La Grange last season, and am hoping to see the Chicago Symphony one day. But since I have heard your music, about a years ago, at first, I have told my husband that one day I *am* going to Boston, just to hear you perform with that marvelous group.

I know of not a single soul interested in this music, therefore, I cannot talk with anyone about it, nor listen to it with anyone, which would make it an even richer experience. The first four of our children dislike the classics; the nine-year-old boy enjoys it, and has attended the symphony with me, but is not really driven in that direction. The four-year-old girl is absorbing it, and likes much of it, but not all. . . .

I hoped I am not giving you the impression that I am some dramatic person, or something. I am just "people," who has found the one thing in life that gives pleasure, as nothing else can do, for me. Which makes me wonder—how do all the great men feel about having created, with all their hearts, and souls, to be appreciated by the likes of me? Well, I am very thankful they lived, to pass on to us this beauty and powerful emotion.

I wish you the best of luck, and hope you continue making such beautiful music, for many more years. Thank you for listening.

Sincerely,
Mrs. Margaret Stejskal

Mr. Leinsdorf responded.

September 29, 1966

Dear Mrs. Stejskal:

Your good letter was awaiting my return from our annual post-Tanglewood vacation, and thus I hope you will forgive my delay in replying. We were of course delighted to learn that you had enjoyed the Boston Symphony's concert that was broadcast from Tanglewood by NBC. We were pleased that through the modern medium of television we could, for an afternoon, share our summer home with you and your neighbors in Brookfield. I was especially glad to hear from someone such as yourself who obviously enjoys music so much.

Thank you for having taken the time to write us.

Sincerely yours,
Erich Leinsdorf

Mrs. Stejskal responded to Leinsdorf saying, "Your letter is going in with my most precious possessions, and I will derive great pleasure from rereading it from time to time."

Two scenes from the opera department production of *Idomeneo*, the "new" Mozart opera Goldovsky discovered. (Boston Symphony Orchestra; Howard S. Babbitt Jr.)

he opera department cast of Paisiello's *King Theodore in Venice*, staged y Goldovsky in 1961. The young Sherrill Milnes is seated second om left, and Justino Diaz is in the back. (Whitestone Photo; Heinz eissenstein)

Boris Goldovsky making one of his many memorable speeches at Tanglewood on Parade. (Boston Symphony Orchestra; Will Plouffe Studio)

With the new BSO music director Charles Munch (at right), Gertrude Robinson Smith felt comfortable returning to Tanglewood. Pierre Monteux (left) was a frequent guest conductor. (Boston Symphony Orchestra; Gus Manos)

Heinz Weissenstein has captured the dignity of Erich Leinsdorf on the podium in the Shed. (Whitestone Photo)

Concertmaster Joseph Silverstein is Maestro Leinsdorf's soloist in this rehearsal. (Whitestone Photo; Heinz Weissenstein)

Erich Leinsdorf (center) congratulating trumpet soloist Roger Voisin with concertmaster Joseph Silverstein in total agreement. (Whitestone Photo; Heinz Weissenstein)

A Tanglewood business meeting on the porch of Heaton Hall in Stockbridge, where Erich Leinsdorf always stayed. From left to right: Leonard Burkat, Leinsdorf, and Tod Perry. (Boston Symphony Orchestra; Boris and Milton)

Erich Leinsdorf (far left) conferring with conducting fellows. (Whitestone Photo; Heinz Weissenstein)

Richard Forman (left) and Stanley Silverman (right), director and composer, respectively, of the "occult" opera *Elephant Steps*, stand on the stage of the Theatre-Concert Hall. Behind them is the infamous bed from which Reinheart fell several times. (Whitestone Photo; Heinz Weissenstein)

After Serge Koussevitzky's death, his widow, Olga, spoke every year at the Berkshire Music Center's Opening Exercises. Aaron Copland is seated behind her. (Boston Symphony Orchestra)

Legendary Tanglewood photographer Heinz Weissenstein (second from left) posing with some of his favorite subjects (left to right) Leonard Bernstein, Gunther Schuller, and Seiji Ozawa. (Boston Symphony Orchestra; Mary Smith)

A picnic on the lawn before a concert in the Leinsdorf era. (Boston Symphony Orchestra; Howard S. Babbitt Jr.)

Paul Fromm, the major financial supporter of new music at Tanglewood, chats with Erich Leinsdorf and the conductor's first wife, Anne, on a chilly evening in the Shed. (Whitestone Photo; Heinz Weissenstein)

Elliott Carter teaches a composition class at the Music Center in 1964. (Whitestone Photo; Heinz Weissenstein)

Aaron Copland (left) tells Gunther Schuller (right) a good joke.
(Whitestone Photo; Heinz Weissenstein)

Gunther Schuller (right) congratulates composer Hans Werner
Henze after a student performance at the Festival of Contemporary
Music in 1983. (Boston Symphony Orchestra; Walter Scott)

Oliver Knussen (left) works with his mentor Gunther Schuller
(right). (Whitestone Photo; Heinz Weissenstein)

Composer Betsy Jolas acknowledges the applause after the premiere performance of her work *Tales of a Summer Sea* on August
16, 1977. Jolas was a guest teacher of composition in 1967 and
1977 and was the first woman composer on the Berkshire Music
Center faculty. (Boston Symphony Orchestra; Walter Scott)

The Tanglewood new music movers and shakers get together. Left
to right: Paul Fromm, Aaron Copland, Lukas Foss, and Gunther
Schuller. (Whitestone Photo; Heinz Weissenstein)

Ozawa conducting the Tanglewood Festival Chorus in one of his signature pieces, the Mahler Symphony no. 2, *Resurrection*. Soloists (left to right) are soprano Barbara Bonney and mezzo-soprano Florence Quivar. (Boston Symphony Orchestra; Walter Scott)

Camp Mah-Kee-Nac boys rehearsing for a performance of the Berlioz *Te Deum* with Charles Munch for a concert in the Shed. (*Berkshire Eagle*; Gus Manos)

Robert Shaw sitting on the lawn, with the Shed behind. (*Berkshire Eagle*)

John Oliver conducting the Bach *Passion According to St. Matthew,* step-ping in for the ailing Seiji Ozawa in 1985. (*Berkshire Eagle*; Walter Scott)

Would-be Tanglewood Festival chorister James Taylor, here giving his own 1996 Popular Artists concert in the Shed. Nobody draws a bigger audience at Tanglewood than James Taylor. (Boston Symphony Orchestra; Walter Scott)

Leonard Bernstein conducts the Beethoven *Missa Solemnis* with soloists (left to right) Sherrill Milnes, William Cochran, Maureen Forrester, and Phyllis Curtin. Note Miss Forrester's now-sleeveless attire. (Boston Symphony Orchestra)

Ms. Curtin demonstrating the proper way for a singer to breathe from the diaphragm. (From the personal collection of Phyllis Curtin; Eugene Cook)

Singer Elsa Charlston gets encouragement from her teacher, Phyllis Curtin. (From the personal collection of Phyllis Curtin; Eugene Cook)

Tenor Kim Scown gets his posture corrected, 1975. (From the personal collection of Phyllis Curtin; Eugene Cook)

Phyllis Curtin in costume for Boris Goldovsky's opera department performance of *Pique Dame*, 1951. (Boston Symphony Orchestra)

Composer George Crumb at the piano with Phyllis Curtin around the time of his 1976 performance of *Echoes of Time and the River (Echoes II)* conducted by Seiji Ozawa. (From the personal collection of Phyllis Curtin; Eugene Cook)

Curtin works with soprano Cheryl Studer, who signed the back of this picture, "For Phyllis Curtin—In deepest appreciation for all the inspiration you have been and continue to be to me. Your admirer, Cheryl Studer." (From the personal collection of Phyllis Curtin; Eugene Cook)

1965 Tanglewood Guides and Guidesses (as they were designated in this official photograph). Left to right: Lee Barton, Larry Shapiro, Marion Polsky, Terry Pope, John Davis, Walter McBeth, Phyllis Bryn Julson, Bob Miller, John Seegal, Bof Silberman, Mike Lotz, Toby Fairbank, and Dan Gustin. Yes, Dan Gustin! (Whitestone Photo; Heinz Weissenstein)

A Tanglewood ground crew member goes about his appointed rounds aerating the lawn. (*Berkshire Eagle*)

Yes, sometimes it rains at Tanglewood. (*Berkshire Eagle*)

Lots of traffic at concert time, but almost always handled smoothly. (*Berkshire Eagle*)

Rock 'n' roll comes to Tanglewood at the Contemporary Trends concerts. Janis Joplin (center) and Sly and the Family Stone (left) got the audience going and caused quite a commotion. (*Berkshire Eagle*)

Audience on the lawn for the Sly and the Family Stone concert. (*Berkshire Eagle*)

The Jefferson Airplane was another Contemporary Trends concert that raised the decibel level way beyond what was considered acceptable in the Berkshires. (*Berkshire Eagle*)

Leonard Bernstein wearing Koussevitzky's cape. For one of Koussevitzky's birthdays, he composed a song called "Koussevitzky Blues." One verse will give you the idea.

> I've got those Koussevitzky blues, and baby,
> That ain't good:
> 'Cause he's the best-dressed man in all of Tanglewood.
> We wear dungarees, we dress like apes,
> But comes the Revolution, we'll all wear capes.

(Whitestone Photo; Heinz Weissenstein)

Aaron Copland (left) and Leonard Bernstein (right) share a laugh in the Tanglewood garden. (Boston Symphony Orchestra; Walter Scott)

Leonard Bernstein requests a little more *piano* while rehearsing with the BSO. (Boston Symphony Orchestra; Plouffe Studio)

Leonard Bernstein gives one of his many inspirational Opening Exercises speeches. (Whitestone Photo; Heinz Weissenstein)

Leonard Bernstein takes a break. (Boston Symphony Orchestra; Gus Monos)

Madame Olga Koussevitzky awards Ozawa with the Tanglewood conducting prize named after her husband. (Boston Symphony Orchestra; Heinz Weissenstein)

Seiji Ozawa and his wife, Vera, attend Opening Exercises in 1971 during the Tanglewood Troika period. (Boston Symphony Orchestra; Heinz Weissenstein)

The student conductor at the Berkshire Music Center in 1960 with conductor Eleazar de Carvalho (left) and BSO music director Charles Munch (right), who considered Seiji to be his protégé. (Boston Symphony Orchestra; Heinz Weissenstein)

This maestro doesn't just conduct—he plays golf, too. It's all about body language. (*Berkshire Eagle*; Heinz Weissenstein)

Contemporary music has many friends, but only a few lovers.

—Igor Stravinsky

CHAPTER 8

Wild New Sounds

Paul Fromm and Gunther Schuller

Contemporary music had always been encouraged and fostered at Tanglewood. Regardless of some reluctance on the part of audiences, Koussevitzky would not have had it otherwise. After his death, an unlikely avatar appeared in the person of Paul Fromm, whom Aaron Copland described in Vivian Perlis's Copland: Since 1943.

One major difference sparked a fresh and lively atmosphere [at the Berkshire Music Center]: the involvement of philanthropist Paul Fromm, a successful wine and liquor importer and merchant from Chicago, originally from Germany. Fromm had a passion for contemporary music. Just the man we needed! He had set up a foundation in 1952 to assist the performance of contemporary music and to commission new works. Paul Fromm had written to me (February 17, 1956) saying, "You can plan boldly since we do not intend to sponsor contemporary music in economy size over the thrift counter." The Fromm Foundation's two concerts of "modern chamber music" took place on Monday evenings in July in the theater–concert hall with members of the BSO. Four Fromm-commissioned works were played. Enthusiasm ran high; Fromm was so pleased that he promised to continue his support. It was a big step forward for contemporary music. We began to talk about adding a seminar to the contemporary concerts the next season.

Paul Fromm, addressing a panel of music critics at Tanglewood, gave his rationale for his "expertise" in the field.

The only excuse I can offer for what might otherwise seem presumptuous—a discussion of music criticism—is my eagerness to promote and improve the cultural climate for music. My credentials consist simply of forty years spent listening to music and my desire to increase my own capacities and awareness as a listener. Also, I have a profound longing to live in a community where the significance of music is recognized as an integral part of our cultural and intellectual life, where the sustenance and development of the music of our own time is a deeply felt responsibility.

Fromm elaborated on his own involvement with music in an article in the 1982 program book of the Festival of Contemporary Music, titled "Reflections of a Musical Critic."

I grew up in Kitzingen, a small Bavarian town in Germany. My formal education, if one can call it that, ended at the age of sixteen when I began working in Frankfurt-am-Main. There I came into contact with a great variety of music of the past and the present. In those days Bartók, Berg, Hindemith, Krenek, Milhaud, Schönberg, Stravinsky, and Webern were the younger-generation composers. American composers, even those of the stature of Ives, Copland, and Sessions, were unknown to us. . . .

The turning point that, musically speaking, brought me into the twentieth century, came in 1927. I heard Stravinsky's *Rite of Spring* for the first time. This was music unlike any I had known. Its impact made me understand what the Spanish painter Juan Gris meant when he said that no work destined to become classic would ever resemble the classic works that preceded it.

I never imagined then that in 1959 I would meet Stravinsky in America and, in that year, sponsor the American premiere of *Threni.*

When I arrived in the United States as an immigrant in 1938, I found the peculiarly American rift between artistic values and commercial values far more troubling that the relatively simpler schism between old and new in Europe. I became particularly concerned about the anomalous position of composers in a society that was not only musically conservative, but also insistent that music make its own way in the market-place as if it were a commodity of some kind. Although their creativity is the source of music and musical culture, composers were excluded from giving direction to musical life, from influencing the musical taste of the public.

For years I pondered these problems and finally, after I had achieved economic security, I was ready to put my ideas into action. That's how in 1952 the Fromm Music Foundation came into existence.

In a speech, "Commitment to the American Composer," given at a Tanglewood panel discussion on August 13, 1964, Fromm turned his attention to the needs of the younger generation of composers.

One of the first steps in this direction was the formation of the Fromm Fellowship Players in Tanglewood in 1957. By attaching these young musicians to the composition department, we hoped to enrich the learning experience of both young composers and performers by direct and immediate contact with sound demonstrations of compositional concepts, as well as by making possible authentic performances of the music of the mature composers who lectured at Tanglewood as our guests.

Copland continues his story.

Tanglewood became an exciting place again for composers, because of Paul Fromm and his foundation. Beginning in 1957, the Fromm Players (ten instrumentalists and one singer) were in residence and responsible for playing and demonstrating new music in the weekly Composers' Forums, the Aspects of Music lecture series, and the Seminar in Contemporary Music envisioned by Fromm in 1956. Ralph Berkowitz, Tod Perry, Gail Rector, and I met during the winter months to choose the Fromm Fellows. Our job was to find top players with an interest in contemporary music who would become a homogeneous ensemble. They had to be able to read almost anything at sight. We were lucky on all counts. The players included a woodwind quintet plus a string quartet, a pianist, and a soprano: All were outstanding performers. I wrote to Leo Smit (July 25 1957), "Tanglewood is hectic as usual, but we have been having lots of fun with our Fromm Players—at our very beck and call—playing oodles of modern music from Varèse to Webern to V. T. [Virgil Thomson] and S. Revueltas.". . .

The atmosphere for composers had never been more stimulating. Having Paul Fromm as our patron was like having our own Prince Esterházy! The Fromm Players gave composers the rare opportunity to have performers right on hand to test out their works. Student composers could hear their pieces played by instruments separately or in combination. They could hear what happens, for example, if a tune is doubled by five instruments rather than four, or hear a five-note chord for woodwind quintet in twenty different ways before deciding the final way. Students don't often get a chance to hear their works before the ink is dry! . . .

Paul Fromm took pleasure from the fact that the composer was again the central figure, a rare occurrence in the twentieth century. As I told a newspaper critic, "Paul Fromm is the ideal patron. He doesn't mix in or give orders, and when he gets enthusiastic about something, he gives money to support his enthusiasm. The Fellowship Players, for instance. It is a vast luxury. Ask anybody. Ask me."

When I went to visit the Fromm Foundation in Chicago in 1958, I did not know what to expect, but whatever it was, I did not find it. Paul Fromm was an importer of liquor, and the foundation offices were in the wholesale wine district. To get there, one walked through the storerooms of crates filled with wine and whiskey. Paul Fromm had a strong German accent; he was not always easy to understand, but what he said about contemporary music was always so passionate that he got his ideas across in no uncertain terms.

In an interview, contemporary composer Oliver Knussen told me that Fromm "was an idealist of quite an amazing kind. He was quite a character—a big, elegantly dressed man. He had a sort of Marty Feldman look and a thick German accent, really *thick, which remained to the very end of his life. He was around for everything. He used to give a speech at the beginning of the Festival. He was obviously interested in what was going on and profoundly aware of cultural developments."*

In a 1966 speech at Tanglewood, Fromm summed up the first ten years of his sponsorship of modern music at the Berkshire Music Center.

In the 1950s the performance of new music was still thought of as a philanthropic activity, undertaken on principle against all odds, and not, as it should have been, as an act of faith in the intrinsic quality of the new music. Here at the Berkshire Music Center, where Aaron Copland and his fellow composers made composition a significant aspect of the Center's activity, we found the ideal milieu in which we were able to present new music without any sense of apology.

Now, in the '60s, we seem at last to have reached the point where it is no longer necessary to insist on the obvious, that the composers of our time must be given their place in our musical life—not because of any moral imperatives, but because of their achievements. Surely no one needs to be reminded again that the first six decades of the twentieth century have already produced a musical literature as rich and vital as any produced at any time in history.

Can't you just hear Koussevitzky applauding!

In 1964 the newly arrived Erich Leinsdorf instituted a major innovation at Tanglewood: the Festival of Contemporary Music, to be directed by composer Gunther Schuller. Over the course of a week, students and faculty would perform in a series of contemporary music concerts with a few old-timers like Bartók and Schönberg thrown in for good measure.

This became a major place to hear new music, and Fromm had much to thank Leinsdorf for.

Erich Leinsdorf is a man who knows that things do not happen if one does not make them happen. He sensed the opportunity and realized its potential with the inception of the Festival of Contemporary Music in 1964, the second year of his directorship. With his commitment to constant renewal he has given our program an impetus that rescued it from threatened institutionalization. Through the appointment of Gunther Schuller as director of this festival within a festival, we are assured that this new momentum will continue with undiminished enthusiasm, professionalism, and creative energy.

The first season, in August of 1964, was memorable and well covered by the press. According to the New York Times, *"a large audience turned out for the opening concert, and judging from the positive reactions to the works, it was a sophisticated and knowledgeable one."*

One of the most impressive aspects of this new endeavor was how many soon-to-become-famous composers were included. Composer and critic Eric Salzman raved in the New York Herald Tribune *that it was a festival of music by young composers who, for once, really were* young.

Monday night's opening program was a fair sample of what's going on, a long, wild and not-so-woolly kickoff.

Three of the pieces were commissioned by Fromm for the series, and two turned out very well indeed. One of them, Synchronisms no. 2 for flute, clarinet, violin, cello and tape recorder by Mario Davidovsky, is—unlikely as it may sound—a little gem of a piece. In spite of the implication of the title, the work is based on juxtapositions of inventive live and tape sounds which approach each other in pattern and timbre, often overlapping in time and texture. It is a clever, elegant, and appealing study made with perfect great skill and perfect form.

The big new piece was Charles Wuorinen's chamber concerto for flute and ten players. Wuorinen, an enormously gifted young man, is one of the few younger composers who has doggedly worked at the problem of big gesture and big form. His music has never been short on imagination, but his conceptions have been too inconsistent and his forms too incoherent to bear the weight of the fat content.

But the new piece works. Written for the flutist-composer Harvey Sollberger, it grows right out of the extraordinary range of Sollberger's flute sound and technique, which is made to emerge gradually from the ensemble play of intensities and textures.

But Salzman wasn't all Mr. Nice Guy.

This was Greek tragedy night, courtesy of the Wechsler Foundation, which commissioned the [William] Sydeman and Robert Newell's "The Trojan Women" for soprano, as well. This work also has its share of portentous whispering to the great embarrassment of all concerned. For the rest, the work is a styleless bit of musical mismanagement.

He reserved his biggest kudos for Stanley Silverman's "Canto" for soprano, choirs, and instruments.

[It] was perhaps the most suggestive and imaginative work of the evening in its beautiful use of a big, blocklike choral sound cut across—and sometime under—by the delicate tracery of an ensemble of plucked and percussive instruments. The conception is not just quite complete—as if these were studies or excerpts from a larger work—but the ideas and the way they are set into a careful, elegant, expressive shape give the music real character and style.

The second concert of the series was given by the Lenox Quartet, three of whose members had been Fromm Fellows in 1959. They quickly became a nationally known performing group. On the program this night were string quartets by Arthur Berger, Gunther Schuller, and Leon Kirchner—with the highlight of the evening being Elliott Carter's Second String Quartet. Salzman was impressed.

The Carter quartet was an especially fitting part of the program. The work was one of the ensemble's early triumphs, and it stands at a kind of turning point in the development of recent American music. The influence of Carter's music, although not necessary obvious or overt, has been one of the key factors in the development of a rich new virtuoso music of great character, resource, and expressive coherence, and we've been hearing some of the remarkable latter-day results all this week.

The Carter is an authentic masterpiece of its kind, generating new ideas of form out of a very individual and imaginative use of the instruments and the medium.

Salzman was having a fine time. Friday night, he had this to say.

David del Tredicis' "I Hear an Army" (a Joyce text) for soprano and string quartet is the first piece by a young composer heard so far on this current, continuing new-music festival which is un-avant-garde enough to really escape the usual pigeonholing. It is freely chromatic, with a centrifugal spinning, intertwining impetus that carries the music forward in a series of intense, overlapping cycles of repetition built around the long-lined, expressive vocal part. In its way, it is a very impressive achievement by a talented composer working out his own way of saying things outside the "mainstream."

At the end of the week, from here on in known as Fromm Week, Erich Leinsdorf thanked Paul Fromm for "a six-course festival." Quite an auspicious beginning!

For better or worse, the Festival was a benchmark for what was happening in modern music. This was due in large part because for the next twenty years the Festival would be programmed by an unorthodox polymath, Gunther Schuller. At the age of eighteen, Schuller had performed his own horn concerto with the Cincinnati Orchestra. By nineteen he was first horn with the Metropolitan Opera Orchestra and from there went on to become a conductor, writer, jazz performer, and teacher—all this without the benefit of any formal education beyond high school.

He came originally to the Music Center in 1963 to teach composition. Columnist Milton Bass, in his Berkshire Eagle *column of August 11, was quite awestruck.*

Although he is only thirty-eight years old, Gunther Schuller is the completely well-rounded man in music. He has had years of experience as a performer; there are some sixty compositions to his credit; he has done his stint as a conductor; and lately he has been engrossed in teaching. His official title is acting head of the department of composition, but unofficially he is all over the place.

By 1964 he was teaching composition and was also in charge of the new Festival of Contemporary Music at the Berkshire Music Center. Bass continues.

Gunther feels just as excited and enthusiastic about the ten young composers whose works are being aired at Tanglewood this week. The audience for contemporary music has broadened in the past five years, and Gunther considers what has taken place to be almost a musical revolution.

The works these young men are composing, he says, are all more difficult than anything done by Webern or Stravinsky, still considered too "modern" even after all these years. Gunther admits that the average person would walk out on this music after ten minutes, considering it meaningless noise. But public interest is growing, and the Berkshire Music Center has invited composers from all over the country to hear what is being done in the now-taken-for-granted twelve-tone, or serial, technique and the aleatory or improvisational form.

For several years, the Festival was lively and adventurous, presenting a range of works, from As Quiet As, *by Michael Colgrass, to Elliott Carter's* Double Concerto for Harpsichord and Piano with Two Chamber Orchestras, *as well as Sir Michael Tiplett's* Praeludium.

But by 1972, a certain perceived staleness had set in. According to many critics, the Festival was getting the reputation of a trade fair for university composers.

On the other hand, as Dan Gustin, for many years assistant manager of the 350 and manager of Tanglewood, pointed out, it is important to remember that "this was what the contemporary music scene was in those days. It wasn't just Tanglewood. It's almost unfair to tar Schuller with that brush when he was in some ways reflecting what was happening in contemporary music."

Donal Henahan wrote a piece in the New York Times *with the unfortunate headline "A Festival in Search of Itself." He reported on Fromm's dissatisfaction with the fact that modern music had not become a part of the mainstream, but rather had "become increasingly isolated in the last several decades, until now the works of the most intelligent composers (not necessarily the best) enjoy an audience composed chiefly of themselves and their closest colleague."*

However, there was worse to come from Michael Steinberg, music critic of the Boston Globe. *On August 19, 1973, he wrote the following about the Festival: "Too much of the music is bad, and so are too many of the performances." Some of the adjectives he used were* inept, amateurish, weak, *and* immature. *He criticized the inadequately prepared performances by relatively unseasoned student players and wondered where the old professional Fromm Players of past Festivals were.*

As a result, Paul Fromm decided to cut his contribution to the Festival's budget by 20 percent. Dan Gustin sent Fromm a beseeching letter to rescind his budget cut, and Fromm answered back with, "I told you in Tanglewood that our project was in a state of institutionalization and in need of strong revitalization. All I can say today is: show us what you will do in 1974, and we will show you what we can do."

More interesting was the correspondence between Steinberg and Fromm, both of whom had a deep concern with the problems of contemporary music and with its need of continuing support.

Fromm to Steinberg, in a conciliatory opening:

In your summary article in the *Globe* the urgency of your concern expressed itself quite harshly; but I know that your plainspokenness proves not that you are hostile to the Festival but that you care so much for its quality. In my initial reaction to your commentary I felt that you must believe us to be so completely uncritical that you must shock us into change. But in view of our long friendship I cannot believe that to be the case.

I am not talking out of school when I disclose to you that Gunther Schuller, Dan Gustin, and I put our heads together on the last day of the Festival and that we came up with an analysis similar to yours, at least in its substance. . . . In our post-Festival talks we came to the conclusion that we could make the Festival most representative by presenting more twentieth-century classics and established works of this generation in juxtaposition with works by young composers who deserve a hearing. . . .

In the area of performance the main question seems to be: should students or professionals play these complex new works? The obvious answer is that professionals can do it better, but that only answers the question, who can play these works better? And there have even been times when the students have performed quite brilliantly, as you have yourself observed in the past. What is more important is that the Festival put into active contact with contemporary music students who come to Tanglewood primarily interested in playing on their instruments and looking for jobs. These are the professional performers of the future, and if they perform new music in the setting of Tanglewood with its attendant enthusiasm, they are likely to resist that music less strenuously than have their elders. This is a long-range goal and one that is not always compatible with excellence of performance. . . .

Meanwhile, Fromm had an interesting comment in a letter to Dan Gustin dated November 29.

Finally, please free yourself of the notion that Michael Steinberg has created our problems. We did, and it is imperative that we find ways to solve them. You remember that I gave you my critical views at Tanglewood long before Michael wrote his review.

He added this advice to Gustin in a December 10 letter.

The final program of last summer's Festival makes my point. It had no interesting works and thus served as an anti-climax for the Festival as a whole.

It must be said that we have experienced a massive audience defection in recent years and that we cannot reverse this decline unless we go beyond facelifting in the reorganization and revitalization of the Festival. . . .

Finally, I would advise Gunther to choose an associate with an entirely different musical orientation. This would add a pluralistic dimension to the Festival and relieve Gunther of the obligation to perform music for which he does not feel a special affinity.

In response, some preventative measures were taken. Schuller hired Theodore Antoniou, whom he characterized as an "excellent composer in his own right. He is also an indefatigable organizer and initiator of contemporary music concerts on both sides of the Atlantic. Thirdly, he has boundless energy, and last but not least, having been a student at Tanglewood, he knows the situation quite well. He is a fine conductor and, of all the people I can think of, seems to have the most insight into contemporary performance problems, and with a very broad and stylistic spectrum." And for good measure, Schuller added that Olivier Messiaen and Sir Michael Tippett would be the following year's composers in residence. All was well for awhile.

But by the early '80s the critics had taken up the cudgels again, complaining about the same old thing. John Rockwell, music critic of the New York Times, *was already saying by 1980 that that 'festival within a festival' was "a hard slog through the various swamps of establishment music." In 1981 he reminded them that "there is so much more going on in new music today—tonal, atonal, consonant and dissonant—that the Tanglewood Festival's insistence on its own openness begins to sound either disingenuous or simply uninformed." In 1982 he complained that "it did seem strange that Philip Glass has never been performed in this festival and Steve Reich has been represented by only one short early work." The following year he concluded that "the trouble with Fromm Week in recent years—but also, it should be said, its distinguishing characteristic—has been that it might better be called the Schuller Week."*

Tim Page fired his own salvo in the Soho News *on September 1, 1981.*

Ah, Frommland! Ground zero for academic composers of all stripes, where hope and postserialism spring eternal in the human breast, where inspiration is gauged by résumé, and No-Doz is the drug of choice. . . .

As it is, most of the spectators sat through the Fromm concerts with an awful, Puritan sense of duty—"This is new music, and I know I won't love it, but I *must* try and find it interesting"—reminding me of Pilgrims squirming through an all-day service on a wooden bench. . . . .

By this time Fromm was really getting fed up. He wrote to Dan Gustin on September 17, 1981:

If you have not done so already, please send the *Soho News* article and the *Village Voice* report ("From Here to Timidity") to Gunther. Sheltering him from "the real world" any longer and ignoring the opinions of critics and fellow musicians would be a disservice to him and to us.

If Gunther continues his refusal to share the planning of the Festival with some knowledgeable and enlightened people (call it a committee or what you will), the future of our Festival is bleak indeed.

We are now at the crossroads.

Although the overriding complaint about the Festival in the press was that there was never any minimal music programmed, Richard Ortner, administrator of the Music Center in those days, maintained that "people forget that the first time that [minimalist composer] Louis Andriessen was heard at Tanglewood was when Gunther was there. Gunther was not a great believer in that music either, but he did understand that Andriessen was a serious and worthy composer." Dan Gustin added that Schuller often told him that the minimalists were not represented in the Festival "because they don't need us. They are doing fine!"

Others in the Tanglewood camp agreed, including then-BSO concertmaster and assistant conductor Joseph Silverstein.

I knew Paul Fromm very well. He was a very, very serious devotee of new music. He was wooed away from Tanglewood by John Rockwell. Ultimately, Rockwell got a hold of Paul Fromm and told him that Gunther Schuller was extremely bigoted against the minimalists and one could not have a contemporary music festival without the music of Steve Reich and Phil Glass. And Gunther did not feel convinced about that music, even though Terry Riley's *In C* had its premiere at Tanglewood—the seminal work of the minimalists. Gunther was not willing to give up his autonomy.

There were a number of composers who were being played in the Festival. We had neoclassicism, composers such as Andres Embry. It wasn't all Roger Sessions and Anton Webern and Elliott Carter. There was a lot of contemporary music being played, and composers who ultimately went into a much more neoromantic, neoclassical, and minimal styles—like Fred Lerdahl, for example. Fred was one of the stars of those early years. So it wasn't all twelve-tone music. Gunther's music is not all twelve-tone music either. He was not the "one-tone-Charlie" people tried to make him.

Knowing Gunther, the reviews had absolutely no impact on what he did at all, because he is a man of very great vision and very great conviction. You can argue with him, but you cannot argue with his integrity and his sense of purpose. And as such, that's the kind of mentality that should be running a contemporary music festival in my opinion.

However, by 1983, in a long letter to Schuller, Fromm stated that . . .

. . . at that point I made up my mind that if the 1983 Festival were indistinguishable from those in recent years I would have no choice but to voice my dissenting opinion publicly.

I was fully aware that in doing so I would have to speak as an individual and not as a representative of an institution. My decision to bring our discussion into the open was reinforced by your and Dan's refusal to accept Luciano Berio's offer to serve as one of our advisors. [Berio had directed the very successful 1982 Festival while Schuller was on sabbatical.] If we are serious about wanting the infusion of fresh ideas, where else could we go for advice than to people of Luciano's stature? . . .

Whenever we paid token tribute to composers with whose music you are not in sympathy, you chose their most innocuous works. You remember when we honored John Cage on his sixtieth birthday in 1972: we performed a nondescript short work of 1942 vintage. And how did we introduce Steve Reich to Tanglewood? We performed his

Music for Pieces of Wood for Five Pairs of Tuned Claves, a work that certainly is uncharacteristic of the music for which Steve is known.

By the end of the 1983 season, Paul Fromm had definitely had it. In December Andrew Pincus reported in the Berkshire Eagle *that Fromm could no longer "support the very narrow view of contemporary music" taken at Tanglewood." Fromm and Schuller had parted over "an honest disagreement over repertoire." Pincus went on.*

Fromm said the Boston group of composers has received a disproportionate share of the Tanglewood commissions and performances over the years. In fact, he said, "sometimes our concerts sounded like summer concerts of the New England Conservatory."

The fact that none of the works the foundation commissioned for Tanglewood have ever entered the repertoire, he said, proves that "the selection was much too narrow." There are, for example, groups of composers in California and in the Midwest who have never received a hearing at Tanglewood.

Given that the Tanglewood management would not give him control over the Festival content, Fromm pulled his money out. The following year, "Fromm Week" relocated to the Aspen Music Festival, where it lasted a mere two years and did not meet with Fromm's approval, nor that of the critics.

One could only note with a certain amount of irony that the reviews of what would become the last Tanglewood Fromm Week were in general rather positive. And the following year, Schuller even programmed a whole evening of minimalist music. "And not a bad evening it was," according to John Rockwell.

The Festival found new funding and has changed and grown in subsequent years, mainly under the direction of Leon Kirchner, Oliver Knussen, Reinbert de Leeuw, and John Harbison. A very wide range of composers and music styles have been presented, and the Festival remains one of the premier venues for exploring the contemporary music scene.

Paul Fromm died on July 4, 1987. Sadly, he did not live to see contemporary music become part of the mainstream—his great dream. However, he would, I think, be heartened by the enthusiasm with which new music has been received in recent years.

In the Festival of Contemporary Music program book that year, Dan Gustin praised Fromm warmly.

Mr. Fromm was one of the important figures in music during the second half of the twentieth century, and although he has not been involved at Tanglewood for several years now, nowhere is his rich legacy more in evidence than in the concerts of the Festival.

The following February, composer Luciano Berio also paid him a memorial tribute.

Paul was a tree. A solitary tree. And a friendly one: an oak, perhaps, an olive tree, a cypress—strong and gentle, with deep, intricate roots, its branches full of gifts. Paul had invented his own way to love music: practical and idealistic, aware and emotional. His love for music was made of the same ingredients that endow with meaning any form of creativity.

We believe that music is one art. The chorus, the symphony orchestra, the virtuoso recitalist, and the string quartet are not competitive "attractions" for the public fashion in patronage, but are instruments of a single craft with similar responsibilities.

—Robert Shaw
"A Choral Creed"

CHAPTER 9

Singing
at
Tanglewood

Robert Shaw, John Oliver, and Phyllis Curtin

"An American Salzburg!" That is what Gertrude Robinson Smith envisioned for the Berkshires. But Koussevitzky had a far more idealized notion of what a music festival should be. "Why Salzburg?" he asked. "Why not Tanglewood USA?" For him Salzburg was commercial—everything from Mozart Kugels to overpriced concert tickets and hotel rooms—and not musically innovative. He wanted to bring music to the masses with symphonic concerts, chamber music, and opera available to all. Great music for a great nation.

Singing is the most direct expression of music, and singing was to be very much a part of Koussevitzky's master plan.

In 1946 he discovered a kindred spirit in the choral conductor Robert Shaw and brought him to Tanglewood. Shaw, the son of a protestant minister in California, began conducting his father's church choir while in his teens. Like his father, Shaw had originally planned to be a minister, but discovered while at Pomona College that his real religious vocation was music.

After an unlikely stint conducting the Fred Waring Glee Club on the bandleader's popular national radio show for a few years, Shaw found that he needed a new direction in music. What he wanted to do was "try to extend professional techniques to large groups of interested amateurs, and to build for amateur singing a sounder, more artistic repertory."

With this goal in mind, in 1941 he founded the Collegiate Chorale, a group of some 150 singers. Their repertory was church a cappella literature and modern American music. Four months after the group's first church concert, Leopold Stokowski booked them to sing with the NBC Symphony under his direction. After the performance, Stokowski wrote Shaw: "I am deeply impressed by what you have done as a conductor and by the ideal spirit that is in your chorus. . . . You have an entirely new approach to choral music. It is fundamentally different from the conventional chorus singing and conducting."

Koussevitzky knew Shaw was the right man for Tanglewood, and he spent three very fruitful seasons there. In a 1996 radio interview with Brian Bell of WGBH Radio in Boston, Shaw looked back.

I had furnished a choir for Dr. Koussevitzky for a performance at the Brooklyn Academy of Music and Carnegie Hall. Two or three years later he invited me to come to Tanglewood and share the [choral] conducting responsibilities with Hugh Ross [conductor of the *Schola Cantorum*], who had already been there at that time. The first year, he did most of the chorus preparation for the symphony performances.

I brought up at that time about twenty young members of the Collegiate Chorale, young kids off the streets of New York substantially, along with twenty choral conducting students, who formed a forty-voice chamber chorus. We gave weekly concerts while we were here.

One of his singers was Lorna Cooke de Varon. She later became the director of the choral department at the New England Conservatory of Music, where she prepared her choral forces for many of the BSO award-winning recordings. She joined the faculty of BMC in 1953.

At the Tanglewood Music Center fiftieth anniversary, she recalled that time.

I was fortunate in 1946 to be a student when Tanglewood swung into full speed after World War II. Then the choral department consisted of two branches: the one headed by Hugh Ross, which provided the choral work for *Peter Grimes*, and the branch headed by Robert Shaw, which rehearsed about six hours a day and gave a concert each Saturday afternoon in the Episcopal church in Lenox. Our concerts created a lot of excitement, not only among those who sang (only twenty-two singers), but in the whole Tanglewood community, and the Lenox town community also. We were so excited by all the musical inspiration we even gathered together evenings, when there was no concert, and we sight read Bach cantatas!

Ned Rorem, then a Music Center student, was also impressed.

On the grass, behind the rehearsal hall, Robert Shaw was putting a group of madrigalists through their paces. The work was Hindemith's unaccompanied set of "Six Chansons" on Rilke's French lyrics, sung now in English. Shaw was a handsome hypnotist who, by merely rocking the cradle, could entice lovely tones from shrieking babies.

It was Koussevitzky who gave Shaw his first crack at symphonic conducting—in the Shed, no less, with the Boston Symphony. According to Shaw, "That may very well have been the first time I ever stepped in front of any orchestra."

The next season was '47, and Dr. Koussevitzky asked if I would do one of the concerts in the Shed. I conducted the Mozart *Requiem* and Stravinsky's *Symphony of Psalms*. We preceded it by a short Bach Cantata, no. 50—*Nun ist das Heil.*

The wonderful thing about the *Symphony of Psalms* to those of us who are interested in choral music is that it seems to be as zealously treasured by instrumentalists as it is by singers. I don't think that there is any doubt—certainly not in my mind—that it is one of the gigantic works of our past century. The extraordinary thing about Stravinsky's music is that the dissonances are amazing, and yet at first hearing, it sounds quite familiar. It doesn't hurt anybody until you begin to study it and you realize that he is writing tonal clusters that defy present listening capabilities. It's a very noble, noble piece.

Shaw left Tanglewood in 1948 to study orchestral conducting and form the Robert Shaw Chorale, his professional chorus, which toured the world to great acclaim and made many memorable recordings. Quite incredibly, it took another forty-eight years before Shaw reappeared on the podium in the Shed. He repeated his first Tanglewood program, and in the Boston Globe Richard Dyer reported that "there was a long and affectionate ovation for the conductor when he made his way to the podium, but he did not turn around to acknowledge it. Sentiment, particularly of the self-serving kind, is not part of Shaw's makeup."

In the past, choruses at Tanglewood were mostly pickup affairs, with Music Center students, college choruses, and local singers pitching in. Koussevitzky had even occasionally recruited some young summer campers when children's choruses were needed. But in 1970 the Boston Symphony decided that the orchestra needed a permanent chorus—a notion most American symphony orchestras do not entertain. It is much easier just to hire a local chorus when needed and avoid the costs and logistical problems inherent in a full-time symphonic chorus.

However, all that was to change when the BSO asked John Oliver to form the Tanglewood Festival Chorus. Although the group sings year-round with the orchestra, Oliver chose the name himself to give the ensemble a separate identity from that of the Boston Symphony.

Oliver had been a student at the Music Center in 1963 and 1964 and came back in 1967 to work in the BMC vocal program preparing choruses for performances in the Shed and coaching some of the student singers. For several years he ran the program.

As a student at Notre Dame, Oliver had heard the Robert Shaw Chorale and couldn't wait to call his parents and tell them what a breathtaking performance he had heard of Bach's Mass in B-minor. *Steve Owades, one of the three original TFC members still singing in the group, maintains that Shaw was a major influence on Oliver.*

One of the things that John took from Robert Shaw was the notion that you could put together a group of really good singers and have it become a chorus. A lot of choral directors choose voices that they think will blend together, not wanting voices that have too much distinctiveness of their own. They want a kind of soupy, blended effect. That was not Shaw's way. He would put together a group of really great singers and somehow, by working together and singing intelligently, they would make a chorus without individually giving up what they brought to the performance. And I think that has been very much John's mode of operation.

With these singers, Oliver has created, in my opinion, the finest volunteer chorus in the United States. They are an ideal match both in musicality and professionalism to the Boston Symphony. The chorus reviews are, more often than not, raves. For example, the Boston Globe *had this to say about their Beethoven Ninth at Tanglewood in 2006.*

Best of all was the Tanglewood Festival Chorus, which sang with great power and sweep. Those qualities occasionally came at the expense of clarity, yet one was still immensely grateful for the passion and commitment of these singers. . . . Their depth of experience with this score was palpable. The large audience cheered lustily.

Composer John Harbison is also amazed by them . . .

. . . especially since they performed the premiere of my *Requiem* from memory. It's an interesting dynamic, because volunteers putting in that amount of time is way beyond what other choruses put in. The concentration when they sing and the attention to detail has been enhanced by the requirement that they sing from memory. They know the detail of the scores amazingly well, and I think it has to do with being able to internalize the music and understand what was coming next.

John Oliver described the chorus's early days in Sennets and Tuckets, *a book of remembrances produced in honor of Leonard Bernstein's seventieth-birthday celebration at Tanglewood.*

Our first Tanglewood weekend opened with Seiji Ozawa conducting Composer Bernstein's *Chichester Psalms* and ended with Maestro Bernstein conducting the Mahler Second Symphony. I remember vividly the moment when Lenny came to the West Barn to have the piano rehearsal of the Mahler. He was flamboyant. He chain-smoked. He was kind and considerate to everyone (particularly to this young conductor, whose desire to create the most beautiful chorus ever heard was almost painfully palpable at the time.)

Probably the most memorable experience we had with Lenny was with Beethoven's *Missa Solemnis* in our second Tanglewood season. We gathered in the cold and damp on the Shed stage at six o'clock on the evening of July 21, 1971. I warmed up the chorus and gave a few final notes in the usual way, and Maestro Bernstein joined us at seven. We worked and worked. At ten o'clock we had only begun to rehearse the Credo. Shortly before midnight the bass soloist, Sherrill Milnes, had had enough and left the stage after an extremely colorful exchange with Lenny. Still we worked, the remaining soloists bundled up in scarves borrowed from the management office.

Only when the hour was coursing toward 1 a.m. and after we had promised to reappear at eight in the morning were we released into the chilly night. The Credo was not yet finished.

At 8 a.m. we were back at work. Lenny, looking fresh as a daisy, said, "You are mighty good to come at this hour . . . and so am I!" Three days later we had a performance of this great work of such power and beauty that it remains in my mind, whole and elusive, to this moment.

The audition—that fearsome process—is the first step in creating a great chorus. Because the TFC is so well regarded, Oliver has a large body of singers from which to choose. According to the Boston Singers' Resource News Bulletin (April 28, 2007), here is what the conductor says he is looking for.

The world is full of people with good, reliable technique these days. At this stage in my life, a singer must have a musical personality and a relationship to the music. . . . Technique and very accurate readings of music—loud, soft, tempi—all this is a given. But it really boils down, essentially, to whether they're communicating something. And it isn't so much that they're standing there trying to communicate, it's that they're standing there and the song or aria itself is communicating something to them; and that it comes through their voice. That's essentially the most important thing.

Who are these singers? Oliver answered that question in a 2007 radio interview on "The Round Table," at WAMC-FM in Albany.

There is quite a large turnover in the chorus. These days we get a lot of young people, college or conservatory graduates who have majored in music, or had a double major. Almost all of them play a musical instrument too—the piano, the violin, or oboe. They are almost all type A personalities. They are scientists, doctors, psychologists. In fact, we have the chief psychopharmacologist of McLean Hospital. The energy of the young people is fantastic!

I don't audition the singers every year. I audition them every three years. For the first couple of years, I audition them every year so that I get to know them—what they can do individually as well as a solo singer. I also get to know what they can do when they come to rehearsal, which is a whole different thing.

I make it very clear to them, and it's in the handbook, that we don't teach notes.

For most choruses, the first rehearsal is by and large a tabula rasa. They have learned neither the music nor how to pronounce the text, if the piece is in a foreign language. Not the TFC. Well before their first rehearsal, they get a score of the music and a CD of the performance and its text. It is up to them to familiarize themselves with the details of the music in advance. Rehearsals are not for learning notes, but working on musical nuances.

According to Steve Owades, "John doesn't like rehearsing a lot. He doesn't like drilling. Part of it is his notion—correct or not, I can't say—that you attract more intelligent singers if you ask more of them on their own and less of them in rehearsal."

To add to the workload, the chorus is also expected to memorize almost all the music they perform. In 1982, Seiji Ozawa brought semi-staged opera performances to Tanglewood. The first opera was Tosca *and the lighting was so low that the chorus needed to memorize their part. Oliver calls it their "first lights-out event." Thus began a tradition, which Oliver told me . . .*

. . . takes away the barrier between them and the music. At the point when we started to memorize the music, for the older people the commitment became stiffer and more difficult. There was some resistance to memorization, but now they take great pride in it. The young people coming in take memorization for granted. They say, "Well, the TFC sings from memory; I want to be part of that group!"

This takes a lot of work. Joan Sherman, another veteran of the early years, acknowledges how hard it is when push comes to shove. "I work under pressure. I like to really start the last week to really get it memorized. I know the music to begin with. I know the notes, I know the music, but the last week before the performance, that's when I really concentrate. I really like singing from memory because it means I really know the piece."

Oliver has an interesting take on the different conducting styles of two BSO conductors: Seiji Ozawa and James Levine.

The approaches of the two men are entirely different. Seiji is the kind of conductor who wants to be involved with every note of the music, and, I would say, he wants to control every note of the music. Whereas Levine wants the music to take on a life of its own.

Therefore, he does not ride herd on the individual notes. He hears everything, but he does not try to control everything. In my opinion, he tries to invite a lively participation from the performers so that they generate what's going on. Whereas with Seiji, it's from the top down.

Besides giving beautiful performances, the group also has a sense of humor. The TFC Handbook, normally not a barrel of laughs, has this tip for the singer:

Please be prepared for anything. John Oliver says, "The weather in the Berkshires is always sublime—clear blue skies, moderate days, and starry nights. However, bring allergy medicine, mosquito repellent, every kind of clothing from minimal to arctic . . . and you will be fine."

And stories abound. Founding member Maisy Bennett has a good one.

Once, many years ago, a woman tried to crash the chorus. We were doing the Brahms *Requiem*, and she knew the piece. She was wearing a white dress. We were going onstage. Well, we identified her and she was thrown out.

However, for the record, let it be known that James Taylor has snuck in to sing with them a couple of times.

At the end of the twenty-fifth TFC season, Charlotte Clark Russell wrote a commemorative poem. This little section reflects the pleasure of being a member of the Tanglewood Festival Chorus.

> The gigs we did in pouring rain . . .
> The dorms that had no screens, no floor!
> The scorching heat, the freezing cold . . .
> What keeps us coming back for more?
> We all recall artistic times
> That gave our hearts and souls a wrench.
> For me it's Britten's *Requiem*
> For Sarah Telford, it's our French.
> We each have our performances
> Of which we are especially proud,
> Like when the trumpets turned to me
> And said, with awe, "You sure are loud!"

At the end of the chorus's first full season, its manager, Paul Levy, wrote John Oliver a letter.

For the record, and so it gets said to you in writing at least once, I must express the feelings of this year's chorus toward you. You realize that chorus members often came to me, as manager, with their complaints, suggestions, and feelings about various issues relating to TFC. As in any organization there were quite a number of negative comments, but none of them ever applied to you. Chorus members always spoke of you with the highest regard, not only for your widely acknowledged musical ability, but also for your genuine concern for the singers. To these comments I must add my congratulations for a job beautifully done. It was an extremely difficult season for you in terms of preparing a large amount of difficult music, combining choruses, and keeping morale high, but you accomplished this with the sureness of a master craftsman.

In the 1947 Tanglewood student opera program, Phyllis Curtin sang Eugene Onegin, *and after that, Koussevitzky always called her Tatiana. Almost half a century later, when giving a short faculty speech at the Music Center Opening Exercises—the first with the new music director of the Boston Symphony, James Levine, in attendance—she mentioned that she had first met him when he was a fifteen-year-old piano student of Rosina Lhevinne at Aspen. At that time his mother asked her to "please look out after Jimmy." On hearing this, the now-grown Levine jumped to his feet and listed five songs he had particularly remembered having heard her sing that summer. She was astonished.*

I think it is safe to say that she is the most respected and beloved person on the Tanglewood campus today. And she is also a lot of fun!

A world-class soprano, Curtin had a rather unorthodox training. As a child in West Virginia, she had seriously studied the violin from age seven. Then it was on to Wellesley College, where she majored in political science, with the odd singing lesson thrown in— much against the dean's wishes. After college, in the early '40s she did war work and took a couple of semesters at the New England Conservatory opera program with Boris Goldovsky. "But that was only Boris," she told me ingenuously. After that, as she put it, "No more fiddle for me!"

So when she auditioned for Tanglewood, she said, "I was surprised I got in. That was the Peter Grimes *year, and Mildred Miller and I were chosen to be the nieces. That was my first opera! So Tanglewood was my music school."*

Before she knew it, she was an American diva—the leading soprano at the New York City Opera, who also happened to sing at La Scala, the Teatro Colón in Buenos Aires, the Glyndebourne Festival, and the Vienna Opera. The Metropolitan came later, but after all, to Rudolf Bing, the Met's Euro-centric general manager at the time, she was only an American singer.

   She was a frequent soloist with the Boston Symphony at Tanglewood.

I remember things like the *Missa Solemnis* in the Shed when Lenny fired the soprano soloist in the last couple of days and he got another singer and then he fired her the Saturday morning rehearsal before the Sunday performance. I had sung the *Missa Solemnis*, but I had not brought any of what I called my "Holy Works" dresses. But I did have a pretty thing I had bought in Honolulu—a light pastel thing—but it didn't have any sleeves, but I was otherwise covered up. And Maureen [Forrester] and I sat in Mary [Smith]'s office in the Shed. Maureen had a black dress with chiffon sleeves. She said, "Well, I'll just cut the sleeves out of my dress," so we were both bare-armed. And when I got home, Lenny had sent me two dozen long-stemmed roses.

   When I listened to a live performance of some Sibelius songs I sang with Lenny, I was just carried away with the ease with which it was to sing with him. He could just take that orchestra and have them come off on the final syllable just beautifully. You never had to worry about the orchestra.

She has an interesting take on singing in the Shed.

I loved singing in the Shed. It is acoustically fine. But the first time, looking into that big space, I wondered if I could be heard. Then I decided that my sound would turn on when it got to the porch of the Main House, across the lawn from the last rows in the Shed. That is a mental impulse leading the sound. And apparently it was successful. I sang often in the Shed, and no one ever said I couldn't be heard easily. And I felt happily comfortable.

   I was once a dinner partner of the *New York Observer* critic Charles Michener. He asked me to whom I sang when I performed. And I said that I sang to nobody, but to the universe. That is the same impulse—sending the sound to the porch, through the exit sign, into space.

In 1963, Phyllis Curtin was the soprano soloist in the U.S. premiere of Benjamin Britten's War Requiem *with Erich Leinsdorf conducting when the administrator of the Music Center came to her with a problem.*

Harry Kraut said to me, "Phyllis, we are really up a tree here. The Music Center has auditioned all these singing fellows, and nobody has thought much what to do with them since there is no opera program any more. [Leinsdorf had gotten rid of it that year thinking that he would use the singers in small parts in the Shed with the BSO.]

So they were faced with a little mutiny and some very unhappy singers. I said, "Well, I certainly don't know what to do, but I suppose we can sit around and talk about sing-ing. So the classes started just out of that, and they've gone on ever since. This [2007] is the forty-third year.

And these classes are one of the major "tourist attractions" of the Tanglewood Festival. Andrew Pincus described them evocatively in his book Scenes from Tanglewood.

A singer will come forward, usually with a student accompanist, and perform an aria or song he or she has prepared. The teacher and fellow students greet the performance with applause and praise; at least in Curtin's hands, the class also serves as a support group in which everyone learns from everyone else's travails and triumphs. Then the hard work begins. For the next fifteen minutes to half-hour, Curtin corrects the student on posture, pronunciation, breathing, voice placement, understanding of the music—anything and everything that bears on communication between singer and audience. Touch is important. She places her hands on diaphragm, cheeks, mouth, chest to see how the student's muscles and breath are working. Conversely, students—men as well as women—must reach around from behind her to feel her diaphragm as she demonstrates how to take a breath and let out a pealing, firmly supported tone.

About one point Curtin has always been adamant.

It has been very interesting with the administration because I have insisted that they not charge anybody anything as an admission fee. I said, Look, everybody worries about audiences disappearing for song recitals, but if we keep this open, there are going to be a lot of people learning a lot about singing. It's wonderful! We get people coming back year after year, and I am thrilled to death.

She tells a revealing anecdote about her first full summer of teaching.

There was a story about the class in *Time* and *Newsweek*, and my agent called me and said, "Phyllis, you can't do that. I've had three or four calls today from orchestra manag-ers where you are singing this season who said, 'Well, we read about the teaching. Is she still singing?' You can't afford to have that happen." It's the old business—if you teach, you don't sing.

I said, "Well, that's interesting and I'm sorry it's that way, but I'm not going to give up this class, because it's so good for me." What was really clear to me was that the class kept me in the best possible technical condition. Listening to and diagnosing a student's singing and finding out exactly the way to fix it, is something which, without the class, I would never have taken the time to do for myself. That class was invaluable to my having such a happy singing career with no vocal crises *ever*.

However, after the first four weeks of the newly minted vocal department's existence, there was a big bump in the road: Mr. Leinsdorf did not approve. In a letter to Curtin he stated, "My idea with the vocal department has been to attract to Tanglewood a number of young singers who are actually usable in performances. . . . My dismay was complete when I found that I could not locate anyone in the vocal department to sing the very few words of the Midsummer Night's Dream *vocal solo parts" in the Shed with the BSO.*
   While on tour in Europe, Curtin wrote him back, vigorously defending her classes.

I met with these students for an hour and a half (each one got a half hour of work himself and sat through for the others' lessons). I was overwhelmed at the high level of talent and disconsolate that their instruction, with but a couple of exceptions, was so poor. . . . I care *desperately* about *how* to sing, and I study that daily. I have become a good diagnostician of vocal illnesses and weaknesses and so it was that in such a summer, I ran, in effect, a vocal clinic.

   There were two big classes—open to all and sundry—about the vocal instrument, its nature, how it works, differing techniques, with illustrations by me, vocally and at the blackboard—random illustrations by brave volunteers, etc. These classes caused considerable excitement, and we could have had several more, had the schedule allowed. As was apparent in the later work, students know almost nothing about singing—teaching is deplorably inadequate—and they were simply overjoyed, I believe, to have some clarity, and some facts to clear away the semantics mishmash that muddies up the situation. They could see how the understanding of a basic technique allowed them to really put their minds at work musically.

Leinsdorf's response:

The detail of your letter was not only reassuring to me about certain formerly disturbing things in the vocal department, but I have gained a completely new dimension of admiration for your own enthusiasms and profound attachment to certain values which generally are no longer cherished by performing artists. . . .

   I have no doubt that your own stimulating and inspiring personality, your own devotion and enthusiasm were a great asset; and I can only say that if we again have a vocal department in the near future, it would be the greatest pleasure for us and of the greatest benefit for the young people to have you with us on the faculty.

In 2002, as part of the Festival of Contemporary Music, there was a concert of the American Art Song as a musical tribute to Phyllis Curtin. Some of her former students wrote about her in the program.

Sanford Sylvan was a fellow from 1974 to 1977. He has become a favorite singer of John Adams and Peter Sellars, having sung Chou En-lai in Nixon in China *and the title role in* The Death of Klinghoffer. *Before studying with Curtin, this baritone avoided contemporary music. But, he said, "She insisted that it was incumbent upon us to sing the music of our own time." This is what he learned from his teacher.*

She teaches us that what we are to give is the most honest expression of those words and that music that we possibly can. It sounds so straightforward; it is so difficult.

We are young, and yearn so deeply to express ourselves, but there are so many pitfalls along the way. We feel we have too many artistic choices and too few vocal choices, and we have no idea how to ask for help. Phyllis steps in with her generous heart, beautiful smile, and astounding intelligence (can anyone else in the world actually use the word *behoove* in a sentence and sound completely natural?) and coaxes us, again and again, back to those words and that music that we have been given. From carefully chosen words of encouragement gently whispered into one's ear, to a look of steely reproach from those glittering eyes, she is somehow able to show us, with deepest calm, what is true and what is false in art.

Dawn Upshaw, from the TMC class of 1983, was another grateful student.

There was also the fact that Phyllis demanded that we pay attention to every detail. This wasn't merely an extension of her powers of perception, acute though they were. It was more that she was so intent on conveying that *everything* matters, that *nothing* is incidental.

Then there was the matter of infusing it all with personal conviction—committing ourselves to those elements that each of us, uniquely, individually, could bring.

Eventually I came to realize that these are the very qualities I associate with true professionalism. Phyllis was doing no less than pulling me off the playground and preparing me for the major leagues.

John Kenneth Galbraith, a wise societal observer, once commented to me that he was surprised at how much hard work was involved in a musical life, and that he had thought only farmers worked really hard.

—John Williams
Boston Pops Laureate Conductor

CHAPTER 10

Behind the Scenes at Tanglewood

Location, Location, Location

Work is work, and we will get to that later, but living the good life is part of the Tanglewood tradition too. Just being in residence in the Berkshires is one of Tanglewood's supreme pleasures. Oliver Knussen speaks for us all when he says,

[Stockbridge Bowl] gives me goose bumps just to think about it. You see what looks like flatlands and then there's this huge vista. That's one of the reasons I used to work in the Main House Library, for the view.

But musicians had discovered this special aspect of the Berkshires even before the arrival of the Berkshire Symphonic Festival. Albert Spalding, heir to the Spalding sporting goods fortune and America's first internationally prominent violin virtuoso and one of Koussevitzky's favorite soloists, came to the Berkshires in the 1920s with his wife. He described his delight with the area in his 1943 memoir, Rise to Follow.

In 1925 Mary and I digressed from our usual habit of spending the summers in England. The magnet that deflected us was a small stone house hidden away under tall pine trees on the crest of one of the mountainous ridges of the Berkshire Hills in western Massachusetts. It had been build by Charles Freer of Detroit, the railroad magnate whose business successes had been only an apprenticeship to his real vocation—the study and collecting of Oriental art, chiefly Chinese. The museum in Washington, D.C., which bears his name is the realization of that mission. . . .

Freer never lived to enjoy this home; he died when it was barely completed. It was left to his assistant and collaborator in his great collection, Katherine Rhoades, who is a warm friend of ours, and it was from her that we rented and eventually bought the house. After we saw it we never wanted to live anywhere else.

The house presents a modest appearance but has rooms of generous proportions. Though conveniently near the town, it feels remote from everything but Nature. Its greatest glory is its array of majestic pine trees, carefully stripped of their lower branches and approaching the sky before spreading their canopy of green shade. It is a place around which the circle of contentment has been drawn.

We found that most of our neighboring friends and acquaintances lived about eight miles to the north of us, in Stockbridge. They rather raised their eyebrows at the little industrial town of Great Barrington. . . .

One day at luncheon I found myself next to a charming lady who militantly posed this question: "And just what prompted you, Mr. Spalding, to settle in Great Barrington?"

Having carelessly failed to catch the lady's name, I rashly replied: "I'm not sure—perhaps merely to avoid Stockbridge!"

The temperature dropped suddenly, though I then had no idea why. But when I told Mary of this passage of arms—"And who," she demanded, torn between amusement and horror, "*who* did you think was talking to you?"

I didn't know. Who?

"Only a member of the Inner Circle of Stockbridge—Mrs. Sedgwick herself! Really, you *are* impossible."

In time, owing to Mary's unfailing tact and the Sedgwicks' magnanimity, we succeeded in living it down. We may have been granted, too, some of that special indulgence accorded to people who live in what I call the "Hoboken of the Berkshires."

Then and now, finding the right living accommodations at Tanglewood is not such an easy task. Even the likes of Aaron Copland and Leonard Bernstein had their Tanglewood real estate ups and downs. An undated letter, probably 1940, from Copland to Bernstein:

Dear L****,

I imagine I'll still be here on Wednesday, though I shouldn't be. That is, I mean, I had hoped to be settled up there [the Berkshires] by then, but all is at sixes and sevens. I found a nice barn-studio in Richmond, only four miles away. Now the lady-owner says someone may be buying it, and I won't know until Tuesday. I also had my eye on a bungalow right on the grounds of the Cranwell School, but it appears they will need it for rooming six students, and I would have wanted it alone.

By the way, I can give you a very good idea of the student quarters, because I was given the grand tour by Father Sullivan. The Cranwell School is run by Jesuit priests, just in case you didn't know. And the grounds are simply heavenly, with tennis courts and everything.

If the barn-studio turns out well, I will be able to have soirees! And a Filipino cook! But if not, I'm sort of up a tree, and haven't the vaguest notion what to do next.

Well anyway, this is just a note to say I'm glad you're heading this way.

The dorms and their facilities may have been "simply heavenly" but by 1941, Leonard Bernstein, now in his second year at the Music Center, had that been-there-done-that feeling and was looking for a lifestyle upgrade. In a letter to Aaron Copland, he pleaded his cause.

Aaroncher—

I know you'll get this in Stockbridge. I plan to be up there this Sunday or so to see Kouss and bring Shirley [his sister] home from college. I'll make it my business to see you. There's a great problem concerning quarters. It seems that Raphael [Hillyer] is coming back; still no work from Jesse [?], but there's always [Arthur] Winograd and [Harold] Shapero and I. Is it really impossible to live in your house? You don't work anyway during those six weeks. And think of the fun! We're all feeling rather antidormitory. Anyway, I'll survey the whole situation this weekend. Can I stay with you in Stockbridge? Let me know right away.

Copland passed on this "fun" opportunity in order to have some peace and quiet for his own composing.

The Tanglewood lifestyle included any number of group living arrangements. Verna Fine, wife of composer Irving Fine, described one in her Yale Oral History American Music project interview.

In the summer of 1946, we didn't live near Aaron, but the next summer, we found a little cabin behind a guest home in Richmond owned by a Reverend Cutler. I made lunches for everyone and took them over to the Tanglewood grounds. Aaron rented a suite with a separate entrance near Reverend Cutler, and every night we had elegant dinners together prepared by Mrs. Cutler. At the end of the summer, Aaron arranged to rent the Gettys' barn the next summer, and in 1948, we all had our meals together at the spacious Kelley mansion, which we rented for the summer. I got two helpers, one to take care of our new baby, the other to help in the kitchen. I ran a "restaurant" every night with typed menus.

A few Boston Symphony players really roughed it. In the August 13, 1939, issue of the Boston Sunday Globe, *writer K. S. Bartlett reported on a small group of tents on the shore of Lake Mahkeenac, where a few stalwart players were "getting back to nature" by living in tents.*

Farther down the line was the most ambitious of the camping outfits, three tents belonging to a single family with a big wooden table and benches out in front. Here lived the Voisins, Mr. and Mrs. René Voisin and their son, Roger. Both the Voisin men are trumpeters with the orchestra. One of the tents, a huge affair like an old-fashioned army wall tent, was for René Voisin and his wife, one of the smaller ones for Roger, and the third for guests.

When the *Globe* reporter reached the Voisin encampment, Mrs. Voisin was cooking vegetables on a gasoline stove inside the large tent, and her son was setting the outdoor table. On one bench sat a visiting orchestra member, Hippolhyte Droeghmanns, who smoked and watched with interest.

Yes, he thought camping must be pleasant, but he didn't think a "cellist should risk his fingers in any sort of rough work. The smallest injury, which the ordinary person would hardly notice and which wouldn't, for instance, bother a trumpeter, might end a cellist's career," he pointed out.

Roger Voisin, on his way down to the lake for a couple of buckets of water, grinned cheerfully and remarked that a trumpeter who cut a finger could use a bit of sticking plaster and manage pretty well if he had to. Still, he conceded, there were drawbacks about trumpets, too. You simply couldn't eat salted peanuts.

Nearby a small and highly reserved Scottie wandered about, eyeing the visitors with canny Scottish doubt. No good, he seemed to say, could come of having strangers about. This was Trumpeter, who, Roger Voisin explained, likes camping, too, but doesn't approve of having his picture taken.

Later, when René Voisin, big, ruddy-faced, and smiling, arrived, Trumpeter looked on while his master washed up in the camp "washbasin." This was a rough wooden bowl holding perhaps half a gallon with a hollow wooden spout at one side. Fill the bowl with water and it runs out slowly through the spout and you can wash your hands and face nicely. It came, Mrs. Voisin said, from France, and would be an asset at many camps. Drinking water at the camp comes from a nearby spring; other water from the lake.

But the quintessential group living experience at Tanglewood has always been and remains the student dorms. Thomas D. Perry reminisced about the quality of life in the dorms in an article for Berkshire Week, *written after he retired as manager of the BSO. The Music Center rented any number of boarding schools in the area, plus . . .*

. . . we even bought Wheatleigh to use as a dormitory for men. Wheatleigh was a great Italianate palace, with famous gardens, fountains, and a walled terrace looking over Stockbridge Bowl. It is hard to imagine a greater mismatch of form and function than using this rich man's house as a men's dormitory, or barracks, its great halls and rooms lined with army surplus double-decker bunks. The flower conservatory was made into a shower room, and even with the fountains turned off, it was no time before we exhausted the water supply and found ourselves digging wells. I hate to think what we did about the sewage effluent situation in those days. After only few years and with a great sigh of relief we sold Wheatleigh and have continued since to try to solve the seemingly insoluble problem of summer student housing.

And what would dormitory life be without rules? Here—in a very tongue-in-cheek style, presumably written by Tod Perry—is what was required of the men in 1951.

You're living at Wheatleigh . . .

The 21¼-acre estate is a two-year-old investment of the school and was once owned by a Spanish ambassador named Carlos de Heredia, whose wife, the Countess, became a hostess par excellence in the vicinity with a penchant for twilight religious services held in the gardens.

She also had house rules. She had a wine cellar, but no hard liquors were allowed on the premises. No one came to dinner from tennis without reasonable dress. Even before Massachusetts state fire regulations she didn't allow smoking on any but the first floor. Smoking in bed was strictly verboten—even fireplaces were to remain very black and cool. Though truly a patron of the arts, the Countess called a curfew on all musical instruments from 10 p.m. to 8 a.m. and at midnight softly coaxed darkness and quiet over all revelry.

Furthermore, the Countess was able to increase patronage of the arts by insisting that everyone clean his own room and make his own bed by 11 a.m. She actually had dustpans and brooms available at strategic locations on each floor. Her friends were so numerous that meal cards had to be presented at each meal. You had to be on time for your meal or be a couple minutes late and go hungry.

Really, Countess de Heredia ran this place so efficiently that even with the house full of musicians, as it is today, we could find but one rule to add—female visitors must remain on the main floor and, like Cinderella, leave at midnight.

As for the women, who were lodged in that same year at the Lenox School, the rules were equally strict, although probably not by the standards of the time.

Your dining room opens Sunday, July 1, and is geared to synchronize closely to your schedule and appetite. Note carefully those times posted for meals at Thayer Hall because the help is working on an hourly basis and can keep the hall open. Just so, even if you do arrive, "Gee, only a couple of minutes late!", the cooks and the school can only serve apologies. But on time, you may bring guests if there is room; for breakfast .75¢ and for dinner $1.75. In fact, if there is a bed you may have a guest at $2 a night. You can save a dollar with a sleeping bag, and if you let a guest use your bed while you are away overnight, it costs them a dollar, but be sure you sign the "overnight book," so parents and school officials won't worry their health away about you. . . .

When walking back with your date after 12 a.m. and you have really decided it's time to go to bed, Mr. Howland, the superintendent and incidentally a duly accredited Lenox police officer, will help expedite matters by driving you to your house from the main road. If you're in a gentleman's car, tell him to drop you off at your house and skedaddle, because no men are allowed to walk on the grounds after midnight.

House mothers had their own set of problems. A May 19, 1942, letter of advice from a former supervisor to her successor, Miss Barr:

Your musical and teacher training should help you in the handling of many problems, but I think it might well complicate life for you also. I mean that nine pianos, an organ, two harps, a violin or two, and a flute, along with a few vocal students all practicing at once in a building not constructed for such endeavor (a hollow tile building which echoes!) might well drive you quite crazy.

Dorm life may have been somewhat restricted, but romance was not unheard of. Pianist Claude Frank, then in the conducting class of the Berkshire Music Center, told of his near miss in the affairs-of-the-heart department.

In 1947, among the pianists in the (then) Department II there was a sixteen-year-old Lilian Kallir, who looked like ten and claimed seventeen. There was only an occasional meeting between us. Lilian returned to Tanglewood the following year, and I didn't, so it took me until 1954 to ask her to marry me, and it took her until 1959 to say "yes." I wish I could say that both the question and answer were in Tanglewood. But to describe further the "adagio" tempo of our mutual lives' events: our first and only child was born exactly twenty years after we met in Tanglewood; her first concert was a Mozart sonata Prelude recital, heard from the baby carriage outside the Shed. The violinist was James Oliver Buswell; the pianist was Pamela's mother. No wonder she has become a violinist, and an outstanding one, by the way.

In later years, after their marriage, both Frank and Kallir became faculty members of the Music Center. And Pamela is one of today's most popular soloists.

Even jaundiced music critics have been known to succumb to Tanglewood's charms. Witness Harold Schonberg's rhapsodizing in the pages of the New York Times *over his sojourns* chez *Mrs. Whipple.*

For a long time the major Northeastern newspapers regularly sent their critics to cover the Tanglewood season. There was some grumbling. The main Tanglewood programs were anything but adventurous and often repeated music that the orchestra had played on its visits to Carnegie Hall and elsewhere. Why travel all the way to the Berkshires to hear yet another *Eroica* or *La Mer* or Isaac Stern again playing the Brahms Violin Concerto?

But there was Mrs. Whipple's, where many of the critics stayed. Mrs. Whipple, a widow, owned a large, beautiful house in Lenox (built, it was said, by Stanford White), within walking distance of the festival grounds. She lived there with a bunch of dogs—pulis, the Hungarian breed, as I remember—and a housekeeper who made the best blueberry muffins, the best scrambled eggs with chives, and the most intoxicating coffee that anybody had ever tasted. It was fun getting together with colleagues, gossiping, exchanging shop talk, living a lazy and pampered weekend. The Tanglewood Festival will never know how much it owed to Mrs. Whipple. Without her charm and lovely hospitality there would have been far less coverage.

Nine to Five

Seeing to the summertime care and feeding of a symphony orchestra with its satellite school, large campus, multiple buildings, and various living arrangements—not to mention hundreds of musician needing constant attention—is no mean feat. At the very least, administrating Tanglewood has produced some legendary stories.

Thomas D. Perry, the witty raconteur of the student production of Acis & Galatea, *worked his way up from the Berkshire Music Center to BSO assistant manager under George Judd. From 1954 to 1978, he was its manager.*

In 1946 it had been his job to get the Berkshire Music Center back up and running after the four-year hiatus during World War II. Later, he wrote about the challenges in the Berkshire Eagle.

In all these efforts [reestablishing the Berkshire Music Center after World War II], however, we discovered war surplus, an early recycling plan for using up all the incredible complex apparatus of global war. You could get most anything—a tank, a bomber, a submarine, army blankets, black socks, or mimeograph machines—for almost nothing, take it away. I recall one incredible shopping spree when a chap and I went to an army depot somewhere in Rhode Island and bought all manner of wonderful things, dirt cheap. We bought mess hall tables for the cafeteria, bunks, army blankets. We bought a school bus that went on for years lugging students to and from Lenox, still painted military mud color, with the words *U.S. Army* faintly visible on the sides. We got rowboats to replace the crumbling flat-bottomed vessels that were on the lake when Tanglewood was given to the Boston Symphony, named after the fairies in Hawthorne's *Tanglewood Tales*, with such un-flat-bottomed names as *Cowslip, Periwinkle, Peasblossom*. We bought four navy hospital tents that were put together as a cover for the cafeteria tables at Tanglewood, very ineffective as rain cover, since while they did keep the direct overhead dousing off, they also concentrated it in sluices of water onto the floor, splashing the entire area so that all those at tables got it not only from above but from beneath as well. . . .

Early on, in 1940, the owner and innkeeper of the Curtis Hotel in Lenox, Lester Roberts, was asked to help by getting lunches down to the students and teachers at the Music Center so that they would not have to take their eyes off the artistic ball long enough to go uptown to have a bite, but rather could eat something at Tanglewood without letting the Muse slip away for even an instant. Lester was ingenious and figured out a way to accomplish the above, to make use of the Curtis Hotel kitchens, and do a bit of cycling all at the same time. He bought a retired passenger bus from the New Haven Street Railway—it was blue and white and had *NHSR* painted on the sides and a destination sign over the driver that said nothing—he took out the seats and installed counters along the walls under the slide-up windows, leaving a space in the middle where the serving help worked.

At Tanglewood a sort of ferry boat–landing slip was built just the size for the bus to back into. Every day the bus would load up at the Curtis with sandwiches, milk, coffee, and other goodies; it would drive to Tanglewood and back into the landing dock; the windows were opened and *voilà*! Lunch!

By the time he became the BSO manager, Perry's symphonic scrounging days were probably long gone, but not so his interest in how things could be acquired "at the best possible price." He wrote a memo on December 5, 1977, with a most interesting attachment that he directed be put in the archives.

Re: Furniture around here

Barbara Thompson (Mrs. Richard Thompson) has written out and sent, at my request, a recount of how we came by much of the fancy furniture we have here and at Tanglewood, much of which came from her childhood home on Com Ave., Boston.

The attachment:

SOME FURNITURE IN SYMPHONY HALL AND TANGLEWOOD
When the BSO acquired Tanglewood, the students had nothing but tables from Pops on which to work in the library, and many scores were too large for comfort on these

diminutive squares. About the same time, my mother was in the process of dismantling a too-large house in the Back Bay. My parents had bought the house, rather fully furnished, when we three were young children and wanted lots of space to play in. Much of the furniture was oversize, to be in scale with the rooms. . . .

And so Mr. Judd [BSO manager] was invited to come and look at the tables and perhaps one or two other things. Sensing his growing excitement as he looked around, we asked him if, for example, he could use some nine-foot-high mirrors in appallingly ornate gilt frames. "Yes indeed." How about the cut-velvet-backed armchairs complete with crests? "By all means." The same was true of a real backbreaking chair, heavily carved with cherubs and other pointed, lethal decorations. We toured the entire house before we finally exhausted our gems of rococo tastes, along with several gilded benches covered in gold brocade, a splendid green music cabinet with a golden lyre on each door—the list was long, and the loot took four vans to tote away. . . .

The big round tables are still in use at Tanglewood in several spots; the music cabinet is in the office, filled with typing materials except when it is needed for scenery, as it used to be during Mr. Goldovsky's time as head of the opera department. This is the spot where we saw it again after our parting in Boston, and Boris Gudonov saw it as he died dramatically, falling from the green velvet chair with the overstuffed crest. For the first time it looked appropriate! The cherub-y chair dominates the entrance hall and presumably discourages everyone from loitering. Desks, tables, and mirrors abound.

Barbara Proctor Thompson, 1977

She added this postscript:

Mother was Mrs. Charles A. Proctor, who attended the Friday concerts regularly for nearly sixty years.

Two ninety-seven was on Commonwealth Ave., "the sunny side"

In the hands of Tod Perry, the interoffice memo was elevated to an art form. When he died in 1997, Tom Morris, Perry's protégé and successor as manager, read one of Perry's classic memos at the memorial service at Seiji Ozawa Hall. He described Perry first.

In thinking about Tod these past weeks, the word *class* emerges most often as characterizing my memories. Tod had a classy car, he was a classy dresser, he had a classy demeanor, and he conducted himself professionally and personally with class. He had an extremely classy wife, who had an appellation in memos that was also very classy: the LMP—the lovely Mrs. Perry. He was a classy writer, and he typed on an extremely classy typewriter. The organization with which he was entrusted reflected that class in every way. Just look at this place [Seiji Ozawa Hall].

This is the Perry memo that Tom Morris read aloud at the service:

June 30, 1969
Memorandum To: Tanglewood staff females, and staff males withal

In an ill-considered moment, I said I would shortly emit a ukase on suitable dress for working female staff members at Tanglewood. I have since had a number of conversations on this subject with females, notably my wife. We have discussed skirts, miniskirts, less-than-mini skirts, culottes, body stockings, plunging necklines, pantsuits, no-pants suits, and peekaboo as well as see-through garments.

It's an interesting subject, surely, but complex, and the ukase that emerges is as follows:

That while on duty at Tanglewood, suitable and reasonable attire shall be worn, that the definition of "suitable and reasonable" shall be up to the department head wherein the female works, and that in general, extremes or extravagances of garb are to be avoided—that is, members of the staff are supposed to be helpful, friendly, and not startling, or unwantedly intrusive upon the attention of the people being dealt with.

The same general rules apply to staff males (with the inevitable differences, naturally, occasioned by differences of gender)—that "suitable and reasonable" attire shall be worn, one shall avoid clothing distracting as to its brilliance, informality, or just plain sloppiness, and the department head is to be the arbiter of what's suitable for his department.

This from the man who in the 1950s introduced the loan of a wraparound skirt to cover up ladies who showed up on the Tanglewood grounds lewdly dressed in shorts. The skirts were purchased in bulk from England's Department Store in Pittsfield, handed out to the ladies in question, and instantly stolen. The practice ceased forthwith.

Next to the artists, nothing at Tanglewood takes more "care and feeding" than the lawn, that greensward that many consider to be the crown jewel of Tanglewood. What would you do if your lawn had over 50,000 visitors stomping on it weekly? Such was James Kiley's problem in 1958 when he became superintendent of grounds and buildings. His first official act was to call in an expert from the University of Massachusetts Plant and Soil Department, who pronounced the lawn "cement."

Mr. Kiley explained his solution in a Tanglewood Talks and Walks, fortunately recorded by Robert Wallace, for many years a radio producer and host at WAMC-FM in Albany.

Many years ago we had a very serious problem with our lawns here at Tanglewood. By that I mean that we had a buildup of lots of thatch [a dense, impermeable matting of roots, leaves and stems—essentially dead turf—on the surface of the lawn], and no root system. It was my job to set about correcting that to bring about the situation we have today. It didn't happen overnight. . . .

We had to get rid of the thatch that we had out there; we had to build up our fertility and develop a healthy root system. We have a program that we have established here at Tanglewood that begins in September, as soon as the festival season is over. We go out there with an aerator, which is a gadget on the back of a tractor that has a bunch of spoons. We poke an awful lot of holes in that lawn out there. The reason for this is to break up the compaction that has been created during the summer.

A number of years ago, some visitors came by, and they saw us out there working on the lawns and they said that we were ruining a beautiful lawn by poking it full of holes. It looks bad when we poke it full of holes and the plugs are lying on the surface. The plugs lie on the surface for a day or two, and then we drive over them . . . and break up these plugs. Then we water it thoroughly, which is steady practice here during the course of the summer. Then we'll fertilize it very, very heavily. The fall is the best time of the year to establish a healthy root system.

Then we will drop our lawn units, which are raised during the course of the summer, and cut the grass shorter going into the winter season. We pick up every leaf and every pine needle that falls out there in the course of the fall season. Then, in the fall of the year, we will put down in the neighborhood of twenty-five to thirty yards of top dressing, which we will make up during the course of the summer.

Then we will go into the winter with our turf cut short. I believe that to maintain a healthy lawn and to come out of the winter in good condition, the turf should be short. If you leave it long, you are susceptible to all kinds of winterkill, snow mold, and other diseases that are not helpful to a good lawn.

In the spring of the year, as soon as the temperature reaches about forty-five degrees, we will apply an application of 2,4-D, which is a broadleaf weed killer and with that we will throw in some Select All, which is an insecticide that will kill any ants, flies, or such insects that live in turf out there.

Many years ago we had a lawn in front of the Shed that was completely filled with dandelions. Over the period or three or four years we have eliminated the dandelions to the extent that we also do the same in our parking lot, which is outside the main gate. The reason we do that is that the seeds from the dandelions blow from these parking lots into the main grounds proper and germinate, and we are getting more and more dandelions through that process. So for the extra that it costs us to use the weed killer on our parking lot, we put it out there to prevent that.

After we've mowed our lawns during the month of May, probably the first part of June we will apply a light application of fertilizer to supplement the growth that has started to fall off a little bit from last fall. We do fertilize the main lawn very lightly during the course of the summer, about every three weeks, to maintain our color.

All this would not be possible if we did not have an irrigation system, which we put in ten or twelve years ago. We have a pond down in the back of the Red House from which we pump water onto the grounds, and then we have rain trains, which we use to irrigate our lawns. When we get into our summer seasons here, we raise our lawn mowers and keep our grass height a little bit higher than we do the rest of the year. This helps us to maintain the traffic that we have during the course of the summer.

We have to seed in front of the Shed because the grass gets beaten down during the course of the summer. We will tackle that immediately after the season. The reason why it will not stand up during the course of the summer is that the grass does not have sufficient time to establish a root system. It gets hit again the first of July, not enough time to establish a root system, and they tramp it out there again, so we have to reseed it.

Now you know what to do with your lawn!

The animal kingdom at Tanglewood also needs management. The pesky mouse has found in the Tanglewood piano a tempting residence. Joseph Vitti stalked the creature as described in a July 18, 1998, article by Jeff Donn sent out by the Associated Press.

Inside the piano, a telltale sprinkling of felt bits betray the unwelcome presence of mice gnawing at the instrument's guts. "You could inspect a piano and, overnight, you could have a nest in there," laments the master piano technician [Vitti]. A box of poison stands guard at each corner of the floor. . . .

"It's kind of unglamorous," says tuning apprentice Tracy Tucker, who totes a spray bottle to disinfect piano keys when mice urinate on them. The crew's twice-a-week mice patrolmen and women also wear face masks and rubber gloves. They place mothballs inside pianos and screen off openings on the underside.

But the peskiest of all the animals is the European starling, Sturnus vulgaris. *These are the birds that roost in the rafters of the Shed. Here are a few facts about them.*

Starlings have diverse and complex vocalizations, and have been known to embed sounds from their surroundings into their own calls, including car alarms and human speech patterns.

Far from being considered beautiful, delicious, or beneficial, European starlings in the United States are normally decried as loud, obnoxious, destructive birds.

The campaign to rid the Shed of them began in the 1940s with birdshot. Chemicals were tried in the '50s, and screening in the '60s—all to no avail.

A new attempt to muzzle the birds was tried in the 1970's, and Andrew Pincus poked a little fun at the Tanglewood management in a July 1979 Berkshire Eagle *article.*

Boston Symphony Orchestra members, being musicians, have nothing against birdsong, you understand. But during concerts the squawks and chirps that emanate from the starlings and English sparrows roosting among the Shed's girders are music to the ears of neither musicians nor audiences.

So James F. Kiley, Tanglewood's operations manager, has bought and installed three electronic noisemakers in the Shed. Two sit in the acoustical "clouds" above the stage. One is above the television platform in the center.

All three rotate and go clackety-clackety-clackety-click when the orchestra isn't playing. When the music begins, the machines switch to a high ultrasonic hum.

The sound, Kiley says, is "piercing to the birds and they shy away from it."

What else is new? The starlings and sparrows still fly in and around and out. But Kiley's not squawking.

Another tactic was reported on by Christian Howlett in the July 26–August 1 issue of Berkshire Week *in 1985. The headline was "Bye Bye Birdie."*

It seemed for awhile that the birds had capitulated [to the electronic devices], but before celebration could begin they returned and took up residence again, oblivious to Kiley's efforts. With more than $1,000 for the noisemakers down the drain, it appeared that the starlings had won. The status quo continued for several years.

Now, though, Kiley is claiming that he has been "very, very successful in eliminating the birds. They're nowhere near as much of a problem this year."

The final solution? Twenty-four inflatable owls from a Lenox hardware store. The owls, which in nature are starling predators, were hung in the Shed at the beginning of nesting season and seem to have scared away the birds. The defense has simply involved moving the owl decoys every five or six days, Kiley said, so the starlings wouldn't catch on.

I don't know about you, but the last time I went to a concert in the Shed, the birds were still singing their little hearts out.

Aside from the occasional complaint about "too much modern music," rarely does music programming create a situation that causes a certain amount of administrative angst. It began innocently enough. At the suggestion of Gunther Schuller, the BMC would present a series of Contemporary Trend Concerts on Wednesday evenings. Nothing radical: The Association—a group of six youngish men in suits—Judy Collins, the Modern Jazz Quartet, and the Don Ellis Orchestra, and an Indian music concert, with Ravi Shankar, Ali Akbar Khan, and other musicians playing a selection of ragas. As an educational plus, the Indian musicians would be in residence at the Music Center giving workshops and symposia. Sound like a recipe for trouble? Not at all.

However, the following year there was to be a new protocol. Erich Leinsdorf introduced the series to the press by saying that "the young men and women studying here have grown up with popular music in all its guises and see no reason why it shouldn't coexist amicably with what my colleague, Gunther Schuller, terms 'so-called serious music.'" Mr. Schuller noted that "it is significant and necessary that the Berkshire Music Center shows its awareness of these new developments in music by instituting a series of concerts delineating these new trends."

So, who did Gunther Schuller chose to represent the new trends? Janis Joplin, Iron Butterfly, Joni Mitchell, Mahalia Jackson/Ornette Coleman/Thad Jones, and the Mel Lewis Orchestra. The final concert would be presented by Bill Graham and the Fillmore East. Participating artists were to be none other than the Jefferson Airplane, B. B. King, and The Who.

The BSO management was in hot water, and the water was going to get hotter. The press reports reflect the flavor of these concerts. The Village Voice *thought that the sounds of pop music would "quake the primeval New England countryside." The* Holyoke Transcript-Telegram *reported, "Out of the darkness into a thunderous applause came the former Big Brother and the Holding Company's lead singer, Miss Janis Joplin. After only ten minutes on stage, Miss Joplin left to complain about the state police and Shed officials who were trying to clear the aisles."*

Iron Butterfly appeared and one local boys' camp director was horrified. He wrote Tanglewood, "Not only were my young ones frightened by the appearance, antics, and interruptions of the 'animals' that crowded about, but they did not and could not observe the so-called presentation. There seemed to be little, if any, police action of these horrendous bits of social garbage. . . ." Tod Perry replied, "I think it must fall upon you to decide whether you wish your children to come, knowing the nature of the music and the nature of the people who attend it. If you do decide they should come, then I think you must be prepared not to be upset at some of the side effects."

The Fillmore concert was the last and broke all records for attendance—22,000 as reported in the North Adams Transcript. *"Tanglewood literally exploded last night with frenzied sound, swirling colors, and thousands of young people. . . . The most spectacular part of the program was the Joshua Light Show, which accompanied each piece, flashing swirling colors on a huge screen behind the groups in time to the music. The colors represented virtually every shade in the spectrum and they never stopped."*

The Berkshires had never seen or heard anything like this before. Most newspapers pronounced it a howling success, although scathingly critical letters to the editor poured into *the* Berkshire Eagle.

The Stockbridge town fathers concurred, fearing that there would be a "possible Woodstock at Tanglewood," and the Tanglewood managers changed course—programming only soft rock, folk, and jazz. They lowered the decibel level and limited the audience attendance.

Next year, according to the Berkshire Eagle, "There were no major disturbances among the young people, many of them shirtless and smoking a variety of products."

Now doesn't this just restore your faith in humanity!

A Tanglewood Bestiary

It isn't just the music, musicians, and Woodstock-like performances at Tanglewood that get a lot of "ink." The animal kingdom has received some notice too—and not just the Sturnus vulgaris. *In its August 13, 1938, issue, the* Berkshire Evening Eagle *reported on some amazing statistics about a familiar summer annoyance: the mosquito.*

Just a year ago four zoologists from Harvard, accompanied by Clay Perry, Superintendent Ward J. Gaston, and this writer, went through the attic of the Tanglewood main house, and found, to our amazement, an unbelievably large number of—bats! The countless gables, turrets, nooks, and crannies of this old house embody just the type of architecture bats love to snooze in during the daytime. A little closer reconnoitering indicated to the Harvard experts that there must be close to 10,000 bats in that building. (We banded over 500 of them!)

Mosquitoes are to bats just about what strawberry shortcake is to you. In one night, we were told, one bat eats its own weight in mosquitoes and other night-flying bugs. Let's use a little math, and see what that amounts to.

One average bat, as we know them here, weighs 80 grams before its breakfast. One average mosquito weighs $\frac{1}{1,000}$ gram. (I had several of them weighed by Dr. H. F. Miller of the GE Laboratories on a scale so fine and accurate that it can weigh a comma). The bat's weight in mosquitoes means, therefore, 80 g. divided by $\frac{1}{1,000}$ g., or the unbelievable amount of 80,000 mosquitoes consumed in one night by one bat. Ten thousand of them, therefore, theoretically, may gobble up 800 million mosquitoes in less than eight hours. . . .

Then there is that fellow in the black and white suit that Andrew Pincus filed a story about in 1977.

During the second of five selections in a Festival of Contemporary Music concert, a young skunk ambled out of the nearby woods and into the theater. While pianist Gilbert Kalish played on, the visitor walked quietly down the aisle, like any polite late-comer, and took a chair about a third of the way back in the center section.

The trouble was, he was sitting under somebody's chair. And only a couple of chairs away sat Paul Fromm, head of the Fromm Music Foundation at Harvard, which cosponsors the annual weeklong showcase of new music. . . .

Things began to get malodorous during the intermission after [Yehudi] Wyner's piece, however. Word spread among the chatting concertgoers that there was an uninvited guest in the house. And when the bell sounded for the second half of the concert to begin, there was no way of getting people to sit down in the center section.

Repeated dimmings of the houselights failed to stop the chattering and clear the aisles. House manager James Whitt tried next, coming out onto the stage and begging the audience to sit down. . . .

Next, David Alpert, head of the guides who assist Tanglewood musicians and audiences, was dispatched from the stage with a corrugated box to try his luck. Alpert looked brave, but he was saved by a woman who stood up near the bushy fellow and addressed the crowd.

"That skunk was under my seat the whole first half of the concert and he minded his business," she said. "I say let's be quiet and get on with the show."

She sat down and so, with hardly a murmur, as did the rest of the crowd. When the concert ended, the skunk was still under the chair. And, except for those who didn't like the products of contemporary composers, nobody had any excuse to say that the concert stunk.

Even man's best friend has a point of view. Fifi, the pet poodle of conductor Pierre Monteux and his wife, Doris, had a yen to express herself.

Across the years I have known all the great and near great in music. (The fact that Maître Pierre Monteux is a leader of symphony orchestras may have had something to do with this.) I have looked upon a queen from close quarters. I have sat in a box with an internationally famous and beloved actor. I have been decorated by an airline.

My picture has appeared in every leading newspaper in Europe and the United States. I have lived in great hotels on three continents; I have even created something of a *cause célèbre* on being ejected by two hotel managers.

And so it was that with all this material—and with the invaluable help of Mme. Monteux— Fifi brought forth her book, Everyone Is Someone.

As I am talking of the Boston Symphony, I must tell about the wonderful reception we received from Mr. Zino Francescatti, his wife, and his dear mother during one of Maître's summer engagements with the Boston orchestra at Tanglewood, in the Berkshire Hills of western Massachusetts. . . .

We were invited to luncheon and, as it was the home of a Frenchman, Madame Doris took special pains with my toilet. . . .

Oh, the memory of that delicious luncheon, which I was offered on a handsome pink plate on the floor. Chicken and green peas from their garden, and then a bit of dessert to top it off. I was delighted, and after it was over I lay on the polished floor and listened to Maître and Francescatti discuss violins and violin music.

I learned that Maître prefers the tone of a Guarnerius violin to that of the Stradivarius, though he did admit that the latter suited more violinists than the Guarnerius. He said that he could not imaging Isaac Stern playing a Strad, but he thought that the beautiful instrument on which Zino played was like silk in his hands. . . .

Maître said he had accompanied the Mendelssohn violin concerto seven times that year, in different cities, and the Madame said she hoped never to hear it again for ten years, at least! (She said the same thing about the Fifth Symphony of Beethoven, and two months after that heard Mr. Bruno Walter conduct it, and shocked me to death by jumping up and down and screaming "Bravo!" at the top of her lungs. Madame is very unpredictable.) The Francescattis served tea, with delicious little cakes, which I think everyone should do when guests appear. It was a lovely day, and we returned to Lenox happy and full of good food and fine conversation, a combination that I find impossible to beat.

Now, from the sublime to the ridiculous. The Berkshire Evening Eagle *reported on an animal mishap that occurred to one of Tanglewood's superluminaries on August 15, 1949.*

Composer Aaron Copland was fined $35 today in District Court for operating to endanger after his explanation of how he happened to hit and kill farmer Leslie Birch's Black Angus steer in Richmond last night failed to satisfy Judge Alberti.

Verna Fine gives the defendant's side of the story.

At the end of each Tanglewood season, Koussevitzky would give a dinner party on Sunday night at the Curtis Hotel in Lenox for the faculty and their wives. It was always very nice but sad—similar to the last days of summer camp. The most memorable of those occasions was in 1949. Aaron, Irving, and I were driving home to nearby Richmond, where we were sharing a house for the summer. Aaron was driving, I was sitting in the middle, and Irving was to my right. In a car behind us were Arthur and Esther Berger, who were staying with us those last two weeks. It was a very foggy night, so we were going very slowly. Suddenly, there was this huge cow standing smack in the middle of the road. Aaron slammed on the brakes, but it was too late. I let out a great scream, and then we all got out of the car. The poor cow was beyond help. Arthur almost fainted; I lost my voice for three days; but Aaron and Irving [Fine] were cucumber-cool. Aaron's Studebaker was badly damaged—undrivable, in fact—so we drove on to the house in the Bergers' car, called the police, and returned to the scene of the "crime."

The police, who were extremely hostile, actually wanted to put Aaron in jail! They took him to Pittsfield, and Irving, as a Massachusetts resident, put up bail. We tried to explain the accident to the police, but they wouldn't listen: "We will talk only to the perpetrator of the crime," they declared. Aaron finally got out and returned home with Irving, who "sprung" him at about 2 a.m. The next morning the news was broadcast on the radio, and the local paper ran the headline "COPLAND KILLS COW!"

I come here for more than twenty-some years and every summer I come gives me something very, very fresh—music and nature, the combination give me energy.

—Seiji Ozawa
Tanglewood Music Center
1998 Opening Exercises

CHAPTER 11

Seiji

Ozawa's Quarter of a Century–Plus at Tanglewood

Seiji Ozawa was the music director of the Boston Symphony from 1973 to 2002—an incredible twenty-nine years, the longest of any BSO conductor. Blockbuster events were one of the hallmarks of his tenure at Tanglewood. Leonard Bernstein's seventieth-birthday celebration, the fiftieth-anniversary production of Peter Grimes *at the Music Center, the Three Birthdays—Ozawa at sixty, Itzhak Perlman at fifty, and Yo-Yo Ma at forty. And let's not forget Ma's innovative Silk Road Project, which had its first performance at a Tanglewood workshop in 2000 and then proceeded on a triumphant tour of Europe, Asia, and North America. Even James Taylor and Garrison Keillor became Tanglewood icons during his era. While Ozawa was there, the Tanglewood property almost doubled, and included a new concert hall named for the maestro.*

There was much to rhapsodize about and not a little to carp about. His insipid performances of Beethoven, Mozart, and Brahms were often noted by the critics and musicians. Consequently, the honeymoon with the BSO players lasted only a few years. He was criticized by Gunther Schuller, Leon Fleisher, and others for making Tanglewood overly commercial. And he was accused of being either the "absentee landlord" or "overcontrolling" at the Tanglewood Music Center.

But he was, always and above all, an audience favorite. Nobody brought audiences to Tanglewood like Seiji. Mark Volpe, the current BSO managing director, put it like this.

There are very few conductors in the world who generate significant box office. Soloists are box office—Yo-Yo, Itzhak, Joshua Bell. There are composers who are box office—Beethoven, Tchaikovsky, and Mozart, for example.

Seiji was a rock star. I was with him at football games, at baseball games, in Paris and Tokyo. It was like being with Madonna or Michael Jordan or Tiger Woods. Seiji is so recognizable. That hair, that face, that walk—he is the most beautiful conductor ever to watch. He transcended classical music, as does Yo-Yo as a cellist. And there are very few conductors in today's world who have that kind of power. We could do a *Turangalîla* of Messiaen with Seiji and sell out five performances. There's no other conductor in the world who can do that.

Where did all this come from?

Seiji Ozawa was born in Manchuria in 1935. His father was a Buddhist and a dentist, his mother a Christian who taught him hymns. He particularly remembers "What a Friend I Have in Jesus." This perhaps was the beginning of the polarity between East and West that has been so crucial in his life. The family returned to Japan in 1944.

John Williams, the former Boston Pops conductor and a Tanglewood favorite, wrote a charming description of young Seiji's musical apprenticeship in the anniversary program book celebrating Ozawa's twenty-fifth year as music director of the BSO.

As a boy, Seiji, his father, and his brother loaded a small piano onto a wheelbarrow and pushed it fifty miles to their home so that Seiji could begin his studies. To me, this story forms a powerful image of Seiji's innate drive and desire. Although his talent quickly made him a prodigy who caught the eyes and ears of Japan's best teachers [notably Hideo Saito], it was, fortuitously, a soccer injury that turned his gifts toward conducting. When he was a little older, he loaded a Subaru motorbike that he'd won in a music competition aboard a freighter and went alone, first to Naples and then to France. . . . His first great stroke of good fortune came in the rather obscure French town of Besançon, where he won a major conducting prize.

There he met a Finnish-born American diplomat, Mr. Piltti Heiskanen, who just happened to be a friend of Olga Koussevitzky. In a letter to her he wrote:

If I say that I was very much impressed by the performance of Mr. Ozawa, it means next to nothing because I am not an expert. I will therefore list the reasons why I think it would be worth while trying to help him. First of all, the seven-man jury unanimously considered him best and I was told that M. Eugene Bigot, the chairman, was very enthusiastic about him. Next, I discussed Mr. Ozawa for over an hour with Lorin Maazel, a conductor who has a very good name here and who was a member of the jury. He said he thought that Mr. Ozawa is particularly talented and that he definitely is worth helping. Mr. Maazel said that he knows of no better place anywhere to learn conducting than at Tanglewood, particularly if one can be one of the three or so who have a special chance to conduct daily. . . .

Knowing that Mr. Munch was coming to Besançon I tried to arrange that Mr. Ozawa would have an opportunity to speak with him. Since I had to leave earlier I do not know if he succeeded. . . . [He did.]

As a person Mr. Ozawa is both extremely charming and modest. He thinks that he needs still much study, particularly of western music. I understand that he has very little money and that his scholarship from Japan is just enough to permit him to live in Paris. As an indication of his modesty and eagerness to learn more, I will mention that he told me the day after his victory that he had heard that it was easy to get a job in the United States as a "dishwasher or playing the organ in a church. . . ."

Olga got right to work, writing Mr. Heiskanen that she was pressing the young man's case vigorously.

Thank you very much, indeed, for bringing the name of the young Japanese conductor, Mr. Ozawa, to my knowledge. I immediately forwarded this information to Mr. Leonard Burkat, administrator of the Berkshire Music Center. I hope that Mr. Ozawa will, in turn, communicate with Mr. Burkat and apply for a conducting scholarship at Tanglewood this summer.

Would you care to pass word of this to the young conductor, since you were so kind as to write to me in his behalf?

Ozawa was accepted at the Berkshire Music Center. In the summer of 1960 he arrived in Lenox, as folklore would have it, either on a Peter Pan or a Greyhound bus with only a modicum of English at his command. According to the diplomat . . .

. . . In 1959 Seiji seemed to know just three (or is it two?) words of English. When I asked how he felt about his victory [at Besançon], he said: "Oh so wonderful. Oh so wonderful? OH SO WONDERFUL!" etc. about six times, always increasing his emphasis.

Although improved today, Ozawa's English remains charmingly original. But he always gets his point across, as in his Tanglewood Music Center Opening Exercises speech in 1998.

It was first time come to the United States day before, and that day, I came to here—second day—a ceremony like this in the old theater—and there was orientation. I remember that, it came back to my mind—I do not speak much English now—but those days I even could not count in English more than twelve or thirteen [laughter]—between seventeen and seventy was a very big problem for me—and, I tell you, they said to me, "Come to orientation,"—I came from Orient [more laughter] so I thought it was something to do with me. Of course, when I was sitting, I did not understand anything. For example, I was supposed not to bring beer can to the dining room. Of course I did not understand that and I have to drink beer every meal, even lunch [even more laughter]. Can you imagine?

In a 1990 interview with the Boston Globe's *Richard Dyer, Ozawa recollected:*

The dormitory was in the Lenox School and my roommate was the Uraguayan conductor José Serebrier. We had bunk beds; I slept up and he slept down. He had a tape recorder, and he owned scores of Mahler and Bruckner symphonies and Verdi's *Falstaff*, and that was wonderful. . . . We conducted a small chamber group—a string quartet, with piano. Many times I played the piano for the other conductors. Charles Munch came only once to teach me, in the finale to Debussy's *La Mer*. Aaron Copland gave me to conduct a short piece by one of the student composers, and in the final concert each of the student conductors led one movement of Tchaikovsky's Fifth Symphony. I conducted the finale. In those days the Music Center orchestra was not as good as it is today—the winds and the brass were good, but the strings were not so hot. I came from Toho [the Japanese music school where he studied], where the strings were already wonderful. After the concert Munch told me I was too stiff, this I must be more *souple*, more supple. Suppleness was very important to him.

Munch did not take a great interest in his duties at the Music Center, preferring to spend his time on the golf course when he wasn't conducting in the Shed. However, he did give Ozawa one lesson and very much considered him to be his protégé.
    On August 15, Harold Schonberg took note of the newcomer in the New York Times.

Here is a name to remember: Seiji Ozawa. Mr. Ozawa is Japanese, twenty-three years old, and he has been studying conducting at the Music Center this summer.
    Yesterday afternoon he led the student orchestra in the last movement of Tchaikovsky's Fifth, and left no doubt that he is a major talent. He has a good deal of temperament, a propulsive rhythm, and thorough command over his forces.
    He also has—and this will do him no harm at all—showmanship. His gestures are à la Bernstein, and that includes the most swivel-hipped action since that great man himself. What with his talent, exotic good looks, flair, and choreographic ability, Mr. Ozawa is a young man who will go far.

Ozawa's reputation was further enhanced when he won the $500 Koussevitzky Prize at the end of the summer. With the proceeds he bought a very "preowned" Oldsmobile he had been coveting all summer and took a short tour around New England before returning to Europe for further study.

In rapid order, Ozawa became Leonard Bernstein's assistant conductor at the New York Philharmonic, music director of the Toronto Symphony, thanks to Charles Munch's recommendation, and then filled the same post at the San Francisco Symphony.

Let us fast-forward to the year 1970. Erich Leinsdorf had gone and the aging William Steinberg had been appointed music director of the BSO. However, Steinberg had no interest in Tanglewood, so a troika took over the running of the operation: Seiji Ozawa was to be in charge of the Festival concerts; Gunther Schuller was to direct the Music Center; and Leonard Bernstein was to be general advisor, or, as former BSO manager Thomas W. Morris put it, "a hovering presence."

Vic Firth, the orchestra's legendary retired timpanist, expressed the feeling of many in the orchestra that Ozawa "brought a youthful exuberance that we hadn't seen in years, because prior to him was William Steinberg, who was in his late seventies when he left us. And prior to him was Erich Leinsdorf, who also was a more mature gentleman. And prior to that were Munch and Koussevitzky. So we had not seen a youthful music director in, I don't know, seventy-five years, let's say. So Seiji came with not one fuse, but twelve fuses, and they were all lit simultaneously, and I think not one of them has burned out to this day."

Ozawa's first Tanglewood program in 1970 was the Bernstein Chichester Psalms, *György Ligeti's* Atmospheres, *and the Berlioz* Symphonie Fantastique—*all in all, quite an adventuresome beginning. According to Morris, during this period, "all the repertoire was fresh. There was little overlap with what Steinberg was conducting in Boston during the winter. If you look at the Munch years, a lot of the Tanglewood repertoire was taken from the winter season."*

The Troika period lasted three years until Ozawa was appointed music director of the Boston Symphony in 1973, and with that an amazing regime at Tanglewood began. Throughout his tenure, many striking musical and historical events were to take place.

For example, national politics rarely take precedence over music at Tanglewood, but in 1974, when Richard Nixon was about to announce his resignation, allowances had to be made. Thomas W. Morris was the orchestra manager then.

I remember being glued to a television set at home. And we had this orchestra concert that night at the Theatre–Concert Hall for the Festival of Contemporary Music. They said that the president was going to address the nation that night at 9 p.m. The concert started at eight-thirty and, of course, everyone knew what was going to happen. I remember talking to Gunther and Dan Gustin. We all wondered whether anybody would come to the concert. And if they did, here was probably one of the most important news events of our time about to happen live. Should we do anything about it, and, if so, what?

What we decided to do was to reorder the program so that there would be a break when the newscast came on. That way we could put it on the PA system. I remember sitting in the concert hall during the first two pieces. And then the president resigned and then we had the next piece. It was surreal. And it was one of the great moments. Everybody applauded after each of the pieces, including the resignation.

There was more drama to be had the following season. Mstislav Rostropovich and his wife, soprano Galina Vishnevskaya, had recently fled the Soviet Union. Ozawa, who considered the cellist to be a musical brother, had invited the couple to come to perform at Tanglewood. During the intermission of one of their concerts, Rostropovich got word from the Soviet Union that Shostakovich had just died. Oliver Knussen was in the audience that night.

There was a concert in 1975 with Rostropovich, one of the most extraordinary psychical events I have ever come across. I forget what was in the first half, but something tells me it was the Tchaikovsky *Romeo and Juliet*. Then Vishnevskaya comes out and does Tatiana's Letter scene—at which point there was applause. She went off and came out again. Everybody went silent and she sang an unaccompanied dirge with no explanation. Can you imagine?

During the intermission the news that Shostakovich had died got out from backstage and traveled around the audience. This strange mood swept over the Shed, which was full, of course. And then we thought, Christ, the Shostakovich Five is in the second half. What is going to happen?

So then Tom Morris came out and announced it. And then Rostropovich, with one of the great acts of emotional bravery I've ever seen, came out and conducted the most staggering performance of the Shostakovich Fifth I have ever heard and proceeded at the end to take just one bow, put a flower on the score as a spontaneous manifestation of collective mourning. And that was it. Everybody burst into tears.

Twenty-four hours later the official Soviet new agency Tass confirmed the news of the composer's death, but Tanglewood audience was the first in America to hear of it.

That same year a new conducting phenomenon with a specialty in Beethoven, Brahms, and Bruckner arrived. Between 1975 and 1982, Klaus Tennstedt made a big splash. Almost no guest conductor there got such rave reviews as Tennstedt. Leighton Kerner of the Village Voice *thought his Beethoven Ninth's Adagio was "simply the most beautiful I had ever heard." Richard Dyer of the* Boston Globe *gushed that "when he is at the BSO, the orchestra sounds more consistently at its best than it does under any other conductor. . . . The crowds fill the night with bravos before the concert even begins when Klaus Tennstedt conducts, and they throng to the front of the stage, applauding still louder, when the concert is done." He even had a clique and a fan club, the International Klaus Tennstedt Society—known familiarly as the Klausketeers.*

What was it about this fiftysomething defector from East Germany that inspired such adulation? The BSO concertmaster at the time, Joseph Silverstein, has some answers.

Klaus Tennstedt created a lot of visceral excitement on the podium. He was very insistent in driving the orchestra, and that certainly came out in the performance. The first couple of times he came, the orchestra almost didn't know what to make of him. He was so energetic and kinetic on the podium and not at all balletic. He was a little awkward, but tremendously intense. One of my colleagues said after rehearsal, "You know, I'm all wrung out and I have to play a concert tonight. I'm so tired from this rehearsal." It was a driving intensity.

But Tennstedt's popularity was short-lived. In 1982 Andrew Pincus wrote: "From the start, however, there were technical difficulties that annoyed many orchestra members. An imprecise beat, which earned him critics' labels such as 'nervous scarecrow' and 'demented stork.' Lapses in accompaniments, which led the orchestra on at least one occasion, to go on automatic pilot and pay no attention to his direction. Tempos and dynamics that disregarded composers' instructions. A growing tendency to talk too much during rehearsals (again like Bernstein). Even those who admired his interpretations suffered disillusionment. After six years of increasingly troubled performances, the BSO decided to give him a rest."

Seiji Ozawa's conducting style, on the other hand, is of quite a different order. He is known for his balletic embodiment of the music, a prodigious memory that allows him to conduct mainly without a score, the ability to learn new and complicated music quickly, and the sensitivity he displays in accompanying soloists. With all this in his portfolio, he has an even greater talent, according to Tom Morris.

One of Seiji's great gifts is conducting spectacular things. For me he is one of the most gifted and natural performers I have ever met. Not only physically the way he conducts, but in terms of delivering a performance. He knows how to do that and how to do that particularly with great big works.

He can marshal complicated forces. For example, the *Gurrelieder*, which we did in 1974 at Tanglewood. It was really the first major performance of the *Gurrelieder* since the '50s. Many orchestras have considered this an unperformable work because of its vast orchestra of 145, four choruses, and five vocal soloists, plus a speaker. It just hadn't been done a lot and it really entered the repertoire thanks to Seiji. He did it once or twice more in my time.

Tanglewood is a vast space. So it is a particularly great and unique place in which to do things like that. From a musical standpoint, I actually think that Symphony Hall is actually too small for the *Gurrelieder*.

This extremely romantic oratorio, first performed in 1913, was written by Arnold Schönberg before he developed the new serial style of music that was to dominate contemporary music for more than half a century. In this 1974 Tanglewood performance, Phyllis Curtin, James McCracken, and George London were the soloists along with the Tanglewood Festival Chorus. The critics were full of praise. Twenty-five years later, two Boston critics, Lloyd Schwartz and Greg Sandow, remembered the concert as Seiji's greatest performance.

The Britten War Requiem *and Berlioz* Requiem *were two more works that made a big splash at Tanglewood. Tom Morris remembered others.*

I can still hear in my head a performance of the Haydn *Seasons*. I had never heard the piece before. It's Haydn, but it's a big, extroverted piece and he just made it alive. I remember the *Damnation of Faust* in the early '70s. He knew how to do that stuff really well. Not only was the music conducted well, but these pieces are collections of movements, and he knew how to go from one to the other. He knew how to build momentum out of a series of episodes.

Ozawa considered himself a conductor but not so much a teacher. And for that reason it was generally understood that he would not be very hands-on at the Berkshire Music Center. Thinking that others could do that much better than he, he once said, "I fired myself," when asked about his limited involvement. Every summer he did conduct the Music Center orchestra in one memorable concert and gave a couple of coaching sessions for the conducting fellows.

Aside from that, until his last few years he left the running of the Music Center strictly to Gunther Schuller, who was in charge from 1963 to 1984. And Schuller was definitely hands-on. He personally traveled around the country auditioning all the prospective fellows. During his last fifteen years or so, that amounted to around 1,500 students annually.

Dan Gustin believes that it was under Schuller's stewardship that the BMC standards were raised considerably.

It was Gunther who brought many of the important non-BSO figures to the teaching staff: Gilbert Kalish, Joel Krosnick, Sol Schoenbach, Rafael Druian, George Perle, Paul Zukofsky, Bruno Maderna, Hans Werner Henze, Donald MacCourt, Maurice Abravanel, Oliver Knussen, Gustav Meier, Betsy Jolas, and Theodore Antoniou among many others. These people and programs helped shape the BMC's contemporary music programs.

He also supported the integration of the singers in Phyllis Curtin's classes into the performance programs of the Music Center. And it was under Gunther's regime that the first renewal of a fellow-based opera program began—with the three-year Music

Theater Project headed by Ian Strasfogel in the '70s, and the concert-staged production of Henze's *Elegy for Young Lovers*.

It was during this period, also, that music of the composer fellows, formerly ghettoized into single evenings called Composers Forums, was integrated into the chamber music and vocal music recitals presented by the fellows throughout the summer.

Gunther also developed the Boston University Tanglewood Institute, the summer music program for high school students. He began to bring jazz and popular music into Tanglewood's ken. These people and programs set the stage for the full flowering of the TMC in the '80s.

The real story of the contemporary music programs during Gunther's period as director is best told by reviewing the incredible variety of composers who taught at Tanglewood and those composers whose works were performed. I believe that overall it is a very impressive record.

That list includes Elliott Carter, Roger Sessions, George Rochberg, George Perle, Ernst Krenek, Luciano Berio, George Crumb, Charles Wuorinen, György Ligeti, Peter Maxwell Davies, Betsy Jolas, Milton Babbitt, Jacob Druckman, Ralph Shapey, Oliver Knussen, and Hans Werner Henze.

Another impressive record is the list of guest conductors at Tanglewood who also worked with the student orchestras. In Helen Drees Ruttencutter's book Previn, *André Previn, a longtime favorite conductor at Tanglewood, said he would never turn down an invitation from Tanglewood because he enjoyed . . .*

. . . working with the absolute cream of music students from all over the world. And I find that it is that kind of division of labor that makes Tanglewood so wonderful. To walk around and hear students practicing, to know that the rehearsals are *full* of music students, of conducting students with scores, eyes *riveted* to the page. So serious, and so ambitious. They *care* so much. I find it absolutely wonderful. To me, it's thrilling to conduct the Boston, but working with the student orchestra and the student conductors is *just* as big a reason for me to come to Tanglewood. I'm not happy working summers, but this is a genuine exception. I'll always come here if they ask me. . . .

Ms. Ruttencutter described a conducting coaching session that André Previn gave in the early '80s at Seranak, Koussevitzky's former home, under the life-size portrait of the maestro.

At the front of the room, the two pianos were placed next to each other, keyboards facing the students, at diagonals, so the two pianists—who were already in place—could see each other.

Also in place, standing between and behind the pianos and facing the class, was the first conductor, Naohiro Totsuka.

Ruttencutter continued her story at the point when Previn stopped the young conductor while he was conducting the Beethoven Seventh and gave him a tip.

"I have a theory, which is just an opinion, that when you have a very *long* crescendo that goes on for a long time, if you start it at the bottom end of the orchestra a little earlier, then upstairs it will really work wonders. You'll find a kind of organic growth coming out. Instead of just the tune or the decoration getting louder, you'll feel the thing it's sitting on getting louder. Very often, I will delay a printed crescendo in the higher register until I make it apparent that it's *going* to happen by strengthening lower strings, lower winds. . . . One thing you'll find when you stand in front of an orchestra—not the Boston—with crescendos, *invariably* they start too soon. Players see a twenty-bar crescendo—especially string players—and within five bars they've already reached what you want from them after twenty bars. So you have to be careful in your gestures not to encourage them"—he make a broad gesture— "Holy Moses. There's no stopping them. In this movement, it should be wildest on the last page, and not before. But it was very, very good. Very fine." Prolonged, loud applause.

Another historic event at Tanglewood took place in 1979. Enormous shock waves went through the classical music world when Gunther Schuller gave an Opening Exercises speech to the newly gathered students of the Berkshire Musical Center. After the usual welcoming remarks and "the holy art of music" statement, he launched into his message.
    It began in the more or less usual way.

For Tanglewood was conceived by an idealist, Serge Koussevitzky, who believed that there must be a place and time where young musicians can pursue the highest ideals of artistry and musicianship, in a setting of musical camaraderie and high commitment to the art, unencumbered by financial worries and the commerce of music, the jobbing and gigging scene—unencumbered, in other words—by some of those aspects of our musical profession which so often make some of us blush in shame.

Ordinarily, one does not hear a lot about "blushing in shame" at Tanglewood. Schuller then got to the crux of the matter.

Frankly, I am worried about our present-day musical climate, and because you, who represent the future of our profession and art, *can* make a difference if you care enough and if your commitment is unassailable, incorruptible, impregnable.

Then he went to town on what was wrong with American symphony orchestras.

I want to pursue the point a few steps further, although it gives me no great pleasure to do so. As we look around our orchestras in the United States, that joy of which I speak has gone out of the faces of many of our musicians. Apathy, cynicism, hatred of new music, are rife and abound on all sides. . . .

This cynicism is spreading like a cancer through our orchestras—I know only a handful that aren't in an irreversibly malignant state—creating an environment into which it is downright dangerous for young people, like yourselves, to step lest they also be instantly infected. Indeed, as I travel around the country guest-conducting various orchestras, it is often former students—whom I knew here at Tanglewood or elsewhere—and who once had that shine in their countenance when they heard or made music, but who long since have lost that spiritual identification with music. The light has gone out of their eyes. For young, innocent musicians, it is often hard to resist such peer group pressures as exist in our orchestras nowadays, and there is unfortunately much in our modern union mentality, what I call the ISCOMization [International Conference of Symphony and Orchestra Musicians] of our orchestras, that turns our profession more and more into merely a business—not even a creative business, for business, too, can be creative—and in which union mentality at its worst constantly undermines any attempts to preserve music as an art.

I am speaking out in this public forum because I see that musicians, by and large for fear their livelihood may be jeopardized, are afraid to speak out—if they are not already corrupted. And so the cancer spreads and takes its grim toll. . . .

There are those that will try to tell you that the ills of the modern symphony orchestra are entirely financial. If only the board could raise more money or people would support symphony orchestras more or if the NEA grant could only be tripled, all our problems would disappear. Not so, my friends. The problems of the symphony orchestra are by now mostly *within*. In fact, orchestras have become in some ways too much successful businesses; their techniques of survival are now those of the American corporation, including the full panoply of managerial and public relations accoutrements, as well as absentee music directors, and orchestras run not by artists, but by committees.

When Schuller made a reference to "absentee music directors" the audience gasped, as Seiji Ozawa was not there because he was conducting in Tokyo. Typically Ozawa spent only about half the season at Tanglewood, relying on guest conductors for the remainder of the concerts.

This was not the first time that this had been spoken of publicly. Richard Dyer of the Boston Globe *and other critics had been lambasting Ozawa for being away so much from the orchestra. However, let it be said that he was spending more time in Japan because his family was living there so that the children could get a Japanese education.*

Schuller's speech lamenting the over-commercialization of orchestras was widely quoted around the country and in national publications like the New Yorker. *It was reprinted in the December issue of* Symphony News *and again in the June 1980 issue of* High Fidelity, *where he elaborated on his views. He argued that orchestral management and trustees should have less to say about musical matters. "Artistic decisions should not be made by nonartists. Period. They can be arrived at in collaboration and consultation with nonartists, but not made solely by them." As a result, "many orchestras have become directionless, amorphous aggregations with no personality, style, or point of view." He even went so far as to say that there should be "obligatory training courses for prospective trustees." Ouch!*

Five years later, Schuller resigned as artistic director of the Berkshire Music Center. He cited "fundamental artistic differences with the music director of the Boston Symphony Orchestra" as well as "a desire, after more than twenty years of service at the BMC, to have my summers and a substantial portion of the winters for myself to devote to composing and conducting." Privately he admitted his deep dissatisfaction with the direction in which Ozawa was taking the orchestra, and publicly he told the New York Times's *John Rockwell that he "wanted to preserve the purity of Koussevitzky's original vision of Tanglewood as a training center where gifted young musicians could work free of the commercial interests of the real world."*

Many people believe that Schuller left Tanglewood because he could not take the criticism of his Festival of Contemporary Music programming. Nothing could be farther from the truth. He is a man of great conviction and vision, and not deterred by outside disapproval.

However, contemporary music at Tanglewood continued to flourish. It took another interesting direction in 1986 when Oliver Knussen became composer-in-residence. He also programmed the Festival of Contemporary Music, which he continued to do until 1993. Olly, as everyone calls him, was an old Tanglewood hand, having been more or less Gunther Schuller's protégé in composition in the early '70s. Since then, many of his pieces had been performed there.

A few years ago, in England, he told me that in the Festival "I tried very carefully to balance American music and European music and to ensure that there would be no terrible disproportion between the new pieces and modern classics. But you also had to make sure that the balance was good for the students themselves, that they were exposed to different and reasonable challenges."

He had a great story about his last year running the Festival, in 1988.

We did the Stockhausen *Gruppen*, which was me deciding that I was going to tear the place apart! Dan [Gustin] had these two extra stages built in the theater and it was the last TMC concert in the old theater. The idea was since the first piece that was ever played in the theater, in 1940, was *Eine Kleine Nachtmusik*, the last piece played should be Stockhausen's *Gruppen*, which is 120 people divided into three orchestras with three conductors. That's why Reinbert [De Leeuw] first went there, because I said I wanted to do it with him. The other conductor was the young Robert Spano. And part of the entertainment that summer was the three of us sitting around tables desperately rehearsing, doing it in different tempos—shouting and yelling at each other. It was very funny—three lunatics practicing simultaneous conducting without orchestras!

The last thing that happened—this will give you some idea of the atmosphere of the thing—was that, unbeknownst to us, there was enormous friendly rivalry between the three orchestras. The three orchestras had arranged to do that ballpark thing, the wave. And this wave went all the way around—180 degrees. It was wonderful!

It's one piece in one program of a half an hour. We did it twice so that the audience could move around a little bit and get a different perspective on it.

Richard Ortner, former longtime administrator of the Music Center, has some interesting observations about Knussen's influence at Tanglewood.

The musical taste that Olly brought to programming contemporary music was—despite his reverence for Gunther and Bruno Maderna and the other Tanglewood lights as teachers and composers—entirely different than what had come before. Olly was of a different generation and was hearing not only the new generation of American composers who were Fellows at Tanglewood (David Lang, Osvaldo Golijov, Michael Gandolfi—so many others!) but of European composers as well. He programmed their music, and also wanted Tanglewood to be the place where Americans first heard the newest new music of Europe.

Olly had Seiji's ear. The bridge between them was, at first, a mutual regard for Tōru Takemitsu, a close friend of Seiji's whose music Olly genuinely admired. (I think there was also something childlike or playful about Takemitsu as a person that Olly responded to especially.) But Seiji certainly recognized Olly's gifts as a composer, and came to respect the quality of Olly's thinking about contemporary music. Olly is also an unusually precise and accurate conductor . . . another gift which Seiji recognized.

Another composer who has made a deep imprint on contemporary music at Tanglewood is John Harbison. A longtime member of the Tanglewood family, he was a fellow in the Music Center in 1959. He talked to me about his experiences then.

In those days there was structurally a freer form. I came into the program as a conductor. I wasn't an active conductor. I simply asked if I could move into these other areas and no one raised any objections. They said, Look, you can probably learn more about conducting by sitting in the viola section. I was literally a yard from the conductor. Then I sang in the chorus. They said, If you can do it, we need you, and we have all these works to perform. So I was busy all the time; I was young and learning a huge amount. It was really one of these compressed, diversified education experiences. I try and tell my fellows—the composers—that it is good to resist being too specialized. I think it makes for a better composer.

As composer-in-residence in 2007, Harbison had a chance to put his theories into practice.

I'm very proud of the composing fellows this summer [2007] because they are so interested in seeing what else is happening. It's not like, "If it's not a composition activity, we don't care." It's if they have a moment, they will turn up at a rehearsal. They're all really trying to get a lot out of what is going on.

When I had come here in the past as a guest composer, it was a little remote. I would come in and try to figure when I was supposed to be where, and everyone was running around preoccupied with something. Other visitors in composition to Tanglewood had often reported that they were not really guided through their experience here. They were just dropped on the campus and that was kind of it. We were getting a reputation of being a little offhand, so I thought this might be a way to make them feel that we are keeping track of them better. In some cases it was very intense.

So we tried an experiment. We told each of the composing fellows that they would be a shepherd for at least three of the visiting composers at the FCM. They were supposed to get in touch with them about three weeks before they got here, introduce themselves, say they were going to help them find their way around when they got here. Then they tracked the rehearsals of the composers' pieces before they came, helping to solve certain kinds of problems. They would sit in the early rehearsals and see how the performers were coached. Some of the fellows were reporting back to the composers as to how the rehearsals were going and how the piece was taking off. In some cases, some very good exchanges developed.

Harbison also put a new spin on the Festival of Contemporary Music's programming.

Jessye Norman, a favorite Ozawa soprano, receives audience accolades with Seiji. (*Berkshire Eagle*; Walter Scott)

André Previn conducts from the piano in 1982. A favorite Tanglewood conductor, he especially appreciates working with the TMC orchestra. (*Berkshire Eagle*; Walter Scott)

Seiji conducting the Haydn cello concerto in 2000 with his and Tanglewood's good friend, Yo-Yo Ma. (*Berkshire Eagle*)

Conductor Klaus Tenndstedt, who brought audiences to their feet and had his own fan club, the Klausketeers. (*Berkshire Eagle*; Walter Scott)

Timpanist John Wyre, composer Tōru Takemitsu, and Seiji Ozawa in 1971, when Takemitsu's piece *Cassiopeia*, which was commissioned by the Tanglewood Music Center, was performed. (*Berkshire Eagle*; Heinz Weissenstein)

Three close-ups of Seiji conducting. (Boston Symphony Orchestra; Walter Scott)

Kathleen Battle and Tom Krause are the 1983 soloists in one of Ozawa's signature big works, *The Creation* by Joseph Haydn. (*Berkshire Eagle*; Walter Scott)

Ozawa rehearses with the student orchestra. (*Berkshire Eagle*; Walter Scott)

Kimono-clad Seiji Ozawa backstage with Russian friends: conductor Maxim Shostakovich, son of the late composer Dmitri Shostakovich (left) and his "big brother," cellist-conductor Mstislav Rostropovich. (*Berkshire Eagle*)

Ozawa works with conducting fellow Grant Llewelyn and two student pianists, standing in for an orchestra, at Seranak. (*Berkshire Eagle*; Walter Scott)

Seiji conducting a semi-staged production of Gluck's *Orfeo ed Euridice* in the Shed, August 6, 1983. Singers (left to right) Erie Mills, Marilyn Horne, and Benita Valente. (*Berkshire Eagle*; Walter Scott)

A parking lot full of television satellite trucks broadcasting Tanglewood concerts to the world. (Boston Symphony Orchestra; Walter Scott)

Seiji (left) helps ground crew member Jim Sturma (right) get ready for the TMC fiftieth anniversary. (*Berkshire Eagle*; Walter Scott)

Walter Scott documents the last concert Leonard Bernstein conducted, appropriately enough at Tanglewood. (Boston Symphony Orchestra)

The two Tanglewood "historians" at their administrative duties. Dan Gustin (left) and Richard Ortner (right). (*Berkshire Eagle*; Walter Scott)

Seiji Ozawa Hall under construction. (Boston Symphony Orchestra; Walter Scott)

Ozawa speaking at a press conference with half-finished hall behind him. (Boston Symphony Orchestra)

Seiji in a moment of reflection, in front of his new concert hall. (Boston Symphony Orchestra; Walter Scott)

A last minute meeting before Ozawa Hall opens. Left to right: Seiji Ozawa, William Rawn, Harry Shapiro, and Dan Gustin. (Boston Symphony Orchestra; Walter Scott)

Frank M. Costantino's architectural rendering of Seiji Ozawa Hall.
(Boston Symphony Orchestra)

Cultivating the audience of the future at Seiji Ozawa Hall.
(*Berkshire Eagle*; Walter Scott)

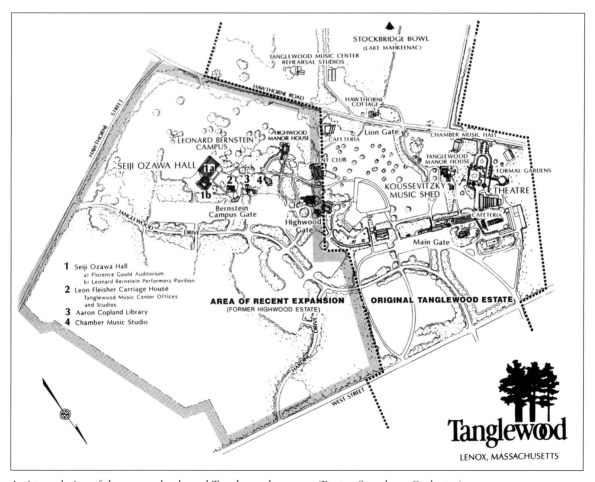

Artist rendering of the new and enlarged Tanglewood campus. (Boston Symphony Orchestra)

Coproducers of the Leonard Bernstein seventieth-birthday gala Humphrey Burton (left) and Dan Gustin (right) confer in the Tanglewood Formal Gardens, 1988. (Private Collection of Dan Gustin)

Stafford Turner (left) and Anthony Dean Griffey singing *Peter Grimes* in the acclaimed fiftieth-anniversary production. Griffey has become the Peter Grimes of our time. (Boston Symphony Orchestra; Walter Scott)

Leonard Bernstein arrives in the Shed for his seventieth-birthday party. (*Berkshire Eagle*)

One of the celebratory concerts for the Bernstein birthday. (Boston Symphony Orchestra; Walter Scott)

Lenny Bernstein (right, standing), in the audience, gets a bear hug from his old friend Slava Rostropovich (left, standing). (*Berkshire Eagle*)

Deep appreciation from Lenny. Left to right: Louise Edeiken, Adrienne Albert, Patricia Rutledge, and Kitty Carlisle Hart. Behind them are John Mauceri and John Oliver. (Boston Symphony Orchestra; Walter Scott)

Bobby McFerrin singing "Somewhere" from *West Side Story*. After hearing him perform, Bernstein agreed to give him conducting lessons. (Boston Symphony Orchestra; Walter Scott)

Some final bows for the performers. (Boston Symphony Orchestra; Walter Scott)

Oliver Knussen conducting the TMC orchestra. (Boston Symphony Orchestra; Walter Scott)

Gunther Schuller giving an Opening Exercises speech in 1976, just three years before he gave the speech that sent the classical music world reeling. (*Berkshire Eagle*)

Karlheinz Stockhausen's *Gruppen* for three orchestras is rehearsed by the Tanglewood Music Center Orchestra for the 1993 Festival of Contemporary Music. Leading the three orchestras are (from left to right) Reinbert de Leeuw, Oliver Knussen, and Robert Spano. (Boston Symphony Orchestra; Walter Scott)

Composer John Harbison conducting the BSO at Tanglewood in a performance of his Symphony no. 1, July 29, 1984, at the Festival of Contemporary Music. This work was commissioned by the BSO for its centennial in 1981. (Boston Symphony Orchestra; Walter Scott)

Yo-Yo Ma and James Levine accept accolades after an August 2007 performance of the Dvořák cello concerto. Levine had stepped in at the last minute to substitute for an ailing Edo de Waart. (Boston Symphony Orchestra; Hilary Scott)

James Levine rehearsing for a concert in the Shed with the BSO on July 30, 1972. This was the only time he conducted at Tanglewood before he was made music director of the orchestra. (Whitestone Photo; Heinz Weissenstein)

Levine conducting the TMC orchestra in a 2006 concert performance in the Shed of Strauss's *Elektra*. Soloists are Christine Brewer (left) and Lisa Gasteen (right). The *New York Times* critic Anthony Tommasini said that after seventeen hours of rehearsing the student orchestra in this "blazing, complex, and still shocking score," the hard work paid off. He had rarely heard a more frenzied and deserved ovation. At the invitation of James Levine, Raymond Gniewek, the retired concertmaster of the Met orchestra in New York, coached the strings and participated in the program as part of the first-violin section. (Boston Symphony Orchestra; Hilary Scott)

Elliott Carter is one of Levine's favorite composers, and he was able to bring the American stage premiere of *What's Next*, Carter's antiopera about six characters who did or did not survive an automobile accident. Levine conducts the TMC students in a production that received rave reviews. (Boston Symphony Orchestra; Hilary Scott)

The following summer the TMC orchestra performed *Don Carlo* in the Shed with another all-star cast of soloists from the Met. Here Levine rehearses with the orchestra. (Boston Symphony Orchestra; Hilary Scott)

In 2005, Levine gave two coaching sessions for the students working on sections from act 1 of *Don Giovanni*. Here he works with the student singers accompanied by piano. In the second section, the student orchestra and student conductor accompanied the singers. (Boston Symphony Orchestra; Walter Scott)

Chamber music has always played a major role at the Music Center. Levine convinced three of his favorite composers, (left to right) Milton Babbitt, Elliott Carter, and John Harbison, to take the speaking roles in Stravinsky's *The Soldier's Tale*, which Levine is coaching. (Boston Symphony Orchestra; Hilary Scott)

My plan was essentially was to have composers who had not been here before. The idea was, Let's discover these people for Tanglewood. In '92 I felt that we needed to react heavily away from the Europeanization of the Festival. There had been a huge amount of English and continental music the previous two years, so I wanted to represent American composers, particularly ones who had not been here for a long time. In '92 there were some discoveries—the first Tanglewood appearances of [Oswaldo] Golijov, Christopher Rouse, the first big piece here by Nicholas Maw. Things that were for Tanglewood, completely new.

The most lavish special event of the Ozawa era had to do with Tanglewood's most famous contemporary composer, Leonard Bernstein. In 1988 he celebrated his seventieth birthday and Tanglewood gave the party. A fundraiser for the Music Center, it was the biggest bash in the Festival's history, as you can see from this letter written on February 1, 1998, by the Center's then-administrator, Richard Ortner, to the director of conducting from the Royal Academy of Music in London, who was innocently inquiring about local accommodations.

Thanks for your letter of January 19. I hasten to reply in order to give you "fair warning" about the special nature of activities at Tanglewood this summer. We want to welcome you in any event, but it may be a bit like walking into a maelstrom.

You will surely be hearing about Leonard Bernstein's seventieth-birthday celebrations, which will occupy us fully during the last two weeks in August 1988. Mr. Bernstein will be with us, as will be 750 of his closest friends and associates, and untold thousands of concertgoers. Everyone from the King of Spain to Elizabeth Taylor has been invited, and many have already cabled their acceptances. In anticipation of this event the Boston Symphony has reserved every room in every decent hostelry in the area (some 320 rooms to date). Hotel accommodations, therefore, will be nearly impossible to come by, and I regret that I'm not in a position to offer any help on that score.

Andrew Pincus described some of the logistics in the August 25, 1998, Berkshire Eagle.

A fleet of forty cars loaned, without charge, by General Motors to ferry the stars and nabobs wherever they want to go. Forty drivers supplied by the Tanglewood Association of Volunteers.

Fourteen extra full-time employees assisting the BSO staff. Ten Winnebago trailers as dressing rooms. Two hundred hotel rooms. Three thousand yards of blue and green ribbon for place settings. Sixty-five waitresses. Eleven thousand invitations, 15,000 brochures, and 2,500 posters. Three musicians arriving by Concorde, two other celebrities by private helicopter. . . .

The Tanglewood cafeteria has hired twenty-five extra food handlers for the weekend. The press office hired a full-time assistant to handle the expected international press corps of seventy-five, all of whom will be issued laminated identification badges. Women in the cast will have their personal hairdressers.

As if that were not enough, Pincus continues.

As the celebration grew, so did the related activities to attract national attention and support. Prices for the birthday concert were pegged at benefit levels—$50 to $5,000 in the Shed, $20 on the lawn.

To make the program more attractive to big givers, the BSO scheduled a preconcert dinner for 550 at its newly acquired Highwood mansion for patrons ($1,000 apiece) and benefactors ($5,000) and a cast party for 350 afterward at Blantyre for benefactors. . . .

Giant television screens—five inside the Shed, three on the lawn—and extra loudspeakers outdoors guarantee that no one, however small or big his contribution, will miss the action.

And, according to the Tanglewood budget, $4,998.50 was spent on stamps alone.

Maybe after hearing about the logistics, you would like to know about the festivities themselves. Humphrey Burton, the longtime head of the BBC arts programming unit and director of over 150 of Bernstein's television programs, chronicled the proceedings in his book Leonard Bernstein.

At the Sunday afternoon concert—the final event in the four-day-long marathon—Seiji Ozawa conducted *A Bernstein Birthday Bouquet, Eight Variations on a Theme by Leonard Bernstein.* The theme was "New York, New York" from *On the Town.* The variations were composed by Luciano Berio, Leon Kirchner, Jacob Druckman, Lukas Foss, John Corigliano, John Williams, Tōru Takemitsu, and William Schuman. For Bernstein it was a heartwarming demonstration of the affection in which he was held by his peers. He had been equally touched on Friday by a "Prelude" event (in the Shed) of songs commissioned in his honor by a dozen other composers: David del Tredici, George Perle, Ned Rorem, Peter Schat, Stephen Schwartz, Harold Shapero, Bright Sheng, Alvin Singleton, Stephen Sondheim, Michael Tilson Thomas, Yehudi Wyner, and his daughter Jamie.

Saturday was given up to tributes from young people. In the morning, an orchestra of high school students from the Boston University Tanglewood Institute gave a stirring performance of the *Jeremiah* Symphony, conducted by Eiji Oue. In the evening, a new production of *Mass* was presented by students of the Opera Theater of Indiana University. By an extraordinary feat of preplanning and rehearsal back home, the show was built, lit, and rehearsed in a single day. Dean Webb had been determined to have Bloomington represented at the party.

Three conductors—Seiji Ozawa, Michael Tilson Thomas, and Leon Fleisher—shared the Tanglewood student orchestra's Friday evening concert of music especially loved by Bernstein: the Brahms Double Concerto with Midori and Yo-Yo Ma, Stravinsky's *Capriccio* with Peter Serkin, Ive's choral *Thanksgiving* and the choral movement from Mahler's *Resurrection* Symphony with Roberta Alexander and Christa Ludwig as the soloists. The choice of young Midori was appropriate: not only had she traveled with Bernstein to Hiroshima, she had made front-page news the following year when she twice broke a violin string while performing his *Serenade* at Tanglewood. Yo-Yo Ma also had special reason to be indebted to Bernstein: part of his Harvard education had been paid for with a Bernstein scholarship. (Bernstein stopped adding to the scholarship's endowment in 1985 in a much-publicized dispute with President Bok concerning the university's policy toward nuclear disarmament. He renewed his funding in 1989.)

And all this was only the prelude to the main event on Saturday night, August 25th—his actual birthday. Burton continued.

An audience of 8,000 gathered for the birthday concert. Beverly Sills was a genial moderator: the entertainment she introduced had been devised to reflect every aspect of Bernstein's musical life, interspersed with videotaped greetings from Bernstein's orchestras in Israel, Bavaria, Schleswig-Holstein, Vienna, London, and New York, and from friends unable to be present, such as Jerome Robbins and Barbara Cook. Michael Tilson Thomas, John Mauceri, and John Williams shared the conducting with Seiji Ozawa. From the opera world Gwyneth Jones flew in from Canada to sing Leonora's great aria from *Fidelio*, and Christa Ludwig launched a new career in operetta, singing "The Old Lady's Tango" from *Candide* with much hip-swaying and the clatter of castanets.

"Slava" Rostropovich had been in Sicily early that same morning: by a combination of private jet and Concorde he arrived in time to play the epilogue from Strauss's *Don Quixote* in memory of Bernstein's 1943 debut with the New York Philharmonic. Afterward he strode into the audience to greet his friend with a giant hug. Lukas Foss accompanied Dawn Upshaw in *I Hate Music*, first sung in public down the road at Lenox exactly forty-five years earlier. Yo-Yo Ma played the cello obbligato in "To What you Said" from *Songfest*—sung by Robert Osborne—and Barbara Hendricks, Jennie Tourel's favorite pupil, sang the lullaby from *Kaddish* with a chorus of schoolgirls from Boston. Stephen Sondheim wrote biting new lyrics for Kurt Weill's "Poor Jenny" retitled "Poor Lenny"—the man who could never make up his mind what he wanted to be.

"Keep it that way" was Sondheim's conclusion. Perched on a bar stool to deliver the song, the raspingly elegant Lauren Bacall brought the house down. The camera showed Bernstein, seated next to his mother, gamely laughing his head off at Sondheim's digs. Jamie, Nina, Alexander, and David Thomas kept up the family tradition of gentle mockery with an a capella song called "The Seven-Oh Stomp" [written by Jamie]. Jamie and David were also in the backing group when Phyllis Newman did the "Swing" number from *Wonderful Town*. Patti Austin, Victor Borge, Betty Comden, Quincy Jones, Bobby McFerrin, and Frederica von Stade were among the other stars.

After four hours the gala concluded with a greeting from Seiji Ozawa. "Tanglewood was your legacy," he said, addressing Bernstein in his box across a sea of faces. "We love you, Lenny: you helped to make our Tanglewood garden glow." Then the entire company came onstage to sing the closing number from *Candide*.

Bobby McFerrin no longer remembers how he came to sing at the Bernstein bash. He thinks it was Lenny's children who invited him. He sang "Somewhere" from West Side Story, *complete with his superhuman range of vocal percussion improvisations and body-drumming. He said, "I was more nervous singing those four minutes than anything I had ever done in my life." During the performance, the look on Bernstein's face was that of utter delight and amazement.*

Bernstein was so enthusiastic about McFerrin's talent that he agreed to give him a conducting lesson at Tanglewood the next summer. McFerrin talked about it in Tim Page on Music.

I went up to Tanglewood to participate in the [Bernstein] celebration. After it was over, I wrote him a letter and asked him if I might have a lesson. And he said, Yeah, sure, come on out next year, and we'll get together. So I spent three weeks in the summer of 1993 at Tanglewood, hanging out with the student conductors, attending the master classes, and finally having my private lesson with Bernstein.

There we were, looking at the score of Beethoven's Seventh Symphony together, and I'm trying to find my way into this new discipline. I read music and all, but singers only have to follow one note at a time, and my piano-playing was done by ear, so looking at this score, with all these instructions for different instruments playing different melodies at the same time, was really *formidable*. And Bernstein sensed my discomfort and said, "Bobby, it's all jazz, it's all just *jazz*, you know." And for some reason that clicked with me. He was teaching me that music was music, and it made me feel better about where I was coming from as a musician, about my background. He was giving me permission to look at those compositions from my own viewpoint.

Seiji Ozawa followed suit, and McFerrin went on to further study with Gustav Meier. Then Phyllis Curtin invited him to teach the Boston University Tanglewood Institute students his version of rhythm, harmony, and melody. She considers him one of the best and most imaginative teachers she has ever encountered. One day, while he and his students were waiting to get into the Chamber Music Hall, he took the kids over to the sundial in the garden behind the Main House. He divided them into two groups, one singing in duple time, the other in triple. Each group walked in opposite directions around the sundial singing in their particular meter. Ms. Curtin thought that was the most inventive way of teaching and experiencing rhythm she had ever encountered.

McFerrin comes from a musical family. His parents were both classical musicians. His father, the baritone Robert McFerrin, was a fellow at the Berkshire Music Center Opera Program under Boris Goldovsky in 1949. He then went on to win the Metropolitan Opera "Auditions of the Air" and become the Met's first African-American male soloist.

In 1990 the Tanglewood Music Center had a summerlong celebration of its fiftieth anniversary, and Robert McFerrin was one of the many alumni and supporters on the Opening Night Gala honorary committee, which was headed up by Phyllis Curtin and Leontyne Price.

To kick off the festivities there were two concerts featuring former students in the vocal department: Dawn Upshaw, '83; Rosalind Elias, '50–51;Margaret Cusack, '80; Shirley Verrett, '56; Evelyn Lear and her husband, Thomas Stewart, both '54; Sherrill Milnes, '60–61; Richard Cassilly, '53; Marni Nixon,'50; Sanford Sylvan, '75–77; and so many more. In between was a dinner honoring Boris Goldovsky, who had jump-started many of their careers.

Also over the summer instrumentalists Christopher O'Reilly, '76–78; Claude Frank, '47; and his wife, Lilian Kallir, '47–48, were soloists at Tanglewood.

Conductors included Seiji Ozawa, '60; Charles Dutoit, '59; Lukas Foss, '40–42; Carl St. Clair, '85; and, of course, Leonard Bernstein, '40. To end the season, Zubin Mehta, '58, brought his New York Philharmonic to perform the last weekend.

Quite a dazzling array of star talent, but enough PR already!

Probably the most moving celebration was the picnic for all the alums and a TMC collection of reminiscences, Tanglewood Remembered: The Music Center, assembled by volunteer Barbara Mandell, who spent two years putting it together. One entry in the reminiscences, written by Janice Weber, '76, from Boston, says it all.

One of the most terrifying and thrilling moments of my life occurred during my first summer at Tanglewood, [in] 1976. Prior to this, my orchestral experience had consisted of playing the um-chick parts in my high school orchestra (there were never enough violas) and occasionally swashbuckling through piano concertos in which the conductor's duty was to follow me, not vice versa. Gilbert Kalish had assigned me the piano part in Carl Ruggles's *Men and Mountains*, which contained on its first page a craggy descending passage for piano marked "solo." No problem, I thought in the practice room. Not until the first rehearsal with Gunther Schuller (who doesn't scare me as much now as he used to) did I discover that I not only had to follow the conductor's beat, but a bassoonist was doubling my part! Unless we were absolutely together, the passage would sound awfully inept. As the entire BMC orchestra sat in ominous silence, Gunther, Wendy Large (whose name will forever remain with me), and I went through this tortuous passage several times. For reasons beyond my comprehension, Wendy and Gunther were always together and I was always in outer space. I needed three eyes: one for the conductor, one for the music, and one for the keyboard! I went over the passage hundred of times, counting out loud, listening to a recording in the library, rehearsing with Wendy behind the theater: nothing helped. Finally, at the dress rehearsal, when the situation appeared hopeless, Gunther sighed, "Jan, just leave your part out," and proceeded.

Before the concert, near death, I knocked on the door of Gunther's dressing room and begged him to go over this satanic passage with me just one more time. I couldn't go down in history "leaving it out" at Tanglewood! We sat at the upright in the corner; Gunther sang the preceding bars . . . here came my lick . . . blew it! "One more time," he said, fixing me wit that Gorgonian stare. Again, again . . . "I think you got it," he finally said. I was not so sure.

Cool as a cuke, Wendy (plus bassoon) seated herself a few feet away from me on the theater stage. Gunther walked to the podium, bowed, surveyed the orchestra, then stared at me. I could almost hear him willing me to play that damn part right. With each passing bar, my heart began thumping harder and harder. . . . Here it came. . . . I lost comprehension after the first few notes. Some hidden automatic shift took over, overriding thought; Wendy and I were perfectly together from first note to last. To the audience it probably sounded easy. Fun. To me it was an out-of-body experience like going over Niagara Falls without a barrel. To this day, I don't know which guardian angel to thank. Besides Gunther, of course.

Years later, I played the same piece with the American Composers Orchestra in New York. That bassoonist and I clicked the first time . . . but I don't remember his name.

On the weekend of August 19–22, on Sunday afternoon, Leonard Bernstein conducted the BSO in the annual Serge and Olga Koussevitzky Memorial Concert. At the beginning of his review of that concert, John Rockwell noted that "Leonard Bernstein has long been the most intensely emotional, the most nakedly human of conductors. That means all his concerts are suffused with a power of personality that focuses attention on himself. In his youth, this insertion of personality could detract from the music; now, in his magisterial maturity—he turns seventy-two this Saturday—it usually augments the impact of his performances."

On the program was his own "Arias and Barcarolles," conducted by Carl St. Clair. Bernstein then conducted, appropriately enough, Britten's "Four Sea Interludes" from Peter Grimes, *followed by the Beethoven Symphony no. 7. According to Rockwell, "he looked drawn, and his trademark flamboyance was muted. His habit of abstaining from actual baton-waving for a minute or two is a familiar Bernstein stunt. But he started coughing into a handkerchief during the Beethoven third movement. And he seemed truly exhausted, even in pain, as he walked off the stage amid the concluding ovations."*

This was to be the last concert that Bernstein would ever conduct. He died a few months later.

During the concert Walter Scott, the Tanglewood staff photographer, took the last picture of Bernstein in performance from atop a backstage ladder with a mirror to help him frame his shot. In a WGBH Radio interview with Brian Bell, Scott told the story.

That was very dramatic. It was kind of scary, as a matter of fact. I saw Bernstein coming onto the stage and going to the green room, and we all knew that he was ill—that was comparatively obvious.

I noticed that he started that concert very high, with very open motions. Then I noticed that as things went along, he began to bring his elbows much tighter into his body. At one point, when I pushed my little mirror back down, he wasn't there. He had vanished as far as I was concerned so I instantly thought, My God, he's collapsed. I also noticed that the orchestra suddenly sounded different. I realized that he had backed up against the railing and was simply nodding at the orchestra. The sound became harsh and everybody thought, Is this it? But he finished the concert.

At that point I sensed that I was not going to see him out here again. And I managed to get down my backstage ladder and around to the side to take that one other shot, which to me is one of the most feeling shots of Lenny, walking off the stage for the last time. It was mostly staged down here at the foreground—lots and lots of foreground. And Lenny, a small figure walking off. Anyone who knows him, his left elbow was out, he was tucking that little red handkerchief into his breast pocket. And that was that. I never saw him again.

Because the picture was shot with a wide-angle lens, the stage looks huge and Lenny looks very small.

A few years before the reunion celebration and Bernstein's last concert, expansive real estate plans had been taking shape at Tanglewood. In 1986 the BSO bought Highwood, the

120-acre estate next door to Tanglewood, increasing the size of its property by 40 percent. Richard Ortner was involved in the planning process.

Word came to us that it [Highwood] was going to go on the market. Frankly, the board [under the leadership of George Kidder] did exactly the right thing. They understood that unless we wanted to see "Tanglewood Estates"—lovely two-acre suburban homes a hundred yards from the back door of the Shed, which is where the property line ran—the orchestra had to preemptively buy it, even though there was no plan regarding what to do with it at the time.

Planning for the new campus followed quickly and in earnest. Ortner continues.

The plans for the new campus evolved slowly, and Dan and I were at the center of the planning. Dan was a true visionary, and together with some gifted professional planners [not William Rawn's staff] and a great trustee committee, everything was given consideration: every tree that would be saved, how the paths would wind through those beautiful big pines and oaks, how the Highwood estate and manor house would function, the moving of "Mamma's Cottage"—a circa 1770s cottage on the estate where Mason Harding's [the former owner's] mother was installed until her death—onto a new foundation to become the Copland Library.

Dan was also the key contact with the architects who designed the new outbuildings—the "press porch" attached to the Highwood manor house, free-standing practice studios, a couple of new food kiosks for the main grounds, and of course the big carriage house that was completely refurbished to become the Music Center offices and Leon Fleisher's studio.

Ortner noted that other considerations were also at play.

That was also right around the time that we determined that if we were going to do some fundraising for the Berkshire Music Center, that was going to be difficult, because nobody had heard of the Berkshire Music Center. They had heard of Tanglewood. The rather simple expedient was to change the name of the place to the Tanglewood Music Center. The name change instantly clarified for everyone, right across the country, that this was the *school* at Tanglewood, which allowed us to proceed with more vigorous fundraising, both for the annual fellowships that supported young musicians for those eight weeks each year, and for what eventually became Ozawa Hall.

And yes, with Highwood came a great site for a new concert hall, allowing us to return the Theatre–Concert Hall to its original function as an opera theater. We had to contend with the fact that the pit was flooded (had always been in fact flooded—the original orchestra for *Peter Grimes* sat on chairs perched on packing palates and wooden crates to keep their feet dry) and the rigging galleries were *completely* full of raccoon shit.

The great discovery was that, once we reopened and corrected the drainage for the pit and tore down the acoustic backing that supported orchestra performance on stage, exposing the old concrete cyclorama, we discovered that the place functioned *beautifully* as an opera theater! Great natural balance between the voices on stage and the orchestra in the pit, a stage house capable of accommodating modest but adequate technical apparatus, and good sight lines throughout the house.

Planning for the new concert hall had already begun. One dilemma the board faced was whether they wanted to hire a famous architect like Eliel Saarinen, who had designed the Shed. Dan Gustin described their decision-making process.

It was a very interesting selection process because we at the Boston Symphony asked architects from all over the United States to submit their credentials for this project. Then we winnowed the candidates down from sixty to seven.

After hearing twelve hours of presentations by the architects under consideration, the committee decided to take a straw vote. Haskell Gordon, the chairman of the design committee said, "Why don't we each write down two names that we consider to be the top candidates?" So we did that and Bill Rawn's name was on every person's list. It was a unanimous choice.

William Rawn was a young architect—in fact, the youngest of all the candidates and the least well known. And he had never designed a concert hall. However, he and his staff had just designed an affordable housing project on the Boston waterfront, and that was what he presented to the board. He also spoke fervently about his idealistic feelings for the new hall and its site, which became one of the determining factors in the committee's decision to give him the commission. The year after the building was finished, at a Talks and Walks event, Rawn revealed to the Friends of Tanglewood what he had said to convince them.

My reaction was very much about simplicity, directness, restraint—these quintessential New England values that I think pervade Tanglewood. There is an informality—the lack of signs, for example. It's all about a trust of our fellow man, if you will. Everything is open. There's a democratic spirit to Tanglewood. On a day like this, people can walk in absolutely free.

We hope that it also captures the values of the New England meetinghouse, or Quaker meetinghouse. On opening night when they played Randall Thompson's

Alleluia, the chorus and everyone stood up to sing. You had the sense of a New England gathering coming together with a real trust of each other, and I hope the building reflects that. It means a lot to me that it does.

To prepare for the work ahead, Rawn and his team of five spent the following summer at Tanglewood scoping out the place. That winter he went to Europe to visit several small halls in order to . . .

. . . understand the scale and the feeling of these halls. I learned a lot. Typical would be like the day I went into Zurich and they [at the Tonhalle] were expecting me. So at noon they let me into the hall during a rehearsal. They let me take my camera, measuring tapes, and sketchbooks, and I spent the whole afternoon understanding the building and then that night would hear a concert. In fact, they would give me two or three different seats in the hall so I could hear it from different vantage points.

Several considerations played an important part in his design.

Clearly the first and most important issue was designing a building that responded to the landscape. This is a magical landscape, as you all know. Everyone feels that. It was certainly a primary element in our design thinking. The second was the old Saarinen Theatre–Concert Hall. It's a wonderful building, a place to come together for a community of music—some of those Thursday nights are really wonderful in that building. So we knew we had to try and capture that intimacy and immediacy of that hall.

We all knew that a five- to six-story building didn't seem to fit into the Tanglewood landscape. So that was a very important issue we had to deal with, and that's when we came up with the rounded roof form. It was really to soften the edge of the roof to the sky. It also is meant to mimic the rolling hills of Stockbridge Bowl.

Acoustics were of primary importance.

A foremost acoustic opportunity is found in a shoe box–shaped hall, which is very much in the great nineteenth-century tradition of halls and clearly has come back since the early eighties as the shape of choice of major acousticians. We were very happy about that. Larry [R. Lawrence Kirkegaard, responsible for the acoustics of the hall] is a great believer in thick sidewalls. He would tell you that the most important issue acoustically in a concert hall is the thickness of the sidewalls. It's all about keeping the bass notes in the hall and getting the reflections off those walls and off the undersides of the balcony back into the orchestra seats. That was Larry's most important criteria.

At a detail level, every surface area in that hall has been reviewed with Larry and his suggestions have been integrated into the design. The curves in the teak grills are all about acoustics. You'll see that the upper walls slope back at about two degrees. The ceiling at the edges—the cornice—slopes at about five degrees. He wants everything almost square, but not exactly, so it was kind of eighty-nine degrees everywhere in the hall. Many of the things you can't see visually, and yet they are important to the acoustics.

Larry is, of course, the hero on this question of the open door to the lawn. We do not know of a single other case where there has been an enclosed concert hall that suddenly has a fifty-foot-wide door opening onto the lawn and the acoustic qualities are maintained inside the hall while those doors are open. That is the invention, in my mind, that is extraordinary about Larry's work.

Rawn also addressed some other architectural issues.

One is the question of windows. You can imagine it would have been very easy to build a hermetic box, maybe with a barn door on one end, with no windows. Larry would have been happy. That would have been easy. But we're at Tanglewood, and the idea of building an urban concert hall at Tanglewood made no sense at all. So we not only had the windows behind the stage, but more important are those windows in the doors along the sides. From just about every seat in the hall—perhaps every seat in the hall—you can see the trees, the green grass or the sky. You know that you are in a place different from an urban concert hall, and that was fundamentally important for us. From certain seats you also get to look out the big barn doors in the back. The windows on the side and behind the stage were critical in my thinking about what this hall should be.

On the exterior, one of the important issues was the slope. You've heard me quoted, I'm sure, that the slope is just steep enough so that the wine goblet will stand upright. That is Tanglewood! If you go to other outdoor venues in this country, they have steep outdoor slopes, and that's not what Tanglewood is about. When you are on a steep slope, you are all sitting in a row like in chairs. At Tanglewood, you're sitting as a group around a blanket. We thought it was incredibly important to get that slope as gentle as we could but still let there be sight lines.

Our office is right near the statehouse in Boston on the Common. So we got the whole office out testing slopes. Fortunately, it's very steep at the top and very shallow at the bottom. And it worked. You can do all the drawings in the world, but unless you can really make it work personally, you're never sure.

All of the big, heavy timbers have been salvaged and retrimmed from old piers and train trestles. They don't look like they've been used before; but they've already dried out and won't shrink any further. Also, of course, this means they've been recycled, so fewer trees were cut down.

If you think of most concert halls when they are full of people, the one architectural detail that is most evident is the balcony rail. We wanted to make ours memorable, and that's when we came up with this teak grill. That becomes a major memorable thing, we think, in the building. It's meant to capture that sense of cool summer breezes wafting through the space.

The hall was definitely full of people on July 7, 1994, opening night. The inaugural concert was a three-hour affair, with all the Tanglewood luminaries performing. Norio Ohga, the head of the Sony Corporation and a musician in his youth, was one of the conductors. Mr. Ohga had donated $2 million to build the hall and the BSO told him he could name the building. Instead of Ohga Hall, he decided to honor his old friend and fellow Japanese by calling it Seiji Ozawa Hall.

The critics loved the hall. New York *magazine's Alan Rich, himself a fellow at the Music Center in 1957, enthused.*

Although the interior echoes various architectural themes, they are all relevant: the communality of a Quaker meeting house, the shoe-box design of Vienna's patrician Musikvereinssaal, the delicate paneling of a Japanese teahouse, the down-to-earth efficiency of a New England barn, and the woodsy warmth of the Maltings concert hall in Aldeburgh on the North Sea. . . . I have seldom sat in a new concert space more sensitive to so many different needs, nor one that accommodates them all so successfully and comfortably.

But nobody loved the hall more than Seiji. As he told the fellows at the 1994 Opening Exercises, the first in the new hall,

I must tell you of my personal feeling, because this is not a usual summer because of this hall. This morning I came in, first time, I work with you and hearing the sound and looking at this hall, this beautiful hall—I came here even in the wintertime when the snow was here—but now it is so beautiful, on the outside is nature, and I feel Koussevitzky's dream. We are doing it in the beautiful nature, and working with young people here, and especially this morning with the Brahms [the work he had been rehearsing with the student orchestra].

You know, it is very emotional for me, a very big morning I spend with you [rehearsing]. And I thank you very much, all of you here, for this wonderful day and this wonderful start for me. I am very honored that I see my name on the outside—it's a very strange feeling.

But this hall is not for me. It is for you. And as a caretaker, you will be the caretaker of this place from now on. For you, very important, what you do, using this facility, using this nature.

Now that Tanglewood had its new concert hall, the question of what to do with the newly refurbished Theatre–Concert Hall still remained. Richard Ortner:

Dan and I had been talking for a long time about opera at the Music Center. There was not much participation from Seiji, because opera was still largely terra incognita to him. But Dan and I were both Tanglewood history buffs, if you will, and we understood that the thing that put the Music Center at the center of American musical culture in the '40s and early '50s was indeed the opera program with Goldovsky, with Leontyne Price, Sherrill Milnes, and Phyllis Curtin and so many others.

There had been a couple of fitful attempts to restart an opera program—notably Ian Strasfogel's music-theater project. It was largely sequestered in the West Barn. They did small-scale but interesting things [some examples are Brecht/Weill's *Mahagonny*, Erik Satie's *Socrate*, Harrison Birtwistle's *Down by the Greenwood Side*, and a new opera by BMC student Robert Selig, *Chocorua*, about a New Hampshire Indian who fell in love with the wife of an English colonist].

Occasionally the students would do a concert staging of an opera. I remember producing *Elegy for Young Lovers* the first time Henze came to the Music Center as composer-in-residence. Lisa Saffer played the madwoman and was fantastic. I think Dominique Labelle was the ingénue. It was a wonderful piece and Gusti Meier conducted. The pit was not usable, so the orchestra had to be onstage, but behind a scrim. I think that was the first time we used TV monitors to provide a virtual conductor to the singers on stage. The orchestra and conductor were behind the singers, but the singers could look out at the audience and get their cues on the monitors. Quite a good success.

Ozawa, too, had begun to take a heightened interest in opera, which in the past he had conducted very infrequently. Until the '80s, he had done only occasional operas in Europe, so there remained a huge amount of repertory that he had never tackled.

Margo Garrett, the collaborative musician and well-known accompanist of singers such as Dawn Upshaw and Kathleen Battle, came to the TMC in 1979 as a vocal coach and later became the head of the vocal department. She understood Seiji's dilemma.

He needed to train himself in the repertory that he was increasingly being asked to do and the repertory he was fascinated by. He adores singers. He came to singers late. He has made a huge growth at a time when he was a very mature, world-renowned, and superb conductor.

As Ozawa became increasingly interested in opera, he wanted to bring it to Tanglewood. Because of the enormous expenses involved, the only way to do it was to present semi-staged productions in the Shed. In 1980 the BSO mounted Puccini's Tosca *with Shirley Verret and Sherrill Milnes. The New York and Boston critics were less than enthusiastic, but many were impressed, including the then–BSO concertmaster, Joseph Silverstein. "I found it particularly exciting. Ozawa has a great gift for opera—musical drama. He has, I think, a wonderful theatrical sense. That is his greatest strength, dealing with music that has a story line. He's very, very good at that."*

In the years to follow, Boris Godunov, Fidelio, Oedipus Rex, Orfeo ed Euridice, Béatrice et Bénédict, Oberon, Elektra, *and* Pique Dame *were presented in the Shed. There was even a semi-staged version of the* St. Matthew Passion.

At the same time, the Music Center administration was also thinking of how to celebrate the fiftieth anniversary of Peter Grimes, *the Benjamin Britten opera that Koussevitzky had commissioned and first presented in America in a student production at Tanglewood.*

Phyllis Curtin had been in the original Tanglewood production of Peter Grimes. *She was very determined that the anniversary of this opera, the story of an English fisherman pitted against smug, hypocritical townspeople, should be celebrated with a new student production.*

Peter Grimes had become one of one of the great operas of the twentieth century and I felt we really should do something to mark the occasion. There hadn't been any opera at the Music Center for a very long time. So four years before the anniversary, I began talking to Dan and Richard.

Richard Ortner also thought it was a great idea.

Dan and I were moving in that direction with no agreement from Seiji that he would do it. Dan went to him four years before 1996, because putting on an opera on at the TMC—especially *Peter Grimes*, which is huge, three acts and four different sets—was a gigantic undertaking. And remember, we weren't paying the singers and we weren't paying the orchestra [because they were students], but I still think we spent about $400,000 to get things up and running. And that is not counting what we had to do to the theater.

Most of the trustees were not against it, but opera was simply not the first thing on their radar screen as an important educational or concert activity.

But Leon [Fleisher, artistic director of the TMC] felt, as did all of us in the administration, that if this was going to be a special place for training, it had to include opera. And it had to be opera not conducted by student conductors, but opera conducted by the music director of the Boston Symphony or by the best guest conductor that we could find for that. It had to be at the highest possible level. So it happened, but not without a lot of tearing of hair.

Once committed to the opera, the problem was to cast the difficult role of Peter Grimes. In fact, they had to find two Peter Grimeses, because the opera was going to be double-cast, to give many students a chance to participate. As Richard Ortner has so rightly pointed out, "Peter Grimeses don't just grow on trees."

Margo Garrett went to the auditions.

I knew about Tony [Anthony Dean Griffey] because we are both from North Carolina and when he first came to Juilliard, there was an awful lot of talk about him. I was not at Juilliard in those days, but Beverley Johnson was his teacher, and we were always very close. When Seiji told me he wanted to do *Peter Grimes*, he said, "We must find Grimes—hard to find Grimes."

The minute I saw Tony I felt, Oh my God, if he can sing it, that's him. Beverley said he was very young and thought it might be too much. But she got busy and helped him learn the role.

He came and auditioned and I remember him walking across the stage at Symphony Hall. Seiji was two seats down from me. And when he looked at Tony, I saw the awareness on Seiji's face that he thought Tony looked like Peter Grimes. He had on a double-breasted blue jacket with gold buttons, and there was just enough sense of the sea about him. And when he opened his mouth, that was it. I will never forget it. Seiji was so grateful. "I so grateful. I so grateful." I said, "I don't know if his teacher is going to let him do it," and Seiji was very respectful of that. He said, "Oh he must do it. We be very careful. We take care of him. Not too much singing."

Griffey did get the role, as did the Canadian tenor Thomas Doherty.

I think Seiji enjoyed working on the opera more than anyone. He conducted most of the staged piano and orchestra rehearsals himself. One day, before the rehearsal, the singers were out on the lawn doing physical warm-up exercises with their acting coach. Seiji just naturally joined them, becoming part of the group doing the exercises.

The performances were a triumph. In the audience were conductor Sarah Caldwell, who had worked on the original production, and tenor Jon Vickers, one of the greatest Peter Grimeses of them all. He pronounced the production "extraordinary."

Beverley Johnson came to the premiere and told Margo Garrett that she felt "it was so emotionally right for Tony. He has a tremendous amount of pathos that he had even then, as a very young man." Garrett felt that Griffey was the Peter Grimes of our time. He has sung it since to great acclaim at the Santa Fe Opera, at the Paris Opera, and at the Glyndebourne Festival. He had a huge success at the Metropolitan Opera in 2008.

As Phyllis Curtin rightly said, "It got Seiji really deeply into the opera, and he did it beautifully. It did bring opera back to Tanglewood."

Yes, Peter Grimes *was a triumphant tour de force, but it had the very unfortunate outcome of exacerbating an ongoing conflict between Seiji Ozawa and the TMC staff. It had begun in 1994 during the Sony production of* Marsalis on Music, *a television series recorded at Tanglewood for PBS to teach music appreciation to young people. Wynton Marsalis was the host, and Ozawa conducted the student orchestra in music illustrating Marsalis's points.*

As a result, the student instrumentalists spent an entire two weeks of their eight-week stay at the Center in a hot barn playing—to them—not particularly stimulating music over and over again to the exclusion of all their other activities. The fellows expressed their dismay to Dan Gustin, Richard Ortner, and Gilbert Kalish, who passed this news on to Seiji. Ozawa, who cared a great deal about the project, seems to have taken this as a sign that the TMC personnel were questioning his authority.

Two summers later, when it came time to rehearse and present Peter Grimes, *Ozawa again wanted all the singers to work only on the opera during the rehearsal period. The singers were upset because they had signed up for the song program with Phyllis Curtin and for performing in the Festival of Contemporary Music. This time Ozawa backed down. But the fact that the staff was again questioning his authority did not go down so well with him.*

Other considerations were also in play. Ozawa had been the BSO music director for over twenty years—a long time for any conductor—and the players were getting restless, many feeling that he had overstayed his time. Some devastating remarks concerning superficial performances had been heard from them and some very unpleasant comments about the maestro posted on the orchestra bulletin board.

In the last few years, Ozawa had been getting great satisfaction from working with the TMC orchestra, particularly during the Peter Grimes *period. There was no longer much fun to be had with the BSO, but the TMC was a different matter entirely, and Ozawa wanted control.*

The first thing he wanted was for Richard Ortner, the longtime and universally respected TMC administrator, to step down. This would put Ozawa in the driver's seat. Ortner was offered another job with the orchestra, but instead posted a letter of resignation at Symphony Hall that December. Sixteen members of the TMC faculty, including Phyllis Curtin, sent Ozawa a letter protesting the firing. They had worked at the Music Center a long time and resented Ozawa's dismissing Ortner for insufficient reasons without consulting them first.

Ellen Highstein, then the executive director of the Concert Artists Guild in New York, was hired as acting administrator of the Center for the following summer. Basically, according to Highstein . . .

. . . at the time that I joined [the TMC], Seiji had been expressing some concern about whether the highest standards were being represented at the Center, and whether, though everything seemed to be going along basically well, it could be even better. He recognized that institutions evolve and require periodic review and reevaluation to make sure they are still operating at the highest level.

I said that it seemed that what was needed first was an evaluation of what was going on there. He agreed, and asked several people to help him do this—with myself as a full-time consultant during the summer, covering the administrator's job as much as I could.

It was hard. I was brand new to the workings of the Center. My job was to talk to everyone and discover what—in everyone's view—was and was not functioning well; and to learn about Seiji's main concerns and find out how real they were, as he hadn't been all that hands-on before this.

Seiji also asked Yo-Yo Ma for help in this evaluation. Isaac Stern, with whom I spent about four or five days that season, was also a major advisor to Seiji during this period; Seiji trusted him completely, and Isaac knew all the present and past cast of characters—and had opinions about all of them.

At the end of the summer, when her report was turned in, Ozawa, in consultation with Mark Volpe, decided the way to make the school work better was, as Highstein put it, "to have a central person responsible for oversight of the educational and artistic mission of the school, as determined to a great extent by the music director." This gave her far more power than Ortner had ever had. "It was particularly difficult to get through this period because there was so much publicity—everything was being done in a fishbowl, with very extensive media coverage of what should, ideally, have been an internal reorganization."

A " fishbowl" is putting it mildly. Practically every newspaper in America reported on what happened next.

Leon Fleisher, artistic administrator of the TMC, and Gilbert Kalish, chairman of the faculty, wanted an administrator, not a director.

On October 29, 1997, Gil Kalish submitted his resignation "with deep regret" in a highly publicized letter to Ozawa.

My decision is the consequence of more than a year of turmoil in which decent, loyal, and distinguished members of this community have been dismissed and humiliated. You have leveled the vague charge that this group of artists and administrators is a self-congratulatory "club" that has failed to lead the Tanglewood Music Center with vision. Yet you are either unable or unwilling to communicate your own vision.

While we struggled this past summer to understand and respond to your dissatisfaction, with endless meetings, discussions, memos, surveys, and mission statements (some of which, of course, had fruitful results) and strove to provide our students with an inspired level of teaching, you were following a seemingly predetermined agenda that made a mockery of all of our efforts. . . .

You told the faculty at the one meeting in which you addressed us (artists such as, Phyllis Curtin, Leon Fleisher, Raphael Hillyer, Joel Krosnick, and all of the rest of this superb faculty) that the summer would be a "test." When Leon later suggested that such language was demeaning to artists of this stature, you responded by saying that "a little fear is a good thing." When you were asked respectfully to help us by articulating the ways in which our program was failing, you stated that such a question was "dangerous."

On December 1, Leon Fleisher also sent Ozawa his letter of resignation. Keep in mind that for many years Ozawa and Fleisher had been close friends and musical colleagues.

I am writing to you in response to our phone conversation of November 2 and 8 and to our meeting in Firenze on November 22.

As then, let me start by thanking you for the joy and privilege of working, for the past twelve years, as artistic director of Tanglewood. It has been, without a doubt, one of the most rewarding and intense involvements of my life. Let me continue by saying that this sorry mess in which we presently find ourselves need never have happened. How much simpler and cleaner it would have been had you but said to us: "Off with your heads! I want a whole new team, administrative and artistic!" This is your prerogative, you know; we serve only at your discretion. It is not necessary to negate years of loyal, loving, and creative work to effect a change. You don't have to destroy the past in order to build the future.

Let me state at this point what I deem to be the present situation. I have not resigned. I consider myself to have been relieved of my position as artistic director by you, and to have been replaced by Ellen Highstein. You have asked me to stay on as a coach of chamber music and as a sort of "gray eminence," in effect reporting to Ms. Highstein. A rather curious position for me to be in, wouldn't you say? Somewhat akin to having my legs chopped off at the knees, you then gently taking me by the arm and inviting me for a stroll. I must decline your invitation.

Enter Mark Volpe in November of 1997 as the newly appointed managing director of the BSO. During his interviewing period, no one had mentioned anything to him about the problems at the TMC.

I played a lot of tennis with Seiji and I could tell something was really wrong. In the interview process, he didn't really get into it. But he did say, "Problems, big problems—what you do?" I said I wouldn't do anything until I understood more about the nuances, the intricacies, the history, the context of the situation. And Seiji said, "Ah, I can't wait!"

Soon after I arrived in Boston, Seiji showed up at my house and said, "We go over to your office. I have Leon waiting." So my first meeting as the managing director of the BSO was with Seiji Ozawa and Leon Fleisher, for three hours in my office.

Seiji didn't fire Leon. He basically told Leon he couldn't conduct the orchestra—TMC or BSO. He could coach, he was a fantastic musician, one of the greatest pianists of our time, but Seiji didn't want him to conduct the orchestra. That was one of the big issues.

The other issue was that Seiji felt that the TMC faculty were a tight clique, and he had to let people know who the number-one music man was.

Seiji, I think, was at that point thinking about his legacy. When he conducted *Peter Grimes*, he remembered what it was like to work with the students. He started at the TMC, so it's been an important part of his life.

Ozawa had two major concerns. The first one was getting the BSO players more involved in the school, as he felt they had been in his day. The players still gave master classes and coached chamber music as they always had, but Ellen Highstein said that . . .

. . . the BSO players now also teach from within the TMC orchestra, playing alongside the fellows in major works on the concerts, adding to the section—not substituting for a fellow. They never play principal chairs; a BSO string player might play inside second stand, for example, or a wind player might play assistant. So they are not taking an opportunity away from a TMCer, but rather adding their expertise to the section—what might be thirty or forty years of knowledge of this repertoire. They play several of the rehearsals, often discussing with that section the specific challenges involved.

Conversely, each year we have auditions for violins, violas, and cellists from the TMC to get to play with the BSO. This year, for example, five of our cellists got to rehearse and play in a concert in the Shed with the Boston Symphony. Since there are only seven of them, our double basses all get to play in one BSO Shed concert each year. The TMC fellows are added to the orchestra, rather than substituting for a BSO musician, thus making sure that union regulations are respected; for the same reason (that is, needing to add rather than substitute for BSO musicians) TMC wind, brass, and percussion players can't play in with the BSO, but they can sit onstage in their respective sections during BSO rehearsals.

Almost all of the BSO players want some contact with these very interesting young artists; if we find the right format for them to work in, they are delighted to participate in the TMC program.

For a long time Ozawa had been concerned that the conductors' seminar was not as good as it had been in the past. Although he rarely attended any auditions, he was dissatisfied with many of the young conductors chosen. Gustav Meier was removed as head of the program and replaced briefly by Robert Spano, then the dynamic young conductor of the Brooklyn Philharmonic and a former BSO assistant conductor. The program took a year off for reevaluation and resumed the following summer.

Mark Volpe addressed some other problems the TMC faced.

We had workload issues, we had scheduling issues, logistics activities. There are 2,000 TMC activities in the course of the season.

Ellen Highstein elaborated.

Before, program planning and scheduling was all done during the summer, week by week. There were players—particularly strings—who, because there was no advance planning, had schedules that were too heavy, and too many went home exhausted and injured. (Many string teachers were not sending their best players to us for this reason.) Other students had summers with very little to do. We needed to get a handle on the problem and figure out a way to make assignments balanced and equitable, to keep the summer intense without making it dangerous. And the solution was advance planning, done preseason.

Volpe:

We decided that the TMC was going to be a priority. We raised some money, and there is a fair amount of the BSO endowment that is earmarked for the TMC. So we felt we had to give it a bigger staff, a scheduler, and a computerized scheduling program.

After all this, is the Music Center all that changed? Certainly the significant increase in its budget and staff has had a salutary effect. Unlike previous summers, Ozawa was actively engaged in all the school's activities and spent most of the summer at Tanglewood, having forgone conducting at Salzburg.

Has the quality of the students gone up? Mark Volpe says, "It was always very good. We're talking about a difference of 94 percent and 96 percent. That difference is important to people like [Christoph von] Dohnányi and [Bernard] Haitink." Hard to prove, though.

Have lives been ruined? Well, Gil Kalish is still the great pianist he always was. Dan Gustin now heads up the Gilmore Foundation that supports young pianists and promotes the art of the piano. Richard Ortner is president of the Boston Conservatory, and Leon Fleisher has received a Kennedy Center Honor, the nation's highest award for the arts.

As Dan Gustin once remarked, "I remember something that Andy Pincus used to say about Tanglewood almost every year: 'The more things change at Tanglewood, the more they remain the same.'"

Tanglewood now has a wonderful new tradition. Beginning in 2000, Garrison Keillor's radio program, A Prairie Home Companion, *has been broadcasting the last show of their season from the Shed at Tanglewood. It probably didn't hurt that Keillor's wife was once a violin student at the Boston University Tanglewood Institute.*

Not to be missed is his audience warm-up before the show goes on the air. He sings a few songs with Guy's All-Star Shoe Band, and before you know what's happening, he is out cruising in the audience with everybody singing "You Are My Sunshine" with him. He has been known to stand on a back bench—permitting the Shed audience a good look at the red running shoes he wears with a very proper blue serge suit, white shirt, and red tie—and serenade the fans on the lawn. You can imagine the reaction.

Over the years the guy from Lake Woebegone has had a lot of fun in his opening monologues at the expense of the good people of the Berkshires. As Keillor tells the story:

Tanglewood is a place the Indians called Tanglewood after they saw the settlers playing golf. Such a beautiful part of the country with mountains, woods, and lakes. A lot of thunderstorms and lightning don't bother the orchestra here [just before he went on the air there had been a doozy of a storm]; they just keep on playing and switch over to Bruckner. Orchestra members don't worry about lightning because that's what they have a conductor for.

He is never at a loss for a joke. When rehearsing the Beethoven Ninth, there was a problem. "It was the bottom of the Ninth and the basses were loaded." As far as real estate goes, "Some New York developer is talking about putting in a twenty-story high-rise at Tanglewood—a retirement home called the Dotted Rest." Said Sam Rhodes, Julliard String Quartet violist, "We'll sit onstage and look out and see old violists lining up for their medications, elderly oboists doing stretching exercises, geezer horn players playing pinochle. Depressing."

On one year's show Joel Smirnoff of the Julliard String Quartet called Guy Noir to see about the death of a conductor in the Shed. "One of the cellists had smiled at him and he fainted away and the baton pierced his heart."

Another year Emanuel Ax visited Guy Noir, who definitely had his number. Guy could tell that Manny was from the Upper West Side of New York because of "the span of the hands and the small indentations on the forefinger from making glissandos. A smudge of cream cheese on your lapel and a sesame seed between your upper incisors. And the fact that you're carrying a volume of Chopin Polonaises in a Zabar's shopping bag."

Garrison told Mark Volpe that he does his show all over the country, but said Tanglewood is unique. He just doesn't want the show to end. Neither does the audience, although they know he will be back next year.

But there would be no next year at Tanglewood for Seiji. On June 23, 1999, the Boston Symphony sent out a press release stating that Ozawa was resigning from the position of music director of the Boston Symphony and would be assuming the music directorship of the Vienna State Opera following the completion of the 2002 Tanglewood season. This is the reason Ozawa gave for leaving.

I would never leave the Boston Symphony for another orchestra. However, in my own growth as a musician, I increasingly have come to love the operatic repertoire. It is with great mixed emotion that I have decided to accept the position with the Vienna State Opera and to resign my position with the Boston Symphony.

This has been one of the most difficult decisions of my life. I look forward to continuing my association with you for a long time to come, both in Boston and particularly at Tanglewood. I hope most of all that our work together of the next three years and beyond will be our best yet. I am forever grateful to you for your artistry and support.

Ozawa's last weekend with the orchestra was at Tanglewood. In many respects Seiji is a very sentimental man and according to Mark Volpe, "he wanted to have his whole Tanglewood experience summarized in one weekend. Slava [Rostropovich] was involved. The students had to be involved." They gave a gala concert in his honor on Friday, July 12. Saturday's concert was Seiji and Friends with Rostropovich conducting works by Takemitsu and Shostakovich, and performances by Gil Shaham, John Williams, Jessye Norman, and Seiji's last Tanglewood student conductor, Federico Cortese. Seiji himself conducted the Marcus Roberts Trio in Gershwin's Rhapsody in Blue *and the Boys Choir of Harlem sang spirituals.*

Volpe said that the final moments brought tears to everyone's eyes.

He wanted to end with a prayer. It was the Randall Thompson *Alleluia* and we printed out the music so everyone could sing. He wanted that to be his last official act as the music director of the Boston Symphony.

In his good-bye message for his last weekend, Ozawa made a bow to the future for Tanglewood in the concert program book.

I also want to say how really pleased I am to be turning over this special place to my old friend and colleague James Levine. I know he understands and deeply values the Boston Symphony tradition and will do wonderful work with the orchestra. I wish him much happiness.

I haven't felt such excitement in the Shed since a certain relative of mine was there.

—Jamie Bernstein

CHAPTER 12

The New Era at Tanglewood

James Levine

*S*eiji Ozawa's last Tanglewood concert was in 2002, and James Levine had already been appointed the next music director of the BSO. But it would be another two seasons before he came to Tanglewood. In the intervening time, rumors were rife in the Berkshires that Levine was only going to do concerts in Boston and skip Tanglewood completely. This turned out not to be true.

So after two summers of numerous guest conductors, by 2005 the concertgoing public and the press were definitely psyched about entering the age of Levine at Tanglewood. James Levine had visited the Festival when he was thirteen years old and had guest conducted the Boston Symphony once in the summer of 1972. Apart from that, he had had no connection with the Festival.

Before his appointment as music director of the BSO, there had been a lot of speculation in the press as to whether or not Levine would be the new director. However, the BSO management was for his appointment very early on. Mark Volpe, the orchestra's manager, was an active supporter of his candidacy.

I was involved in recruiting him to be the music director. We started talking to the players, talking to the various internal constituencies, the board, the committee. It was perfectly clear to all that the conductor to succeed Seiji was Jim Levine. This was true on many levels. I sat with him and talked for hours and hours and hours about what was possible in Boston, given his commitment to the Met. I think what especially intrigued him was being the music director of an important American orchestra, and what was especially compelling to him was a great tradition, a great hall, one of the better cities in America for music, if not the best. And then you have this thing called Tanglewood.

And this thing called Tanglewood turned out to be one of the most absorbing and satisfying aspects of Levine's work with the Boston Symphony. As he told me,

When I was asked to become the music director of the BSO, which meant being the music director of Tanglewood, I thought to myself, This is the most natural thing in the world for me to try to do because, at least emotionally, psychologically, intellectually, I am completely at one with Koussevitzky's vision—particularly about that which concerns the purpose, the mission, and the function of Tanglewood and of new music.

I think that Tanglewood is a legendary, magical atmosphere, which nurtures itself in the most phenomenal way. There is such a unique combination of established content and constantly reinventing development and progress there.

All my life I have been very happy in my work from one day to the next, and I have worked a lot of summer outdoor music festivals, from seventeen summers in Salzburg and fifteen in Bayreuth and twenty in Chicago, to Aspen and Marlboro when I was a kid. Many formative things took place for me in those places in tandem with great winter music making in great halls in big cities. But I think that everything about the Boston and Tanglewood situation, as it connects with visionary artistic goals and Boston and Tanglewood's musical history, appeals to the core of me infinitely.

Levine is very much a hands-on music director, involved in the big picture as well as the minutiae of programming for the BSO. Anthony Fogg, the orchestra's artistic administrator, works closely with Levine.

When Jimmy first agreed to become music director—and even before, in preliminary discussions with him leading up to his appointment—it was obvious that he had a very clear concept of what he was going to do with the Boston Symphony. He had ideas about the directions he wanted to go, and about all sorts of repertoires that he wanted to explore. For him, the history of the Boston Symphony was something that was vivid—almost second nature to him. It had been a fascination since his childhood.

Some of the programs he brought that first summer for the BSO included a couple of his signature works. The Mahler Eighth Symphony opened the season, and then he did the four Brahms Symphonies in two consecutive concerts. He had famously recorded the Brahms Symphonies with the Chicago Symphony Orchestra and the Vienna Philharmonic.

James R. Oestreich reviewed the Brahms cycle in the New York Times *on July 25, 2005.*

What he and the orchestra achieved was no small feat: consistently engaging and often fresh performances of overfamiliar works. It is clear not only in the newly rich sound of the Boston Symphony but also in its attentive demeanor how effectively Mr. Levine has drawn the orchestra together in his first year as music director.

A change that Mr. Levine had made that first year accounted for the new rich sound. One of the first things the audience noticed in the Shed was that the orchestra had a new seating configuration. The first and second violins were no longer grouped together on the left side of the stage. Levine explained the change as follows:

In the beginning, the distinguishing feature of baroque orchestras was that they had two groups of violins, and in the nature of the composition of baroque and classical repertoire, the violins functioned as first and second sections. I think it never would have occurred to anyone to actually put them on the same side of the stage. They had independent parts, and they played contrapuntally. This gradually evolved into the classical orchestra of Haydn and Mozart and Schubert and Beethoven. This [seating arrangement] went for all the major big European orchestras until somewhere in the early part of the twentieth century.

Then composers began to write for larger and larger and more and more unusual combinations of instruments. For example, in Debussy's *La Mer* there are parts for sixteen cellos. At one point in *Elektra*, Strauss wrote four violin parts—that is, four sections, made up of violinists and violists playing violin parts.

The result is that the seating of orchestras began to go through a trial-and-error phase. And in the trial-and-error phase a lot of conductors tried putting all the violins on one side, because some of the newest music was no longer using them as two separate sections. They were still called first violins and second violins, but they were being composed for as a large group of thirty violins or more. In some of the new music—and I think this was one of the very strong influences—it turned out to be easier to keep the orchestra together by grouping the violins all on one side, where they appeared to collect more power in their sonority.

But a very, very critical thing was lost in this seating. If you put the first and second violins together on the left, the second violins' tone is blocked by the bodies of the first violins. Therefore, you are always asking them for more, and the sonority isn't really two groups. It's one clump, split. There is an unmistakable low string sound all in a clump over here [pointing to his right], and all the violin sound is over here [pointing to his left]. Meanwhile, to get any kind of transparency from the basses, cellos, and violas—all clumped together on the right—is a real job. So the historically correct seating avoids all those unnecessary problems and allows us to concentrate on working on the music and not on spurious balance issues.

However, when it came to the Tanglewood Music Center, Levine was hesitant to make any changes immediately, preferring to take a wait-and-see attitude about the school until he was more familiar with its workings. But he definitely did *want the students to profit from his particular experiences in music. Anthony Fogg describes what Levine did initially.*

The first summer, he made a strong impact on the planning and the programming. He wanted to do projects that he thought would be distinctive to him. When discussing the program for the Bernstein Memorial Concert that he did with the TMC orchestra, he said, "Look, I could easily do a Mahler symphony or Brahms or a big romantic piece, but that's an experience that for them [the TMC students] is not going to be unique to me."

So that first summer he did two acts of Wagner operas [act 1 of *Die Walküre* and act 3 of *Götterdämmerung*] with very distinguished casts, including Deborah Voigt and a number of singers from the Metropolitan Opera. It was something that they had never encountered in their musical careers. They certainly wouldn't have had that sort of opportunity at college where, typically, they wouldn't have access to singers who could sing Wagner. It proved to be a completely fresh and singular event for the TMC.

Richard Dyer, recently retired from the Boston Globe, *was there and reported that "at the first read-through, some of the violinists were visibly stupefied by the length of their parts, and after they had been playing for more than an hour, some were counting the number of remaining pages."*

Dyer went on to quote Katherine Bormann, the concertmaster for that concert, who felt initially that Levine's small beat "took some getting used to, but we caught on fast. He can just wiggle his fingers, and all of us know what color and character he's looking for. Working with singers, you hear tone colors in a different way. He wants us to be self-reliant. After awhile, we tried to know what he wanted ahead of time, without his having to stop and say anything. When we succeeded, he'd lean over and give us a great big smile. That was the most fun."

Levine has his own theory on minimal conducting.

Based on the way I was taught, I used to do a quite busy gestural technique, but I found the more I worked and the older I got and the better the orchestras I was working with, I wasn't happy—and I am not happy—unless the musicians understand what they are trying to do and are empowered in the concert to do it: to play directly to the public without there being some magician with a magic wand in between exhorting and carrying on. I always stay, of course, one hundred and ten percent involved. If they look at me, they will see the same involvement here [pointing to his face] as when we rehearsed. I try to give them what they need. But I am very conscious of not turning conducting into a visual leading for the audience. I want them to be able to take in the music through their ears, the way the composer intended it.

The reviews for the Wagner concert were spectacular. According to Anthony Tommasini in his July 19 review of the concert for the New York Times, *"After nearly 30 hours of rehearsals for this single performance, Mr. Levine drew an assured, inspired, and thrilling performance from the fledgling musicians."*

And what did Mr. Levine and the BSO present for the following Sunday afternoon concert? John Harbison's "Darkbloom: Overture for an Imagined Opera," Charles Wuorinen's Fourth Piano Concerto, Edgar Varèse's "Amériques," and finally George Gershwin's "An American in Paris." It wasn't just the students who were challenged that first season; the public was too.

One of Levine's coaching sessions with the students that same season was to work on excerpts from Don Giovanni. *The first session he worked with the singers and pianists of the vocal department. In the second session, he coached the singers and the student conductors leading a chamber orchestra made up of TMC players. Levine explained what he was after.*

I was trying to find out what they needed. I was trying to get involved in a classical operatic masterpiece and to find out to what extent they understood, to what extent they had technical and psychological knowledge and insight into singing, acting, language, ensemble response and development.

Bass Charles Temkey was spending his second summer as a fellow at the Tanglewood Music Center, having just graduated from the Manhattan School of Music. He was to sing Leporello in the Giovanni *coaching sessions and recalls the event vividly.*

The first session was pretty strictly about the singers themselves. I remember a great deal of it being spent on proper style in *secco recitative*, the dry recitative where the singers are just accompanied by harpsichord.

He worked a lot with us on cadence. There is the element of music in recitatives, when you see notes on the page, but there is a great amount of freedom that you can work with in this kind of singing. You have a rough sketch in front of you where Mozart has said, Okay, this word sounds like two sixteenths and an eighth note—he gives you a guideline as to how the Italian sounds, but if you have done your homework, you know how the language rolls along, and you can do a great deal with it in terms of rushing tempos ahead and getting through information that is not critically important. You can make the drama more exciting by accentuating certain words. It's like art song in a way. You really have a chance to go with the language and the drama rather than just give it musical attention.

Levine knows every word of the opera he is working on. When we came into the middle section of the sextet in act 2, where Leporello says very, very quickly, "*Mille torbidi pensieri mi s'aggiran per la testa,*" and goes on about the fear and foreboding that are going on so quickly that it makes his head spin, I had a lot of trouble. It's a very difficult section, very, very fast. . . . It was incredible to watch him mouth the words. He knew every single solitary word. It is obvious that he has a great musical mind and is a great musical thinker, but the simple fact is that he cares so much about the drama.

When it comes to the TMC, Levine is interested and involved in a whole spectrum of activities. Director Ellen Highstein says, "Jim likes working with 'the compleat musician,' who is in the orchestra one day and in a chamber group the next; where singers, instrumentalists, and composers work together all the time; and where new music is part of everyone's life." Levine maintains that "it's a chance, really, for that extraordinary interaction that makes musicians happy and makes their development thrive."

One of the most interesting TMC interactions was a 2006 performance by the students of Stravinsky's jazzy chamber work, The Soldier's Tale, *scored for violin, clarinet, bassoon, trumpet, trombone, double bass, and percussion plus three actors. Levine, who coached the young instrumentalists, had the brilliant idea of casting ninety-seven-year-old Elliott Carter as the Boy and Milton Babbitt, ninety, as the Devil, with the youngish (then sixty-seven) John Harbison as the Narrator—all of whom conveniently happened to be on the Tanglewood campus that week.*

The Boy and the Devil called each other Elliott and Milton ("Milton, you're a rotten thief!" wailed Elliott), and the "hot and dusty road" they traveled on was reinvented as "the road between Lenox and Back Bay."

That same year (2006), Levine conducted the students in the world premiere of Elliott Carter's new one-act opera What Next? *He very imaginatively completed the program with two other short operas, Hindemith's* Hin und Zurück *and Stravinsky's* Mavra.

Ellen Highstein adds to the catalog of Levine's activities.

Levine also works each year with the fellowship conductors in a variety of formats; they're his assistant conductors for his opera projects (both concert and staged), and he coaches them in work with large and small ensembles. This year he coached a program of major works of Ligeti, Wuorinen, and Schoenberg; and he himself conducted Poulenc on that concert. It was very much a Jim program.

Mark Volpe worries a bit about Levine's intense involvement with the Music Center.

My issue with Jim and the TMC sometimes is trying to protect him from overworking, because he is so energized by the students. When Bill Bolcom and Joan Morris are doing their master classes, there he is. If Elliott is doing a talk, there he is. He has dropped in on the BSO players' master classes. I can't imagine anybody being as committed to and interested in the TMC as Jim is—every aspect of it, the composers, the conductors.

How does a conductor coach fledgling composers? Levine finds this opportunity "fascinating and very exciting."

It's a chance for them to ask me a lot of relevant questions, and they do. They want to know all the things you would think they would want to know: what is it that captures my attention when I look at a new score, what can they do to make their music more available—in other words, is there anything they can do to create more performance opportunities for large new works, which is one of the problems. What about the relationship of rehearsal time to orchestral music when it is at such a premium and yet the score has more moving parts than smaller music does?

Does all this remind you of Koussevitzky? Is Levine deeply committed to the Koussevitzky vision?

Yes! Let me say exactly what I feel. I think Koussevitzky was a kind of ideal of what a civic music director should be. Koussevitzky clearly saw what the responsibility of a musical civic leader is—developing the orchestra itself, developing its relationship to the audience, developing a *sure* presence for commissions and new pieces and the whole idea of an orchestra as a tool for education and development, and I couldn't concur more.

And I think that the work of the TMC—at least everything we have tried to do since I started—has come back many, many times over in every conceivable positive way, and that thrills me. There has always been a mood in summer music that you can't sustain this commitment. Because of the weather, it's just better for the box office to do one pop event after the other. A lot of us have just dug in about this, believing that the whole unique quality of Tanglewood has to be maintained and has to thrive, and that's the only way it will.

After hearing this statement of purpose, one might conclude that "Koussevitzky redivivus." Or, as Andy Pincus is wont to say, "The more Tanglewood changes, the more it stays the same."

Acknowledgments

After working on this book for ten years, I have many people to thank. In the first-and-foremost category, I am forever grateful to the Boston Symphony Orchestra and its administrative personnel (whom I will list individually later). But here I would especially like to single out the BSO's senior archivist, Bridget Carr, and her assistant archivist, Barbara Perkel. These two went way beyond the call of duty to help me discover the treasures in their amazing collection. I thank them for their knowledge and generosity, and for their sense of humor when the going got tough.

I am particularly indebted to the *Berkshire Eagle* and its editor Tim Farkas, the *New York Times*, and the *Boston Globe* for very generously allowing me to reprint articles going back to 1934 that add such a you-are-there texture to the history of Tanglewood. The *Eagle* also gave me free access to its historic collection of Tanglewood photographs.

I take a deep bow in the direction of Jane O'Reilly—my own personal Maxwell Perkins in an era where that position has, alas, become redundant. She and Dan Gustin read my manuscript in several versions and set me straight on plenty of occasions and provided support over many rough bumps. And so did Phyllis Curtin.

Thank you Carole and Gordon Hyatt and Sandy Baron and Greg Diskant, who for years on end provided me with a home away from home in the Berkshires. The same goes for Syrl Silberman and Saul Rubin, my Boston hosts and drinking buddies, and Ann Geracimos who performed the same functions in Washington, D.C. My next-door neighbor in New York City, Caryl Lee Fisher, was and is my computer guru, and Manuela Soares and Loreta Barrett pointed the way to finding a publisher. And to John Cerullo, Carol Flannery, and Polly Watson at Amadeus Press, who put the package together, go many thanks.

I have had help at a great number of libraries and archives. I must have spent months in the Music Division of the Library of Congress researching in the Koussevitzky Archives, the Aaron Copland Collection, and the Leonard Bernstein Collection, where its curator, Mark Horowitz, was most helpful. The Lenox Library and its director Denis Lesieur gave me access to the records of the Berkshire Symphonic Festival in the library's Tanglewood Collection, and the Rockefeller Foundation provided me with a look at the beginnings of the Berkshire Music Center through its correspondence files.

Another volley of thanks go to all the people who graciously gave me their time and insights in interviews: Margo Garrett, Lukas Foss, Joseph Silverstein, Phyllis Curtin, Olly Knussen, Richard Ortner, Tom Morris, Robert Ward, James Levine, Tony Fogg,

Mark Volpe, Ellen Highstein, Charlie Temkey, John Oliver, Maisy Bennett, Joan Sherman, Steve Owades, and Dan Gustin.

Mark Volpe, Anthony Fogg, Kim Noltemy, Ellen Highstein, John Oliver, Marc Mandel, Suzanne Page, Meryl Atlas, Tim Martyn, and Dave Sturma—all from the Boston Symphony and Tanglewood family—helped enormously in countless ways.

Last but not least, and in no particular order, heartfelt thanks go to all the friends and colleagues who helped and supported me along the way: Janet Sternburg, Laverne Berry, Lucie Collins, Kenneth Hunt, Tim Page, Mary Engel, Peter Weissenstein, Carol Dwight Bain, Sarah Schaffer, Marie Carter, Thomas Wolf, Daphne Brooks Prout, Theodore Gross, Jane Polle, Leonard Marcus, Connie Shuman, Yehudi Wyner, William Rawn, Allan Miller, Marie Winn, Neil Herlands, Doug Pomeroy, Frances Heinsheimer Wainwright, Jeanne Betancourt, Barbara Mandell, and Rivalyn Zweig.

And I had better not forget to thank my ancient five-year-old Dell Inspiron 9100, which had the great good grace not to crash on me during the writing of this book.

Notes

CHAPTER 1
Music Under the Moon

3 *"One day he came home"*: Alice Edman, interview with Carol Dwight Bain for the Boston Symphony Orchestra Archives, Symphony Hall, Boston (hereafter cited as BSO Archives).

4–5 *"Dear Mrs. Taylor"*: Gertrude Robinson Smith to potential subscribers, 18 June 1934. All records and correspondence of the Berkshire Symphonic Festival can be found at the Tanglewood Collection, Berkshire Symphonic Archives, Lenox Library Association, Lenox, Mass. (hereafter cited as Tanglewood Collection).

13 *According to writer Edmund Wilson*: Edmund Wilson, "Our Footloose Correspondence," *New Yorker*, 4 September 1948.

13–14 *Miss Robinson Smith recognized early on*: Gertrude Robinson Smith to George Judd, 27 October 1936, Tanglewood Collection.

15–16 *The die was now cast*: Minutes of the Berkshire Symphony Festival board meeting, 24 February 1937, Tanglewood Collection.

16 *Eliel Saarinen did give them*: Eliel Saarinen to Gertrude Robinson Smith, 21 March 1938. All Saarinen correspondence can be found at the Cranbook Archives and Cultural Properties, Bloomfield Hills, Mich.

17–18 *Mrs. Dreyfus also reported*: BSO Archives.

CHAPTER 2
Koussevitzky's Dream

20 *"And the great Koussevitzky was standing"*: Leonard Bernstein, Berkshire Music Center Opening Exercises speech, Tanglewood, Lenox, Mass., transcript, BSO Archives. This speech is also reprinted in *Findings*, a book of Leonard Bernstein's writings (New York: Simon & Schuster, 1982).

21 *". . . a summer school under the aegis"*: Aaron Copland Collection, Music Division, Library of Congress, Washington, D.C. (hereafter cited as Copland Collection).

21–22 *But before he could realize*: Serge Koussevitzky, "Vision of a Music Center," speech given 1939, from *A Tanglewood Dream: The Berkshire Music Center 25th Anniversary Album* (Lenox, Mass: Berkshire Music Center, 1965).

22   *Dr. David H. Stevens was the foundation's*: David H. Stevens, report to Raymond Fosdick, 15 November 1939, Rockefeller Archive Center.

22–23   *"Re: Berkshire Music Festival and School"*: All Rockefeller Foundation material comes from the Rockefeller Archive Center, Pocantico Hills, N.Y. (hereafter cited as Rockefeller Archive Center).

24–25   *July 8, 1940—the great day had arrived*: Serge Koussevitzky, Berkshire Music Center Opening Exercises speech, Tanglewood, 8 July 1940, transcript, BSO Archives.

26–27   *Randall Thompson gave his own account*: Gertrude Norman and Miriam Lubell Shrifte, eds., *Letters of Composers: An Anthology 1603–1945* (New York: Alfred A. Knopf, 1946).

27–28   *The school had begun*: Leonard Bernstein Collection, Music Division, Library of Congress (hereafter cited as Bernstein Collection).

29   *At the end of the summer*: Leonard Bernstein to Helen Coates, Bernstein Collection.

31–33   *This Koussevitzky speech, "On the Art of Conducting"*: Serge Koussevitzky, "On the Art of Conducting," speech given to conducting students at Tanglewood, 1940, transcript, BSO Archives.

34–36   *Hindemith, with his wife, Gertrud*: Paul Hindemith to Gertrud Hindemith, 14 July 1940, Hindemith-Institute, Frankfurt am Main, Germany.

44   *The president of the Rockefeller Foundation replied*: Jerome Greene, besides being a BSO trustee, was also on the board of the Rockefeller Foundation, serving as its first secretary (1913–16) and a two-time trustee (1913–17 and 1928–39) This may account for the familiar tone of the correspondence with Raymond Fosdick.

44–45   *In an informal speech . .* Mrs. Gorham Brooks, speech to BSO trustees, transcript, BSO Archives.

CHAPTER 3
Tanglewood Goes to War

46   *"A rumor is spreading"*: Serge Koussevitzky, statement to BSO trustees, 30 April 1942, transcript, BSO Archives

47   *He expressed his very heartfelt opinion*: Minutes of the Berkshire Symphony Festival board meeting, 4 June 1942, BSO Archives.

48   *The BSO trustees had both patriotic*: Jerome Greene to Gertrude Robinson Smith, 20 April 1942, BSO Archives.

49–50   *In the first two years*: Lucien Wulsin to Serge Koussevitzky, Serge Koussevitzky Archives, Music Division, Library of Congress (hereafter cited as Koussevitzky Archives).

51   *At the Opening Exercises that year*: Serge Koussevitzky, Berkshire Music Center Opening Exercises speech, Tanglewood, transcript, BSO Archives.

54–55   *In this* New York Times *article*: "Koussevitzky Shows Symphonic State of the Nation at Stockbridge," *New York Times*, n.d.

56–57   *Tanglewood Revisited, a remembrance*: BSO Archives.

60–62   *The keynote speech was given*: Dorothy Thompson, speech given at the Allied Relief Concert for British Aid, Tanglewood, 16 August 1942, reprinted in the *Hartford Times*, 17 August 1940.

CHAPTER 4
The Happiest Summer of My Life

68   *For the first time since the war*: Rorem, *Knowing When to Stop*, 292.

69   *That Koussevitzky had survived*: Serge Koussevitzky, Berkshire Music Center Opening Exercises speech, Tanglewood, transcript, BSO Archives

77–78   *"But man proposes, God disposes"*: Charlotte Martinů, *My Life with Bohuslav Martinů*, (Prague: Orbis Press, 1978).

83   *One student, Yehudi Wyner*: Yehudi Wyner to Aaron Copland, 21 May 1947, BSO Archives.

83–84   *According to what he wrote*: Tanglewood Remembered: The Music Center.

85–87   *Over the following winter*: Ruth Orkin to Serge Koussevitzky, 28 April 1947, BSO Archives

88   *Tod Perry sums up the 1947 season*: Tanglewood Alumni Bulletin, BSO Archives.

88–89   *Let's give the last word*: Rorem, *Knowing When to Stop*, 292.

CHAPTER 5
Boris Goldovsky and the Opera Department

90   *"Throughout that time"*: Goldovsky, *My Road to Opera*, 302.

99–100   *This production became the impetus*: Steven Ledbetter, program notes for the Berkshire Music Center's fiftieth-anniversary production of *Peter Grimes*, BSO Archives.

100–101   *Ned Rorem, a student that summer*: Rorem, *Knowing When to Stop*, 293.

101   *An excerpt of that review*: "Mountain Music," *Time*, 19 August 1946.

101–2   *Benjamin Britten made a big hit*: "Mephisto's Musings," *Musical America*, August 1946.

102–3   *"This story is almost unbelievable"*: Charlie Weintraub in Tanglewood Remembered.

103   *"I was a student there in 1946"*: Arnold Fromme in Tanglewood Remembered.

104   *Along with* Don Giovanni, *Mozart considered*: Goldovsky, *My Road to Opera*, 354.

104–5 *So* Idomeneo *became Goldovsky's first*: "Idomeneo at Tanglewood," Erica Perl, *Opera News*, 6 October 1947.

106 *Goldovsky held up high theatrical standards*: Boris Goldovsky, undated letter, BSO Archives.

107 *In a March 23, 1959, letter*: Leonard Burkat to Aaron Copland, 23 March 1959, BSO Archives.

CHAPTER 6
Transitions

108 *"Could Tanglewood exist"*: Koussevitzky Archives.

109 *One of the more subtle signs*: George Edman to Gertrude Robinson Smith, 20 January 1940, Tanglewood Collection.

109–10 *By August 30, 1941. . .* Gertrude Robinson Smith to Mrs. Bruce Crane, 30 August 1941, Tanglewood Collection.

110–11 *Serge Koussevitzky was, of course, deeply involved*: Serge Koussevitzky to Gertrude Robinson Smith, 22 September 1941, Tanglewood Collection.

111 *On September 24, Miss Robinson Smith wrote*: Gertrude Robinson Smith to Stuart Montgomery, 24 September 1941, Tanglewood Collection.

112 *Push came to shove*: Telegram, Getrude Robinson Smith and the trustees of the Berkshire Symphonic Festival to the trustees of the Boston Symphony Orchestra, 4 October 1945.

112 *"Infinitely touched"*: Telegram, Serge Koussevitzky to Robinson Smith, 5 October 1945, BSO Archives.

112 *However, in 1949 a more radical*: Goldovsky, *My Road to Opera*, 370.

112–13 *Koussevitzky let the trustees know*: Serge Koussevitzky, interview with James Fassett, *Your Invitation to Music*, CBS Radio, transcript, BSO Archives.

113–15 *No finer appreciation of Koussevitzky's persona*: Bernstein, Berkshire Music Center Opening Exercises Speech, Tanglewood, 1951, transcript, BSO Archives.

CHAPTER 7
The Leinsdorf Era

118 *I interpret the word* festival *as meaning*: "Leinsdorf and Lenox," *Patriot-Ledger*, 9 April 1963.

119 *In a 1963 speech in London*: Transcript, BSO Archives.

122 *Phyllis Curtin, the soprano soloist*: Phyllis Curtin, interview with the author, Great Barrington, Mass., June 10, 2007.

127 *This resulted in the renaissance*: Harry Kraut to Scott Nickrenz, 24 February 1965, BSO Archives.

128–29 *Leinsdorf's first Opening Exercises speech*: Erich Leinsdorf, Berkshire Music Center Opening Exercises speech, Tanglewood, 1963, transcript, BSO Archives.

129 *Afterwards, a faculty member was heard*: *Berkshire Eagle*, 5 July 1964.

129 *As his parting shot*: "'Wozzeck' Is Offered by Students at Berkshire Center," *New York Times*, 9 August 1969.

130 *One of his pet peeves*: Erich Leinsdorf, Berkshire Music Center Opening Exercises speech, Tanglewood, 1964, transcript, BSO Archives.

130–31 *He elaborated on this*: Erich Leinsdorf, speech to the Musicological Symposium, 1964, transcript, BSO Archives.

131–32 *Leinsdorf was a very serious man*: Margaret Stejskal to Erich Leinsdorf, 30 August 1966, BSO Archives.

132–33 *"Dear Mrs. Stejskal"*: Leinsdorf to Stejskal, 29 September 1966, BSO Archives.

CHAPTER 8
Wild, New Sounds

134 *"Contemporary music has many friends"*: Igor Stravinsky toasting Paul Fromm, quoted in "Paul Fromm, Contemporary' Music's Friend and Lover," *Toledo Blade*, 2 August 1987.

135–36 *Paul Fromm, addressing a panel*: Paul Fromm, speech to Music Critics' Association, Tanglewood, 12 August 1969, transcript, BSO Archives.

136 *Fromm elaborates on his own history*: Paul Fromm, "Reflections of a Musical Critic," 1982 Festival of Contemporary Music, program book, BSO Archives.

137 *Copland continues his story*: Copland, Perlis, *Copland: Since 1943*.

138 *In an interview, contemporary composer*: Oliver Knussen, interview with author, Snape, England, 15 June 1999.

138 *In a 1966 speech at Tanglewood*: Paul Fromm, speech at Festival of Contemporary Music Concert, Tanglewood, 14 August 1966, transcript, BSO Archives.

138 *This became a major place*: Ibid.

139 *One of the most impressive*: "Tanglewood's Youth Week," *New York Herald Tribune*, 12 August 1964.

142 *Donal Henahan wrote*: "A Festival in Search of Itself," *New York Times*, 12 August 1972.

142 *Fromm answered back with*: Paul Fromm to Dan Gustin, 28 September 1973, BSO Archives

142–43 *Fromm to Steinberg, in a conciliatory opening*: Paul Fromm to Michael Steinberg, 31 August 1973, Fromm Music Foundation, Harvard University, Houghton Library (hereafter cited as Fromm Music Foundation).

143 *Meanwhile, Fromm had an interesting comment*: Paul Fromm to Dan Gustin, 29 November 1973, Fromm Music Foundation.

143 *He added this advice*: Fromm to Gustin, 10 December 1973, Fromm Music Foundation.

143 *In response, some preventative measures*:Gunther Schuller to Paul Fromm, 5 April 1974, BSO Archives.

144 *Although the overriding complaint*: Richard Ortner, interview with author, Cambridge, Mass., 25 November 2006.

145 *Others in the Tanglewood camp agreed*: Joseph Silverstein, interview with author, Stockbridge, Mass., 17 August 2006.

145–46 *However, by 1983, in a long letter. . .* Paul Fromm to Gunther Schuller, 6 September 1983, Fromm Music Foundation.

146 *One could only note with a certain amount of irony*: "Music: An Evening of Minimalism at Tanglewood," *New York Times*, 31 July 1984.

147 *The following February, composer*: Lucio Berio, in a booklet of memorial tributes, Fromm Music Foundation.

CHAPTER 9
Singing at Tanglewood

148 *"We believe that music is one art"*: Robert Shaw, "A Choral Creed," written first for Collegiate Chorale newsletter and later reprinted in the Tanglewood Bulletin.

149 *After an unlikely stint*: "Conductor Robert Shaw," Nancy McNally, *Pomona Today*, July 1966.

149 *With this goal in mind*: Mussulman, *Dear People*, 25.

150 *At the Tanglewood Music Center fiftieth anniversary*: Lorna Cooke de Varon in Tanglewood Remembered.

150–51 *It was Koussevitzky who gave Shaw*: Robert Shaw, interview with Brian Bell, WGBH Radio, 1996, audio tape, BSO Archives.

151 *Shaw left Tanglewood in 1948*: *Boston Globe*, 26 August 1996.

151 *As a student at Notre Dame*: John Oliver, interview with author, Symphony Hall, Boston, 26 June 2007.

152 *With these singers, Oliver has created*: *Boston Globe*, 10 July 2006.

152 *Composer John Harbison is also amazed*: John Harbison, interview with author, 2 August 2007.

153–54 *"There is quite a large turnover"*: John Oliver, interviewed on *The Round Table*, WAMC-FM, Albany, audio tape.

154 *This takes a lot of work*: Joan Sherman, interview with author, Tanglewood, 25 July 2007.

154–55 *Oliver has an interesting take on*: John Oliver, author interview.

155 *And stories abound*: Maisy Bennett, interview with author, Tanglewood, 25 July 2007.

155 *At the end of the twenty-fifth TFC season*: unpublished poem, BSO Archives.

156 *At the end of the chorus's first full season*: Paul Levy to John Oliver, 9 September 1971, BSO Archives.

156–57 *In the 1947 Tanglewood student opera program*: Phyllis Curtin, interview with author, Great Barringon, Mass., 30 September 2007.

158 *About one point Curtin has always been adamant*: Curtin, author interview, 30 September 2007.

159 *However, after the first four weeks*: Erich Leinsdorf to Phyllis Curtin, September 1964, BSO Archives.

159 *Curtin wrote him back*: Curtin to Leinsdorf, 29 September 1964, BSO Archives.

159–60 *Leinsdorf's response*: Leinsdorf to Curtin, 13 October 1964, BSO Archives.

CHAPTER 10
Behind the Scenes at Tanglewood

162 *"John Kenneth Galbraith"*: John Williams quoted Galbraith in "A Musical Life" in the Seiji Ozawa Twenty-Fifth Anniversary program

163 *Just being in residence*: Knussen, author interview.

163–64 *But musicians had discovered*: Spalding, *Rise to Follow*, 296.

164 *Then and now, finding the right*: Aaron Copland to Leonard Bernstein, n.d., Copland Collection.

165 *The dorms may have been "simply heavenly"*: Bernstein to Copland, 1941, Bernstein Collection.

166–67 *But the quintessential group living experience . .* "Tanglewood Tales," *Berkshire Week*, 26 July–1 August 1979.

167 *And what would dormitory life be*: Memo to fellows on dormitory rules, BSO Archives.

168 *House mothers had their own*: Internal letter, 19 May 1942, BSO Archives.

168 *Dorm life may have been somewhat restricted*: Claude Frank in Tanglewood Remembered.

168–69 *Even jaundiced music critics*: *New York Times*, 4 July 1990.

169–70 *In 1946, it had been his job*: "Tanglewood Tales."

171–72   *In the hands of Tod Perry*: Audio tape, BSO Archives.

173–74   *Mr. Kiley explained* : James Kiley, *Talks and Walks*, WAMC-FM, Albany, 1958, audio tape, BSO Archives.

175   *Another tactic was reported*: "Bye Bye Birdie," *Berkshire Week*, 26 July–August 1 1985.

176   *However, the following year*: *The Union* (Springfield, Mass.), 13 June 1968, BSO Archives.

176   *The BSO management was in hot water*: *Village Voice*, 19 June 1969.

176   *Iron Butterfly appeared and one local*: Woodcrest Camp director to director of Tanglewood, 18 July 1969, BSO Archives.

178   *Then there is that fellow*: "The Music Nearly Stunk," *Berkshire Eagle*, 16 August 1977.

180   *Verna Fine gives the defendant's*: Oral History American Music, Yale University, New Haven, Conn.

CHAPTER 11
Seiji

183–84   *But he was, always and above*: Mark Volpe, interview with author, Symphony Hall, Boston, 19 September 2007.

184–85   *There he met a Finnish-born*: Piltti Heiskanen to Olga Koussevitzky, BSO Archives.

185   *Olga got right to work*: O. Koussevitzky to Heiskanen, October 1959, BSO Archives.

185–86   *Although improved today, his English*: Seiji Ozawa, Berkshire Music Center Opening Exercises Speech, Tanglewood, 1998, audio tape, BSO Archives.

186   *In a 1990 interview*: *Boston Globe*, 6 July 1990.

187   *Vic Firth, the orchestra's legendary*: Vic Firth, interview with Mark Mobley, National Public Radio, *Weekend Edition*, 14 July 2002, http://www.npr.org.

187–88   *For example, national politics*: Tom Morris, interview with author, New York, N.Y., 7 December 2007.

188   *There was more drama*: Knussen, author interview.

188   *That same year*: "Tennstedt Takes Life at a Fast Tempo," *Boston Globe*, 6 August 1980.

189   *What was it about this fifty-something defector*: Silverstein, author interview.

189   *But Tennstedt's popularity was short-lived*: "The Rite of Summer," *Berkshire Week*, 1982.

189   *Seiji Ozawa's conducting style*: Morris, author interview.

190–91   *Dan Gustin believed that it was under*: Gustin, author interview.

192–93   *It began in the more or less usual way*: Gunther Schuller, Berkshire Music Center Opening Exercises speech, Tanglewood, 24 June 1979, transcript, BSO Archives.

195   *He has a great story about his last year*: Knussen, author interview.

195   *Richard Ortner has some interesting observations*: Ortner, author interview.

196–97   *Another composer who has made*: Harbison, author interview.

203–5   *A few years before the reunion celebration*: Ortner, author interview.

205   *Planning for the new concert hall*: Gustin, author interview.

208   *The critics loved the hall*: *New York*, August 1994.

208–9   *But nobody loved the hall more*: Seiji Ozawa, Berkshire Music Center Opening Exercises speech, Tanglewood, June 1994, audio tape, BSO Archives.

209   *Now that Tanglewood had* : Ortner, author interview.

209–10   *Margo Garrett, the collaborative*: Margo Garrett, interview with author, New York, N.Y., 2 October 2007.

210   *Phyllis Curtin had been in the original*: Curtin, author interview via telephone, 16 October 2007.

213   *Ellen Highstein, then the executive*: Ellen Highstein, interview with author, Tanglewood, 22 August 2007.

213–14   *On October 29, 1997, Gil Kalish submitted*: Gil Kalish to Seiji Ozawa, 29 October 1997, BSO Archives.

214   *On December 1, Leon Fleisher also sent* . . . Leon Fleisher to Seiji Ozawa, 1 December 1997, BSO Archives.

214–15   *Enter Mark Volpe*: Volpe, author interview.

215–16   *Ozawa had two major concerns*: Highstein, author interview.

218   *But there would be no next year at Tanglewood*: Press release from the Boston Symphony Orchestra, 23 June 1999, BSO Archives.

219   *In his good-bye message*: Tanglewood program book, weekend of 11 July 2002, BSO Archives.

CHAPTER 12
The New Era at Tanglewood

220   *"I haven't felt such excitement in the Shed"*: Jamie Bernstein Thomas, WQXR, live broadcast from Tanglewood, 16 July 2005, as reported in the *New York Times*, 22 July 2005.

221   *Before his appointment as music director*: Mark Volpe, interview with author, Symphony Hall, Boston, 17 January 2008.

222   *Levine is very much a hands-on*: Anthony Fogg, interview with author, Tanglewood, 22 August 2007.

223 *A change that Mr. Levine had made*: James Levine, interview with author, 13 February 2008.

223–24 *However, when it came to the Tanglewood Music Center*: Fogg, author interview.

224 *Richard Dyer, recently retired from the* Boston Globe*, was there*: *Symphony*, American Symphony Orchestra League, May–June 2007.

224 *Levine has his own theory*: Levine, author interview.

225 *One of Levine's coaching sessions*: Levine, author interview.

226 *When it comes to the TMC*: Highstein, author interview.

226–27 *Mark Volpe worries a bit about*: Volpe, author interview.

Selected Bibliography

Bookspan, Martin, and Ross Yockey. *Zubin: The Zubin Mehta Story*. New York: Harper & Row, 1978.

Burton, Humphrey. *Leonard Bernstein*. New York: Doubleday, 1994.

Copland, Aaron, and Vivian Perlis. *Copland: Since 1943*. New York: St. Martin's, 1989.

Fiedler, Johanna. *Arthur Fiedler: Papa, the Pops and Me*. New York: Doubleday, 1994.

Gable, David, and Christoph Wolff, editors. *A Life for New Music: Selected Papers of Paul Fromm*. Cambridge, Mass.: Harvard Univ. Press, 1988.

Goldovsky, Boris. *My Road to Opera: The Recollections of Boris Goldovsky, as told to Curtis Cate*. Boston: Houghton Mifflin, 1979.

Graf, Herbert. *Opera for the People*. Minneapolis: Univ. of Minnesota Press, 1951.

Kupferberg, Herbert. *Tanglewood*. New York: McGraw-Hill, 1976.

Ledbetter, Steven, editor. *Sennets & Tuckets: A Bernstein Celebration*. Boston: Boston Symphony Orchestra/David Godine, 1988.

Leinsdorf, Erich. *Cadenza: A Musical Career*. Boston: Houghton Mifflin, 1976.

———. *The Composer's Advocate: A Radical Orthodoxy for Musicians*. Yale Univ. Press, 1981.

Mahanna, John G. W. *Music Under the Moon: A History of the Berkshire Symphonic Festival, Inc.* Pittsfield, Mass.: Berkshire Eagle, 1955.

Monteux, Doris G. [Fifi Monteux]. *Everyone Is Someone*. New York: Farrar, Strauss & Cudahy, 1962.

Mussulman, Joseph A. *Dear People . . . Robert Shaw: A Biography*. Bloomington: Indiana Univ. Press, 1979.

Nabokov, Nicholas. *Old Friends and New Music*. Boston: Little, Brown, 1951.

Orkin, Ruth. *A Photo Journal*. New York: Viking, 1981.

Page, Tim. *Tim Page on Music: Views and Reviews*. Portland, Ore.: Amadeus Press, 2002.

Pincus, Andrew L. *Musicians with a Mission: Keeping the Classical Tradition Alive*. Boston: Northeastern Univ. Press, 2002.

———. *Scenes from Tanglewood*. Boston: Northeastern Univ. Press, 1989.

———. *Tanglewood: The Clash Between Tradition and Change*. Boston: Northeastern Univ. Press, 1998.

Rorem, Ned. *Knowing When to Stop: A Memoir*. New York: Simon & Schuster, 1994.

Rosenberg, Deena, and Bernard Rosenberg. *The Music Makers*. New York: Columbia Univ. Press, 1979.

Ruttencutter, Helen Drees. *Previn*. New York: St. Martin's/Marek, 1985.

Smith, Moses. *Koussevitzky*. New York: Allen, Towne & Heath, 1947.

Spalding, Albert. *Rise to Follow: An Autobiography*. New York: Holt, 1943.

Grateful acknowledgment is made to the following for permission to use both published and unpublished materials:

The Aaron Copland Fund for Music, Inc.: Excerpt from letter from Aaron Copland to Leonard Bernstein. Reprinted by permission of The Aaron Copland Fund for Music, Inc., copyright owner.

Associated Press: Excerpt from "Dowagers Thumb Ride to Symphonic Concert" (August 12, 1940). Used by permission.

Berkshire Eagle: Excerpts from *Music Under the Moon: A History of the Berkshire Symphonic Festival, Inc* by John G. W. Mahanna, published by the Berkshire Eagle in 1955; photographs; excerpts from articles. Used by permission.

The Boston Globe: Excerpts from articles from *The Boston Globe*, copyright © 1939, 1942, 1990 Globe Newspaper Company: "Boston Symphony Orchestra Members Get Back to Nature in the Berkshires" by K. S. Bartlett (August 13, 1939), "Youth at Tanglewood" by Uncle Dudley (August 4, 1942), an interview with Seiji Ozawa by Richard Dyer (July 6, 1990). Republished with permission.

Bristol Herald Courier: Excerpt from "Among Us Girls" by Lydia from the *Bristol Herald Courier* (August 22, 1940). Reprinted with permission of the *Bristol Herald Courier*.

Columbia University Press: Excerpt from *The Music Makers* by Deena Rosenberg, published by Columbia University Press in 1979. Used by permission.

Conde Nast Publications: Excerpt from "Musical Events" by Robert A. Simon from the *New Yorker* (August 13, 1938). Used by permission.

Cranbrook Archives and Cultural Properties: Excerpts from the correspondence of Eliel Saarinen. Used by permission.

Editio Bärenreiter Praha Ltd.: Excerpt from *My Life with Bohuslav Martinů* by Charlotte Martinů, published by Orbis Press in 1978. © 2003, Editio Bärenreiter Praha. Reproduced by permission of Editio Bärenreiter Praha Ltd., Prague, Czech Republic.

Ann Elmquist: Excerpt from Tanglewood Remembered. Used by permission.

Mary Engel/Ruth Orkin Archives: Ruth Orkin photographs, © Ruth Orkin Archives; excerpt from *A Photo Journal* by Ruth Orkin, published by Viking Press in 1981; excerpt from souvenir book; correspondence with Koussevitzky. Used by permission.

Farrar, Strauss and Giroux, LLC: Excerpts from *Everyone Is Someone* by Doris G. Monteux. Copyright © 1962 by Doris G. Monteux. Copyright renewed 1990 by Nancie Monteux. Reprinted by permission of Farrar, Strauss and Giroux, LLC.

Claude Frank: Excerpt from Tanglewood Remembered. Used by permission.

Estate of Boris Goldovsky: Excerpts from *My Road to Opera: The Recollections of Boris Goldovsky, as told to Curtis Cate* by Boris Goldovsky, published by Houghton Mifflin Company in 1979. Used by permission.

Julian Gorelli: Olga Gorelli's recollection in Tanglewood Remembered. Used by permission.

Henry Holt and Company, LLC: Excerpt from *Rise to Follow: An Autobiography* by Albert Spalding. Copyright 1943 by Henry Holt and Company, © 1967 by Mary Pyle Spalding. Reprinted by permission of Henry Holt and Company, LLC.

Hindemith-Institute Frankfurt/Main: Excerpt from correspondence of Paul Hindemith. Used by permission.

Houghton Mifflin Harcourt Publishing Company: Excerpts from *Cadenza: A Musical Career* by Erich Leinsdorf. Copyright © 1976 by Erich Leinsdorf. Reprinted by permission of Houghton Mifflin Harcourt Publishing Company. All rights reserved.

Koussevitzky Music Foundation: Excerpts from letters, speeches, and telegrams of Serge Koussevitzky. Used by permission.

Lenox Library Association: Excerpts from the Berkshire Symphonic Society papers: Tanglewood Collection, Berkshire Symphonic Archives. Used by Permission.

The Leonard Bernstein Office, Inc.: Excerpts from texts, letters, speeches, and poems of Leonard Bernstein. © Amberson Holdings LLC. Reproduced by permission of The Leonard Bernstein Office, Inc.

Paul Levy: Excerpt from letter to John Oliver. Used by permission.

McIntosh & Otis, Inc.: Excerpts from speech by Dorothy Thompson. Copyright © 1940 Dorothy Thompson. Reprinted with permission of McIntosh & Otis, Inc.

Musical America Archives: Excerpt from "Mephisto's Musings" from *Musical America* (August 1946). Courtesy Musical America Archives. Used by permission.

Domnique Nabokov: Excerpts from *Old Friends and New Music* by Nicholas Nabokov, published by Little, Brown and Company in 1951. Used by permission.

The New York Times Agency: Excerpts from articles from *The New York Times,* copyright © 1936, 1940, 1942, 1963, 1963, 1968, 1974 by The New York Times Company: "Berkshire Symphonic Festival" (August 23, 1936), "Symphonic Festival Local in Origin Attains International Fame" (July 28, 1940), "Review of Shostakovitch's Seventh Symphony" (August 16, 1942), "Music: At Tanglewood" (July 6, 1963), "Music: A War Requiem" (July 29, 1963), "Who Makes Music and Where" (July 14, 1968) "Koussevitzky, the Conductor Who Was a Force of Nature" (August 18, 1974). Reprinted with permission.

Opera News: Excerpt from "Sky Hooks for Opera" by Milton Stansbury from *Opera News* (October 6, 1941). Used by permission.

Daphne Brooks Prout: Excerpt from speech by Mrs. Gorham Brooks. Used by permission.

Random House, Inc.: Excerpt from *Leonard Bernstein* by Humphrey Burton. Copyright © 1994 by Humphrey Burton. Used by permission of Doubleday, a division of Random House, Inc. Excerpts from *Arthur Fiedler: Papa, the Pops and Me* by Johanna Fiedler. Copyright © 1994 by Johanna Fiedler. Used by permission of Doubleday, a division of Random House, Inc.

William L. Rawn: Excerpts from Talks and Walks speech to Friends of Tanglewood (1994). Used by permission.

Rockefeller Archive Center: Excerpts from Rockefeller Foundation correspondence. Used by permission.

Ned Rorem: Excerpts from *Knowing When to Stop* by Ned Rorem, published by Simon & Schuster, Inc., in 1994. Used by permission.

Charlotte C. Russell: Excerpt from Tanglewood Festival Chorus poem. Used by permission.

Eric Salzman: Excerpts from reviews of the Fromm Festival of Contemporary Music at Tanglewood by Eric Salzman from the *New York Herald Tribune.* Used by permission.

Harold Shapero: Excerpts from Oral History American Music interview. Used by permission.

Robert Shaw Family: Excerpts from WGBH Radio interview with Robert Shaw. Used by permission.

University of Minnesota Press: Excerpt from *Opera for the People* by Herbert Graf, published by University of Minnesota Press in 1951. Copyright © 1951 by Herbert Graf. Used by permission.

Janice Weber: Excerpt from Tanglewood Remembered. Used by permission.

WGBH Educational Foundation: Excerpts from WGBH Radio interviews: Brian Bell's interviews with Robert Shaw and Walter Scott. Used by permission.

Yale University Press: Excerpts from *The Composer's Advocate: A Radical Orthodoxy for Musicians* by Erich Leinsdorf, published by Yale University Press in 1981. Copyright © 1981 by Erich Leinsdorf. Used by permission

The author also expresses gratitude to the following for quoted materials:

Fromm Music Foundation: Excerpts from letters of Paul Fromm.

St. Martin's Press: Excerpts from *Copland: Since 1943* by Aaron Copland and Vivian Perlis, published by St. Martin's Press in 1989. Excerpts from *Previn* by Helen Drees Ruttencutter, published by St. Martin's Press/Marek in 1985.

Every reasonable effort has been made to contact copyright holders and secure permissions. Omissions can be remedied in future editions.